W9-CUZ-800

AESCHINES

THE ORATORY OF CLASSICAL GREECE
Translated with Notes • *Michael Gagarin, Series Editor*

VOLUME 3

AESCHINES

Translated by Chris Carey

 UNIVERSITY OF TEXAS PRESS, AUSTIN

Publication of this book has been generously assisted
by grants from the National Endowment for the
Humanities and the Gladys Krieble Delmas
Foundation.

Copyright © 2000 by the University of Texas Press
All rights reserved
Printed in the United States of America

First edition, 2000

Requests for permission to reproduce material from
this work should be sent to Permissions, University
of Texas Press, Box 7819, Austin, TX 78713-7819.

⊗ The paper used in this book meets the minimum
requirements of ANSI/NISO Z39.48-1992 (R1997)
(Permanence of Paper).

Library of Congress Cataloging-in-Publication Data

ISBN 0-292-71222-7
ISBN 0-292-71223-5

Aeschines.
    [Works. English. 2000]
    Aeschines / translated by Chris Carey. — 1st ed.
       p.   cm. — (The oratory of classical Greece ; v. 3)
    Includes bibliographical references (p.   ) and index.
    ISBN 0-292-71222-7 (alk. paper) — ISBN 0-292-71223-5 (pbk. : alk.
paper)
    1. Aeschines—Translations into English.   2. Speeches, addresses,
etc., Greek—Translations into English.   I. Carey, Christopher.
II. Title.   III. Series.
PA3823.A36   2000
885'.01—dc21

                                                     00-008419

In Memory Of My Sister,
Pauline Carey/Reffould
1954 –1997

CONTENTS

SERIES EDITOR'S PREFACE

This is the third volume in a series of translations of *The Oratory of Classical Greece.* The aim of the series is to make available primarily for those who do not read Greek up-to-date, accurate, and readable translations with introductions and explanatory notes of all the surviving works and major fragments of the Attic orators of the classical period (ca. 420–320 BC): Aeschines, Andocides, Antiphon, Demosthenes, Dinarchus, Hyperides, Isaeus, Isocrates, Lycurgus, and Lysias. This volume contains the three surviving speeches of Aeschines, an orator traditionally overshadowed by his main adversary, Demosthenes, but whose considerable talents have recently been attracting interest in their own right, not least for his attack on the sexual immorality of Timocrates in Oration 1. Aeschines won the first two rounds of his struggle against Demosthenes before being overwhelmingly defeated in their final contest.

I am again grateful for the full support of the University of Texas Press, especially from Director Joanna Hitchcock, Humanities Editor Jim Burr, and the production staff, especially Managing Editor Carolyn Wylie.

—M. G.

TRANSLATOR'S PREFACE

〜〜

The present volume has benefited enormously from the aid of several colleagues and friends. Two debts in particular need to be acknowledged. The series editor, Michael Gagarin, offered countless corrections and improvements, and his guidance has made its presence felt on every page, especially in the area of idiom, where his intervention has resulted in a more fluent version; in almost all cases I have, and probably in all cases I should have, accepted his suggestions. I am also grateful for his permission to offer a relatively full apparatus of footnotes, necessary in my opinion in a writer as under-researched as Aeschines, whose readers lack even the limited support available for the other orators, since the most recent published commentary material (where there is any) dates to the late nineteenth and early twentieth centuries. I hope that the convenience of having the material at hand will compensate the reader for any distraction caused.

The other *eminence grise* behind the volume is Edward Harris, who generously undertook to comment on the historical introductions and notes and made free with his impressive knowledge of the period. The resultant exchange of e-mail messages has been a source of both entertainment and instruction. His fingerprints are most visible in my note on the meetings of 18 and 19 Elaphebolion at Aeschines 2.66, a subject that continues to perplex me; but scattered throughout the book are paragraphs and notes where his intervention has brought about adjustment. He is, of course, innocent of any misconception I may have introduced in responding to his comments.

I have from time to time thrown questions informally at my learned colleague Lene Rubinstein and have always emerged wiser for her responses. I have also had the opportunity over the past few years to discuss Aeschines with Athanasios Efstathiou, whose Royal Holloway doctoral dissertation, now nearing completion, is a commentary on Aeschines 2. It was the stimulus of supervising his research that induced me to volunteer to cover Aeschines for the series.

I owe a special debt to the British Academy Humanities Research Board (now triumphantly reborn as the Arts and Humanities Research Board) and the Leverhulme Trust for a British Academy/Leverhulme Senior Research Fellowship in 1996–1997. Though the Fellowship was devoted to a new edition of Lysias, I was able to while away odd moments pleasantly in the task of translating Aeschines, a diversion necessary if I was to maintain a broader perspective amid the minutiae of philology, codicology, and papyrology.

Thanks are also due to the staff at the University of Texas Press for their promptness and efficiency, and especially to Sherry Wert for her accurate, thoughtful, and helpful copyediting.

And I should at long last acknowledge my debt to the person who over so many years and through so many projects has done more than anyone to keep me sane amid the competing demands of modern academic life: my wife, Pauline. I don't deserve her, but it would be a grim world if we all got what we deserved.

—C. C.

SERIES INTRODUCTION
Greek Oratory

〜〜

By Michael Gagarin

ORATORY IN CLASSICAL ATHENS

From as early as Homer (and undoubtedly much earlier) the Greeks placed a high value on effective speaking. Even Achilles, whose greatness was primarily established on the battlefield, was brought up to be "a speaker of words and a doer of deeds" (*Iliad* 9.443); and Athenian leaders of the sixth and fifth centuries,[1] such as Solon, Themistocles, and Pericles, were all accomplished orators. Most Greek literary genres—notably epic, tragedy, and history—underscore the importance of oratory by their inclusion of set speeches. The formal pleadings of the envoys to Achilles in the *Iliad*, the messenger speeches in tragedy reporting events like the battle of Salamis in Aeschylus' *Persians* or the gruesome death of Pentheus in Euripides' *Bacchae*, and the powerful political oratory of Pericles' funeral oration in Thucydides are but a few of the most notable examples of the Greeks' never-ending fascination with formal public speaking, which was to reach its height in the public oratory of the fourth century.

In early times, oratory was not a specialized subject of study but was learned by practice and example. The formal study of rhetoric as an "art" (*technē*) began, we are told, in the middle of the fifth century in Sicily with the work of Corax and his pupil Tisias.[2] These two are

---

[1] All dates in this volume are BC unless the contrary is either indicated or obvious.

[2] See Kennedy 1963: 26–51. Cole 1991 has challenged this traditional picture, arguing that the term "rhetoric" was coined by Plato to designate and denigrate an activity he strongly opposed. Cole's own reconstruction is not without prob-

scarcely more than names to us, but another famous Sicilian, Gorgias of Leontini (ca. 490–390), developed a new style of argument and is reported to have dazzled the Athenians with a speech delivered when he visited Athens in 427. Gorgias initiated the practice, which continued into the early fourth century, of composing speeches for mythical or imaginary occasions. The surviving examples reveal a lively intellectual climate in the late fifth and early fourth centuries, in which oratory served to display new ideas, new forms of expression, and new methods of argument.[3] This tradition of "intellectual" oratory was continued by the fourth-century educator Isocrates and played a large role in later Greek and Roman education.

In addition to this intellectual oratory, at about the same time the practice also began of writing speeches for real occasions in public life, which we may designate "practical" oratory. For centuries Athenians had been delivering speeches in public settings (primarily the courts and the Assembly), but these had always been composed and delivered impromptu, without being written down and thus without being preserved. The practice of writing speeches began in the courts and then expanded to include the Assembly and other settings. Athens was one of the leading cities of Greece in the fifth and fourth centuries, and its political and legal systems depended on direct participation by a large number of citizens; all important decisions were made by these large bodies, and the primary means of influencing these decisions was oratory.[4] Thus, it is not surprising that oratory flourished in Athens,[5] but it may not be immediately obvious why it should be written down.

The pivotal figure in this development was Antiphon, one of the fifth-century intellectuals who are often grouped together under the

---

lems, but he does well to remind us how thoroughly the traditional view of rhetoric depends on one of its most ardent opponents.

[3] Of these only Antiphon's Tetralogies are included in this series. Gorgias' *Helen* and *Palamedes*, Alcidamas' *Odysseus*, and Antisthenes' *Ajax* and *Odysseus* are translated in Gagarin and Woodruff 1995.

[4] Yunis 1996 has a good treatment of political oratory from Pericles to Demosthenes.

[5] All our evidence for practical oratory comes from Athens, with the exception of Isocrates 19, written for a trial in Aegina. Many speeches were undoubtedly delivered in courts and political forums in other Greek cities, but it may be that such speeches were written down only in Athens.

name "Sophists."⁶ Like some of the other sophists he contributed to
the intellectual oratory of the period, but he also had a strong practical
interest in law. At the same time, Antiphon had an aversion to public
speaking and did not directly involve himself in legal or political affairs (Thucydides 8.68). However, he began giving general advice to
other citizens who were engaged in litigation and were thus expected
to address the court themselves. As this practice grew, Antiphon went
further, and around 430 he began writing out whole speeches for others to memorize and deliver. Thus began the practice of "logography,"
which continued through the next century and beyond.⁷ Logography
particularly appealed to men like Lysias, who were metics, or noncitizen residents of Athens. Since they were not Athenian citizens,
they were barred from direct participation in public life, but they
could contribute by writing speeches for others.

Antiphon was also the first (to our knowledge) to write down a
speech he would himself deliver, writing the speech for his own defense at his trial for treason in 411. His motive was probably to publi-
cize and preserve his views, and others continued this practice of writing down speeches they would themselves deliver in the courts and
(more rarely) the Assembly.⁸ Finally, one other type of practical oratory was the special tribute delivered on certain important public occasions, the best known of which is the funeral oration. It is convenient to designate these three types of oratory by the terms Aristotle
later uses: forensic (for the courts), deliberative (for the Assembly),
and epideictic (for display).⁹

⁶The term "sophist" was loosely used through the fifth and fourth centuries
to designate various intellectuals and orators, but under the influence of Plato,
who attacked certain figures under this name, the term is now used of a specific
group of thinkers; see Kerferd 1981.

⁷For Antiphon as the first to write speeches, see Photius, *Bibliotheca* 486a7–11
and [Plut.], *Moralia* 832c–d. The latest extant speech can be dated to 320, but we
know that at least one orator, Dinarchus, continued the practice after that date.

⁸Unlike forensic speeches, speeches for delivery in the Assembly were usually
not composed beforehand in writing, since the speaker could not know exactly
when or in what context he would be speaking; see further Trevett 1996.

⁹*Rhetoric* 1.3. Intellectual orations, like Gorgias' *Helen*, do not easily fit into
Aristotle's classification. For a fuller (but still brief) introduction to Attic oratory
and the orators, see Edwards 1994.

THE ORATORS

In the century from about 420 to 320, dozens—perhaps even hundreds—of now unknown orators and logographers must have composed speeches that are now lost, but only ten of these men were selected for preservation and study by ancient scholars, and only works collected under the names of these ten have been preserved. Some of these works are undoubtedly spurious, though in most cases they are fourth-century works by a different author rather than later "forgeries." Indeed, modern scholars suspect that as many as seven of the speeches attributed to Demosthenes may have been written by Apollodorus, son of Pasion, who is sometimes called "the eleventh orator." [10] Including these speeches among the works of Demosthenes may have been an honest mistake, or perhaps a bookseller felt he could sell more copies of these speeches if they were attributed to a more famous orator.

In alphabetical order the Ten Orators are as follows: [11]

- AESCHINES (ca. 395–ca. 322) rose from obscure origins to become an important Athenian political figure, first an ally, then a bitter enemy of Demosthenes. His three speeches all concern major public issues. The best known of these (Aes. 3) was delivered at the trial in 330, when Demosthenes responded with *On the Crown* (Dem. 18). Aeschines lost the case and was forced to leave Athens and live the rest of his life in exile.

- ANDOCIDES (ca. 440–ca. 390) is best known for his role in the scandal of 415, when just before the departure of the fateful Athenian expedition to Sicily during the Peloponnesian War (431–404), a band of young men mutilated statues of Hermes, and at the same time information was revealed about the secret rites of Demeter.

---

[10] See Trevett 1992.

[11] The Loeb volumes of *Minor Attic Orators* also include the prominent Athenian political figure Demades (ca. 385–319), who was not one of the Ten; but the only speech that has come down to us under his name is a later forgery. It is possible that Demades and other fourth-century politicians who had a high reputation for public speaking did not put any speeches in writing, especially if they rarely spoke in the courts (see above n. 8).

Andocides was exiled but later returned. Two of the four speeches in his name give us a contemporary view of the scandal: one pleads for his return, the other argues against a second period of exile.

- ANTIPHON (ca. 480–411), as already noted, wrote forensic speeches for others and only once spoke himself. In 411 he participated in an oligarchic coup by a group of 400, and when the democrats regained power he was tried for treason and executed. His six surviving speeches include three for delivery in court and the three Tetralogies—imaginary intellectual exercises for display or teaching that consist of four speeches each, two on each side. All six of Antiphon's speeches concern homicide, probably because these stood at the beginning of the collection of his works. Fragments of some thirty other speeches cover many different topics.

- DEMOSTHENES (384–322) is generally considered the best of the Attic orators. Although his nationalistic message is less highly regarded today, his powerful mastery of and ability to combine many different rhetorical styles continues to impress readers. Demosthenes was still a child when his wealthy father died. The trustees of the estate apparently misappropriated much of it, and when he came of age, he sued them in a series of cases (27–31), regaining some of his fortune and making a name as a powerful speaker. He then wrote speeches for others in a variety of cases, public and private, and for his own use in court (where many cases involved major public issues), and in the Assembly, where he opposed the growing power of Philip of Macedon. The triumph of Philip and his son Alexander the Great eventually put an end to Demosthenes' career. Some sixty speeches have come down under his name, about a third of them of questionable authenticity.

- DINARCHUS (ca. 360–ca. 290) was born in Corinth but spent much of his life in Athens as a metic (a noncitizen resident). His public fame came primarily from writing speeches for the prosecutions surrounding the Harpalus affair in 324, when several prominent figures (including Demosthenes) were accused of bribery. After 322 he had a profitable career as a logographer.

- HYPERIDES (390–322) was a political leader and logographer of so many different talents that he was called the pentathlete of orators.

He was a leader of the Athenian resistance to Philip and Alexander and (like Demosthenes) was condemned to death after Athens' final surrender. One speech and substantial fragments of five others have been recovered from papyrus remains; otherwise, only fragments survive.

- ISAEUS (ca. 415–ca. 340) wrote speeches on a wide range of topics, but the eleven complete speeches that survive, dating from ca. 390 to ca. 344, all concern inheritance. As with Antiphon, the survival of these particular speeches may have been the result of the later ordering of his speeches by subject; we have part of a twelfth speech and fragments and titles of some forty other works. Isaeus is said to have been a pupil of Isocrates and the teacher of Demosthenes.

- ISOCRATES (436–338) considered himself a philosopher and educator, not an orator or rhetorician. He came from a wealthy Athenian family but lost most of his property in the Peloponnesian War, and in 403 he took up logography. About 390 he abandoned this practice and turned to writing and teaching, setting forth his educational, philosophical, and political views in essays that took the form of speeches but were not meant for oral delivery. He favored accommodation with the growing power of Philip of Macedon and panhellenic unity. His school was based on a broad concept of rhetoric and applied philosophy; it attracted pupils from the entire Greek world (including Isaeus, Lycurgus, and Hyperides) and became the main rival of Plato's Academy. Isocrates greatly influenced education and rhetoric in the Hellenistic, Roman, and modern periods until the eighteenth century.

- LYCURGUS (ca. 390–ca. 324) was a leading public official who restored the financial condition of Athens after 338 and played a large role in the city for the next dozen years. He brought charges of corruption or treason against many other officials, usually with success. Only one speech survives.

- LYSIAS (ca. 445–ca. 380) was a metic—an official resident of Athens but not a citizen. Much of his property was seized by the Thirty during their short-lived oligarchic coup in 404–403. Perhaps as a result he turned to logography. More than thirty speeches survive in whole or in part, though the authenticity of some is doubted.

We also have fragments or know the titles of more than a hundred others. The speeches cover a wide range of cases, and he may have delivered one himself (Lys. 12), on the death of his brother at the hands of the Thirty. Lysias is particularly known for his vivid narratives, his *ēthopoiïa*, or "creation of character," and his prose style, which became a model of clarity and vividness.

THE WORKS OF THE ORATORS

As soon as speeches began to be written down, they could be preserved. We know little about the conditions of book "publication" (i.e., making copies for distribution) in the fourth century, but there was an active market for books in Athens, and some of the speeches may have achieved wide circulation.[12] An orator (or his family) may have preserved his own speeches, perhaps to advertise his ability or demonstrate his success, or booksellers may have collected and copied them in order to make money.

We do not know how closely the preserved text of these speeches corresponded to the version actually delivered in court or in the Assembly. Speakers undoubtedly extemporized or varied from their text on occasion, but there is no good evidence that deliberative speeches were substantially revised for publication.[13] In forensic oratory a logographer's reputation would derive first and foremost from his success with jurors. If a forensic speech was victorious, there would be no reason to alter it for publication, and if it lost, alteration would probably not deceive potential clients. Thus, the published texts of forensic speeches were probably quite faithful to the texts that were provided to clients, and we have little reason to suspect substantial alteration in the century or so before they were collected by scholars in Alexandria (see below).

In addition to the speaker's text, most forensic speeches have breaks for the inclusion of documents. The logographer inserted a notation

---

[12] Dover's discussion (1968) of the preservation and transmission of the works of Lysias (and perhaps others under his name) is useful not just for Lysias but for the other orators too. His theory of shared authorship between logographer and litigant, however, is unconvincing (see Usher 1976).

[13] See further Trevett 1996: 437–439.

in his text—such as *nomos* ("law") or *martyria* ("testimony") — and
the speaker would pause while the clerk read out the text of a law or
the testimony of witnesses. Many speeches survive with only a notation that a *nomos* or *martyria* was read at that point, but in some cases
the text of the document is included. It used to be thought that these
documents were all creations of later scholars, but many (though not
all) are now accepted as genuine.[14]

With the foundation of the famous library in Alexandria early in
the third century, scholars began to collect and catalogue texts of the
orators, along with many other classical authors. Only the best orators
were preserved in the library, many of them represented by over 100
speeches each (some undoubtedly spurious). Only some of these works
survived in manuscript form to the modern era; more recently a few
others have been discovered on ancient sheets of papyrus, so that today
the corpus of Attic Oratory consists of about 150 speeches, together
with a few letters and other works. The subject matter ranges from
important public issues and serious crimes to business affairs, lovers'
quarrels, inheritance disputes, and other personal or family matters.

In the centuries after these works were collected, ancient scholars
gathered biographical facts about their authors, produced grammatical
and lexicographic notes, and used some of the speeches as evidence
for Athenian political history. But the ancient scholars who were most
interested in the orators were those who studied prose style, the most
notable of these being Dionysius of Halicarnassus (first century BC),
who wrote treatises on several of the orators,[15] and Hermogenes of
Tarsus (second century AD), who wrote several literary studies, including *On Types of Style*.[16] But relative to epic or tragedy, oratory was little
studied; and even scholars of rhetoric whose interests were broader
than style, like Cicero and Quintilian, paid little attention to the orators, except for the acknowledged master, Demosthenes.

Most modern scholars until the second half of the twentieth century continued to treat the orators primarily as prose stylists.[17] The

---

[14] See MacDowell 1990: 43–47; Todd 1993: 44–45.

[15] Dionysius' literary studies are collected and translated in Usher 1974–1985.

[16] Wooten 1987. Stylistic considerations probably also influenced the selection
of the "canon" of ten orators; see Worthington 1994.

[17] For example, the most popular and influential book ever written on the orators, Jebb's *The Attic Orators* (1875) was presented as an "attempt to aid in giving

reevaluation of Athenian democracy by George Grote and others in the nineteenth century stimulated renewed interest in Greek oratory among historians; and increasing interest in Athenian law during that century led a few legal scholars to read the orators. But in comparison with the interest shown in the other literary genres—epic, lyric, tragedy, comedy, and even history—Attic oratory has been relatively neglected until the last third of the twentieth century. More recently, however, scholars have discovered the value of the orators for the broader study of Athenian culture and society. Since Dover's groundbreaking works on popular morality and homosexuality,[18] interest in the orators has been increasing rapidly, and they are now seen as primary representatives of Athenian moral and social values, and as evidence for social and economic conditions, political and social ideology, and in general those aspects of Athenian culture that in the past were commonly ignored by historians of ancient Greece but are of increasing interest and importance today, including women and the family, slavery, and the economy.

GOVERNMENT AND LAW IN CLASSICAL ATHENS

The hallmark of the Athenian political and legal systems was its amateurism. Most public officials, including those who supervised the courts, were selected by lot and held office for a limited period, typically a year. Thus a great many citizens held public office at some point in their lives, but almost none served for an extended period of time or developed the experience or expertise that would make them professionals. All significant policy decisions were debated and voted on in the Assembly, where the quorum was 6,000 citizens, and all significant legal cases were judged by bodies of 200 to 500 jurors or more. Public prominence was not achieved by election (or selection) to public office but depended rather on a man's ability to sway the

---

Attic Oratory its due place in the history of Attic Prose" (I.xiii). This modern focus on prose style can plausibly be connected to the large role played by prose composition (the translation of English prose into Greek, usually in imitation of specific authors or styles) in the Classics curriculum, especially in Britain.

[18] Dover (1974, 1978). Dover recently commented (1994: 157), "When I began to mine the riches of Attic forensic oratory I was astonished to discover that the mine had never been exploited."

majority of citizens in the Assembly or jurors in court to vote in favor
of a proposed course of action or for one of the litigants in a trial.
Success was never permanent, and a victory on one policy issue or a
verdict in one case could be quickly reversed in another.[19] In such a
system the value of public oratory is obvious, and in the fourth century, oratory became the most important cultural institution in Athens, replacing drama as the forum where major ideological concerns
were displayed and debated.

Several recent books give good detailed accounts of Athenian government and law,[20] and so a brief sketch can suffice here. The main
policy-making body was the Assembly, open to all adult male citizens;
a small payment for attendance enabled at least some of the poor to
attend along with the leisured rich. In addition, a Council of 500 citizens, selected each year by lot with no one allowed to serve more than
two years, prepared material for and made recommendations to the
Assembly; a rotating subgroup of this Council served as an executive
committee, the Prytany. Finally, numerous officials, most of them selected by lot for one-year terms, supervised different areas of administration and finance. The most important of these were the nine Archons (lit. "rulers"): the eponymous Archon after whom the year was
named, the Basileus ("king"),[21] the Polemarch, and the six Thesmothetae. Councilors and almost all these officials underwent a preliminary
examination (*dokimasia*) before taking office, and officials submitted
to a final accounting (*euthynai*) upon leaving; at these times any citi-

---

[19] In the Assembly this could be accomplished by a reconsideration of the
question, as in the famous Mytilenean debate (Thuc. 3.36–50); in court a verdict
was final, but its practical effects could be thwarted or reversed by later litigation
on a related issue.

[20] For government, see Sinclair 1988, Hansen 1991; for law, MacDowell 1978,
Todd 1993, and Boegehold 1995 (Bonner 1927 is still helpful). Much of our infor-
mation about the legal and political systems comes from a work attributed to
Aristotle but perhaps written by a pupil of his, *The Athenian Constitution* (*Ath.
Pol.*—conveniently translated with notes by Rhodes 1984). The discovery of this
work on a papyrus in Egypt in 1890 caused a major resurgence of interest in
Athenian government.

[21] Modern scholars often use the term *archōn basileus* or "king archon," but
Athenian sources (e.g., *Ath. Pol.* 57) simply call him the *basileus*.

zen who wished could challenge a person's fitness for his new position or his performance in his recent position.

There was no general taxation of Athenian citizens. Sources of public funding included the annual tax levied on metics, various fees and import duties, and (in the fifth century) tribute from allied cities; but the source that figures most prominently in the orators is the Athenian system of liturgies (*leitourgiai*), by which in a regular rotation the rich provided funding for certain special public needs. The main liturgies were the *chorēgia*, in which a sponsor (*chorēgos*) supervised and paid for the training and performance of a chorus which sang and danced at a public festival,[22] and the trierarchy, in which a sponsor (trierarch) paid to equip and usually commanded a trireme, or warship, for a year. Some of these liturgies required substantial expenditures, but even so, some men spent far more than required in order to promote themselves and their public careers, and litigants often try to impress the jurors by referring to liturgies they have undertaken (see, e.g., Lys. 21.1–5). A further twist on this system was that if a man thought he had been assigned a liturgy that should have gone to someone else who was richer than he, he could propose an exchange of property (*antidosis*), giving the other man a choice of either taking over the liturgy or exchanging property with him. Finally, the rich were also subject to special taxes (*eisphorai*) levied as a percentage of their property in times of need.

The Athenian legal system remained similarly resistant to professionalization. Trials and the procedures leading up to them were supervised by officials, primarily the nine Archons, but their role was purely administrative, and they were in no way equivalent to modern judges. All significant questions about what we would call points of law were presented to the jurors, who considered them together with all other issues when they delivered their verdict at the end of the trial.[23] Trials were "contests" (*agōnes*) between two litigants, each of whom presented his own case to the jurors in a speech, plaintiff first,

---

[22] These included the productions of tragedy and comedy, for which the main expense was for the chorus.

[23] Certain religious "interpreters" (*exēgētai*) were occasionally asked to give their opinion on a legal matter that had a religious dimension (such as the prosecution of a homicide), but although these opinions could be reported in court

then defendant; in some cases each party then spoke again, probably in rebuttal. Since a litigant had only one or two speeches in which to present his entire case, and no issue was decided separately by a judge, all the necessary factual information and every important argument on substance or procedure, fact or law, had to be presented together. A single speech might thus combine narrative, argument, emotional appeal, and various digressions, all with the goal of obtaining a favorable verdict. Even more than today, a litigant's primary task was to control the issue—to determine which issues the jurors would consider most important and which questions they would have in their minds as they cast their votes. We only rarely have both speeches from a trial,[24] and we usually have little or no external evidence for the facts of a case or the verdict. We must thus infer both the facts and the opponent's strategy from the speech we have, and any assessment of the overall effectiveness of a speech and of the logographer's strategy is to some extent speculative.

Before a trial there were usually several preliminary hearings for presenting evidence; arbitration, public and private, was available and sometimes required. These hearings and arbitration sessions allowed each side to become familiar with the other side's case, so that discussions of "what my opponent will say" could be included in one's speech. Normally a litigant presented his own case, but he was often assisted by family or friends. If he wished (and could afford it), he could enlist the services of a logographer, who presumably gave strategic advice in addition to writing a speech. The speeches were timed to ensure an equal hearing for both sides,[25] and all trials were completed within a day. Two hundred or more jurors decided each case in the popular courts, which met in the Agora.[26] Homicide cases and

---

(e.g., Dem. 47.68–73), they had no official legal standing. The most significant administrative decision we hear of is the refusal of the Basileus to accept the case in Antiphon 6 (see 6.37–46).

[24] The exceptions are Demosthenes 19 and Aeschines 2, Aeschines 3 and Demosthenes 18, and Lysias 6 (one of several prosecution speeches) and Andocides 1; all were written for major public cases.

[25] Timing was done by means of a water-clock, which in most cases was stopped during the reading of documents.

[26] See Boegehold 1995.

certain other religious trials (e.g., Lys. 7) were heard by the Council of the Areopagus or an associated group of fifty-one Ephetae. The Areopagus was composed of all former Archons—perhaps 150–200 members at most times. It met on a hill called the Areopagus ("rock of Ares") near the Acropolis.

Jurors for the regular courts were selected by lot from those citizens who registered each year and who appeared for duty that day; as with the Assembly, a small payment allowed the poor to serve. After the speakers had finished, the jurors voted immediately without any formal discussion. The side with the majority won; a tie vote decided the case for the defendant. In some cases where the penalty was not fixed, after a conviction the jurors voted again on the penalty, choosing between penalties proposed by each side. Even when we know the verdict, we cannot know which of the speaker's arguments contributed most to his success or failure. However, a logographer could probably learn from jurors which points had or had not been successful, so that arguments that are found repeatedly in speeches probably were known to be effective in most cases.

The first written laws in Athens were enacted by Draco (ca. 620) and Solon (ca. 590), and new laws were regularly added. At the end of the fifth century the existing laws were reorganized, and a new procedure for enacting laws was instituted; thereafter a group of Law-Givers (*nomothetai*) had to certify that a proposed law did not conflict with any existing laws. There was no attempt, however, to organize legislation systematically, and although Plato, Aristotle, and other philosophers wrote various works on law and law-giving, these were either theoretical or descriptive and had no apparent influence on legislation. Written statutes generally used ordinary language rather than precise legal definitions in designating offenses, and questions concerning precisely what constituted a specific offense or what was the correct interpretation of a written statute were decided (together with other issues) by the jurors in each case. A litigant might, of course, assert a certain definition or interpretation as "something you all know" or "what the lawgiver intended," but such remarks are evidently tendentious and cannot be taken as authoritative.

The result of these procedural and substantive features was that the verdict depended largely on each litigant's speech (or speeches). As one speaker puts it (Ant. 6.18), "When there are no witnesses, you (jurors) are forced to reach a verdict about the case on the basis of the prosecutor's and defendant's words alone; you must be suspicious and examine their accounts in detail, and your vote will necessarily be cast on the basis of likelihood rather than clear knowledge." Even the testimony of witnesses (usually on both sides) is rarely decisive. On the other hand, most speakers make a considerable effort to establish facts and provide legitimate arguments in conformity with established law. Plato's view of rhetoric as a clever technique for persuading an ignorant crowd that the false is true is not borne out by the speeches, and the legal system does not appear to have produced many arbitrary or clearly unjust results.

The main form of legal procedure was a *dikē* ("suit") in which the injured party (or his relatives in a case of homicide) brought suit against the offender. Suits for injuries to slaves would be brought by the slave's master, and injuries to women would be prosecuted by a male relative. Strictly speaking, a *dikē* was a private matter between individuals, though like all cases, *dikai* often had public dimensions. The other major form of procedure was a *graphē* ("writing" or "indictment") in which "anyone who wished" (i.e., any citizen) could bring a prosecution for wrongdoing. *Graphai* were instituted by Solon, probably in order to allow prosecution of offenses where the victim was unable or unlikely to bring suit himself, such as selling a dependent into slavery; but the number of areas covered by *graphai* increased to cover many types of public offenses as well as some apparently private crimes, such as *hybris*.

The system of prosecution by "anyone who wished" also extended to several other more specialized forms of prosecution, like *eisangelia* ("impeachment"), used in cases of treason. Another specialized prosecution was *apagōgē* ("summary arrest"), in which someone could arrest a common criminal (*kakourgos*, lit. "evil-doer"), or have him arrested, on the spot. The reliance on private initiative meant that Athenians never developed a system of public prosecution; rather, they presumed that everyone would keep an eye on the behavior of his political enemies and bring suit as soon as he suspected a crime, both to harm his opponents and to advance his own career. In this way all public officials would be watched by someone. There was no disgrace in admitting that a prosecution was motivated by private enmity.

By the end of the fifth century the system of prosecution by "any one who wished" was apparently being abused by so-called sykophants (*sykophantai*), who allegedly brought or threatened to bring false suits against rich men, either to gain part of the fine that would be levied or to induce an out-of-court settlement in which the accused would pay to have the matter dropped. We cannot gauge the true extent of this problem, since speakers usually provide little evidence to support their claims that their opponents are sykophants, but the Athenians did make sykophancy a crime. They also specified that in many public procedures a plaintiff who either dropped the case or failed to obtain one-fifth of the votes would have to pay a heavy fine of 1,000 drachmas. Despite this, it appears that litigation was common in Athens and was seen by some as excessive.

Over the course of time, the Athenian legal and political systems have more often been judged negatively than positively. Philosophers and political theorists have generally followed the lead of Plato (427– 347), who lived and worked in Athens his entire life while severely criticizing its system of government as well as many other aspects of its culture. For Plato, democracy amounted to the tyranny of the masses over the educated elite and was destined to collapse from its own instability. The legal system was capricious and depended entirely on the rhetorical ability of litigants with no regard for truth or justice. These criticisms have often been echoed by modern scholars, who particularly complain that law was much too closely interwoven with politics and did not have the autonomous status it achieved in Roman law and continues to have, at least in theory, in modern legal systems.

Plato's judgments are valid if one accepts the underlying presuppositions, that the aim of law is absolute truth and abstract justice and that achieving the highest good of the state requires thorough and systematic organization. Most Athenians do not seem to have subscribed to either the criticisms or the presuppositions, and most scholars now accept the long-ignored fact that despite major external disruptions in the form of wars and two short-lived coups brought about by one of these wars, the Athenian legal and political systems remained remarkably stable for almost two hundred years (508–320). Moreover, like all other Greek cities at the time, whatever their form of government, Athenian democracy was brought to an end not by internal forces but by the external power of Philip of Macedon and his son Alexander. The legal system never became autonomous, and the rich sometimes complained that they were victims of unscrupulous litigants, but there is no indication that the people wanted to yield control of the legal process to a professional class, as Plato recommended. For most Athenians—Plato being an exception in this and many other matters—one purpose of the legal system was to give everyone the opportunity to have his case heard by other citizens and have it heard quickly and cheaply; and in this it clearly succeeded.

Indeed, the Athenian legal system also served the interests of the rich, even the very rich, as well as the common people, in that it provided a forum for the competition that since Homer had been an important part of aristocratic life. In this competition, the rich used the courts as battlegrounds, though their main weapon was the rhetoric of popular ideology, which hailed the rule of law and promoted the ideal of moderation and restraint.[27] But those who aspired to political leadership and the honor and status that accompanied it repeatedly entered the legal arena, bringing suit against their political enemies whenever possible and defending themselves against suits brought by others whenever necessary. The ultimate judges of these public competitions were the common people, who seem to have relished the dramatic clash of individuals and ideologies. In this respect fourth-century oratory was the cultural heir of fifth-century drama and was similarly appreciated by the citizens. Despite the disapproval of intellectuals like Plato, most Athenians legitimately considered their legal system a hallmark of their democracy and a vital presence in their culture.

THE TRANSLATION OF GREEK ORATORY

The purpose of this series is to provide students and scholars in all fields with accurate, readable translations of all surviving classical Attic oratory, including speeches whose authenticity is disputed, as well as the substantial surviving fragments. In keeping with the originals, the language is for the most part nontechnical. Names of persons and places are given in the (generally more familiar) Latinized forms, and names of officials or legal procedures have been translated into English

---

[27] Ober 1989 is fundamental; see also Cohen 1995.

equivalents, where possible. Notes are intended to provide the necessary historical and cultural background; scholarly controversies are generally not discussed. The notes and introductions refer to scholarly treatments in addition to those listed below, which the reader may consult for further information.

Cross-references to other speeches follow the standard numbering system, which is now well established except in the case of Hyperides (for whom the numbering of the Oxford Classical Text is used).[28] References are by work and section (e.g., Dem. 24.73); spurious works are not specially marked; when no author is named (e.g., 24.73), the reference is to the same author as the annotated passage.

ABBREVIATIONS:

Aes.	=	Aeschines
And.	=	Andocides
Ant.	=	Antiphon
Arist.	=	Aristotle
Aristoph.	=	Aristophanes
Ath. Pol.	=	*The Athenian Constitution*
Dem.	=	Demosthenes
Din.	=	Dinarchus
Herod.	=	Herodotus
Hyp.	=	Hyperides
Is.	=	Isaeus
Isoc.	=	Isocrates
Lyc.	=	Lycurgus
Lys.	=	Lysias
Plut.	=	Plutarch
Thuc.	=	Thucydides
Xen.	=	Xenophon

NOTE: The main unit of Athenian currency was the drachma; this was divided into obols and larger amounts were designated minas and talents.

---

[28] For a listing of all the orators and their works, with classifications (forensic, deliberative, epideictic) and rough dates, see Edwards 1994: 74–79.

1 drachma = 6 obols
1 mina   = 100 drachmas
1 talent = 60 minas (6,000 drachmas)

It is impossible to give an accurate equivalence in terms of modern currency, but it may be helpful to remember that the daily wage of some skilled workers was a drachma in the mid-fifth century and 2–2½ drachmas in the later fourth century. Thus it may not be too misleading to think of a drachma as worth about $50 or £33 and a talent as about $300,000 or £200,000 in 1997 currency.

BIBLIOGRAPHY OF WORKS CITED

Boegehold, Alan L., 1995: *The Lawcourts at Athens: Sites, Buildings, Equipment, Procedure, and Testimonia*. Princeton.

Bonner, Robert J., 1927: *Lawyers and Litigants in Ancient Athens*. Chicago.

Cohen, David, 1995: *Law, Violence and Community in Classical Athens*. Cambridge.

Cole, Thomas, 1991: *The Origins of Rhetoric in Ancient Greece*. Baltimore.

Dover, Kenneth J., 1968: *Lysias and the Corpus Lysiacum*. Berkeley.

———, 1974: *Greek Popular Morality in the Time of Plato and Aristotle*. Oxford.

———, 1978: *Greek Homosexuality*. London.

———, 1994: *Marginal Comment*. London.

Edwards, Michael, 1994: *The Attic Orators*. London.

Gagarin, Michael, and Paul Woodruff, 1995: *Early Greek Political Thought from Homer to the Sophists*. Cambridge.

Hansen, Mogens Herman, 1991: *The Athenian Democracy in the Age of Demosthenes*. Oxford.

Jebb, Richard, 1875: *The Attic Orators*, 2 vols. London.

Kennedy, George A., 1963: *The Art of Persuasion in Greece*. Princeton.

Kerferd, G. B., 1981: *The Sophistic Movement*. Cambridge.

MacDowell, Douglas M., 1978: *The Law in Classical Athens*. London.

———, ed. 1990: *Demosthenes, Against Meidias*. Oxford.

Ober, Josiah, 1989: *Mass and Elite in Democratic Athens*. Princeton.

Rhodes, P. J., trans., 1984: *Aristotle, The Athenian Constitution*. Penguin Books.

Sinclair, R. K., 1988: *Democracy and Participation in Athens.* Cambridge.

Todd, Stephen, 1993: *The Shape of Athenian Law.* Oxford.

Trevett, Jeremy, 1992: *Apollodoros the Son of Pasion.* Oxford.

———, 1996: "Did Demosthenes Publish His Deliberative Speeches?" *Hermes* 124: 425–441.

Usher, Stephen, 1976: "Lysias and His Clients," *Greek, Roman and Byzantine Studies* 17: 31–40.

———, trans., 1974–1985: *Dionysius of Halicarnassus, Critical Essays.* 2 vols. Loeb Classical Library. Cambridge, MA.

Wooten, Cecil W., trans., 1987: *Hermogenes' On Types of Style.* Chapel Hill, NC.

Worthington, Ian, 1994: "The Canon of the Ten Attic Orators," in *Persuasion: Greek Rhetoric in Action,* ed. Ian Worthington. London: 244–263.

Yunis, Harvey, 1996: *Taming Democracy: Models of Political Rhetoric in Classical Athens.* Ithaca, NY.

There is now a collection of speeches with legal interest and a good brief introduction to Athenian law in Christopher Carey, *Trials from Classical Athens* (London, 1997).

AESCHINES

〰〰〰〰〰〰〰〰〰〰〰〰〰〰〰〰〰〰〰〰〰〰〰〰〰〰〰〰〰〰〰〰〰〰〰

Translated with introduction by Chris Carey

INTRODUCTION
The Life and Times of Aeschines

〰〰

THE TIMES

The Rise of Macedonia

To the modern reader at least, the fifth century, for all its intellectual turmoil, looks like an age of political certainty. For much of the century, in a way familiar to anyone whose horizons were formed by the world between the Second World War and the fall of the European communist regimes, the Greek world was largely divided into two power blocks. This configuration ended with the defeat of Athens in the Peloponnesian War against Sparta, which lasted (with intermissions) from 431 to 404, and which left Sparta temporarily the undisputed leader of the Greek world. Spartan supremacy was not long unchallenged, however, and the first half of the fourth century saw a rapid sequence of changes in the balance of power on the Greek mainland.

The least predictable development in this uncertain context was the rise of Macedonia. In retrospect, this process possesses a deceptive appearance of inevitability. But during the fifth and early fourth centuries, Macedonia was at the mercy of the great powers of Greece and its immediate non-Greek ("barbarian") neighbors, and in the decades preceding the accession of Philip II to the throne in 359, Macedonian kings could only maintain a precarious hold over their territory. With Philip, all this changed. After consolidating his position within Macedonia, he began to extend his power and influence into neighboring territories, a necessary move if he was to ensure the security of the Macedonian state from foreign interference.

Since Athens had possessions, allies, and ambitions in the north, friction between the two powers was inevitable. Philip was helped at first by the so-called Social War between Athens and its allies of 357–355,[1] which distracted Athenian interest and energy. Athens was in fact technically at war with Philip from 357, when, with a duplicity that was to serve him well throughout his career, he captured the city of Amphipolis in the far north, which Athens regarded as Athenian property (though Athens had lost control of it over six decades earlier). But even after the Social War ended, there was little popular appetite in Athens for an adventurous foreign policy, and the dominant political group, headed by the enormously influential Eubulus, pursued a pragmatic policy of ensuring a military capacity to defend Athens' interests while avoiding commitments that might prove expensive, logistically difficult, and dangerous.

There were, however, politicians who favored a more vigorous response to Macedonian expansion. One of these was Demosthenes, who was then in his thirties. An opportunity to thwart Philip came in 349. In the north, the city of Olynthus, which was the head of a confederation of Greek cities, had come into conflict with Philip. The Olynthians appealed to Athens for assistance, and under the influence of Demosthenes and others, Athens sent aid. Philip took the city in 348. The destruction of a potentially valuable ally close to Macedonian territory had serious implications for the future of Athens' war against Philip. Athens was further isolated in 348 when its attempts to create a Greek coalition against Philip were rebuffed by other Greek states. A further blow came from Athens' Phocian allies. In 356 Thebes had manipulated the Amphictyonic League, which existed to protect Delphi, into imposing a fine on Phocis. The Phocians responded by seizing the temple of Apollo at Delphi, and thus began the decade-long Third Sacred War, which wore down both Phocis and its enemies, the former more gradually because of its access to the temple treasures as a source of pay for mercenaries. Athens was allied with Phocis (as was Sparta, now considerably weakened by the Theban invasions of the Peloponnese and the liberation of Messenia), while Philip sided with Thessaly, Thebes, and most of the other Amphictyonic states. Phocis

---

[1] The (to the modern reader) paradoxical title given to this war is derived from the Latin word for ally, "socius."

played a vital role in keeping Philip out of central Greece. But after the Phocians had offered in 347 to hand over to Athens several fortified positions controlling the pass at Thermopylae, the gateway to central Greece from the north, they reneged on the offer in early 346.[2] Thus the cumulative effect of developments between 348 and 346 was to leave Athens isolated and exposed.

The Peace of Philocrates

The Peace of Philocrates is a complex, and in places obscure, issue, owing both to our limited sources of evidence and to the fact that our two most important sources, Aeschines and Demosthenes, offer conflicting accounts. Here only a basic account is offered.

In view of Athens' current isolation, politicians with quite different agendas began to look seriously at the possibility of peace with Macedonia. Probably for some the aim was a lasting peace, for others a breathing space during which Athens could prepare for the next stage in the conflict. The short-term convergence was not total. Some influential politicians opposed the peace. But its proponents were in tune with the mood of the people. Philip had made overtures to Athens in 348 before the fall of Olynthus. Athens had responded positively, but serious negotiations never commenced, possibly because of the fall of Olynthus to Philip.

The process was resumed early in 346. In response to fresh indications that Philip wanted peace, Athens sent an embassy (the first of several that year) to Philip. This delegation included both Aeschines and Demosthenes. The envoys on their return gave a positive report. The Assembly debated the issue on two successive days in the spring of 346, and five days later another Assembly meeting swore Athens and the members of its maritime league to peace and alliance with Macedonia. Athens' ally, the Thracian king Cersobleptes, sent a representative to Athens seeking permission to swear to the treaty along with the members of Athens' league, but his request was rejected.

A second embassy was sent to receive the oaths of Philip and his

---

[2] For the power struggle within Phocis that led to this reversal, see 2.130n, 2.133n.

allies. Philip was at this time in Thrace on a campaign that reduced Cersobleptes' kingdom to the position of a Macedonian dependency. On arriving at Pella, the Macedonian capital, the Athenian envoys found representatives from all over Greece, all seeking to influence Philip; it was clear that he was preparing a major expedition to terminate the Sacred War, but he kept everyone guessing about the nature of his intended settlement. The uncertainty continued during Philip's march south, on which he was accompanied by the Athenian envoys. In the event, the Sacred War was settled without a fight. Philip may have been negotiating with the Phocians in secret; at any rate, the Phocian leader Phalaecus made an agreement under which he and his mercenaries were allowed to depart. After a vigorous debate in which more severe punishments were canvassed, the Amphictyons decided for the destruction of the Phocian cities and the resettlement of the population in villages, together with the imposition of a schedule for repayment of the funds stolen from the Delphic temple. By this time, Athenian suspicions of Philip had resurfaced. Athens had been invited to contribute troops to Philip's forces but, under the influence of politicians hostile to Philip, had refused to participate.

The Aftermath

From the outset the peace was unsatisfactory from an Athenian perspective. The terms reflected the bargaining positions of the two powers. The conclusion of peace on the basis of the territorial status quo confirmed Athenian losses to Macedonia, while conferring no consolatory gains. The fact that the peace was confined to Athens and the members of its league automatically excluded Phocis from the treaty; this, together with the conclusion of peace with alliance rather than peace alone, left Athens powerless to intervene either for Phocis or for Cersobleptes, even if the Athenians had spared a thought for either in the rush for peace. In Cersobleptes and Phocis, Athens lost important allies against Philip in the north and Thebes in the south. Resentment smoldered in the years after 346, fanned by groups hostile to the peace. Philip made some attempts to meet Athenian complaints; these included sending a delegation headed by the distinguished orator Pytho of Byzantium in 344/3 with offers to amend the treaty. But there was a large gulf between what Philip was prepared to concede and what the Athenians wanted, and Athens lacked any means to apply pressure to him. By the late 340s it was clear that hostilities would recommence sooner or later, and Athens and Macedonia found themselves in a state of cold war. Philip continued to extend his sphere of influence, either militarily or by giving support to pro-Macedonian factions; Athens countered by making alliances with anti-Macedonian factions and with states alarmed by Philip's policy. In 343 Philip supported, or at least was believed to have supported, attempted revolutions in Elis and possibly in Megara; by late 343 Athens had concluded alliances with a number of states in the northern Peloponnese. In 343/2 Philip invaded Epirus; Athens sent troops to defend Acarnania and embassies to other states in the region. From 343 Athens and Macedonia were engaged in a struggle for influence in Euboea that was ultimately resolved in Athens' favor when negotiations with Callias of Chalcis resulted in an alliance between Athens and an independent league of Euboean cities led by Chalcis. Athens also engaged in an aggressive policy in Thrace in the north. In 340 matters came to a head: Athens supported Byzantium and Perinthus when they were attacked by Philip. In the absence of the Athenian commander Chares, Philip seized the Athenian Black Sea grain fleet, and Athens declared war.

The war was initially a fairly desultory affair. But hostilities escalated significantly after an incident at Delphi in 339. The Athenian delegation to the Amphictyonic Council meeting was privately informed of an attempt by Amphissa to accuse Athens of sacrilege at Delphi, thereby raising the prospect of a new sacred war, this time against Athens. One of the Athenian representatives was Aeschines. His response to the Amphissaean attack was devastating. He countered the charge by accusing Amphissa in turn of impiety. The outcome was that a collective campaign was declared against Amphissa, in which Athens was expected to participate. Had it done so, Athens would have found itself on the same side as Philip, and one possible outcome would have been a cessation of hostilities between Athens and Macedonia, however temporary. It was rash, though, to incite armed conflict in this way, especially since Aeschines could not guarantee that his intervention and its practical implications would be approved in Athens. In the event, he could not persuade the Assembly that Athens should participate in the conference to decide the fate of Amphissa, thanks to the opposition of Demosthenes. After a lack-luster Amphictyonic campaign against Amphissa, Philip was once more chosen to lead the Amphictyons in defending Delphi. Athens now sided with Amphissa, and Demosthenes created a coalition based on an alliance for which he had long been hoping between Athens and Thebes, which had reason both to resent Macedonian influence in central Greece and to fear for its own independence from Macedonia if Athens were eliminated as a military force. The decisive battle was fought at Chaeronea in Boeotia in 338, where the Macedonian army, though attacking from an inferior position, was able to use its superiority in cavalry to advantage. Philip was victorious. The Athenians lost 1,000 dead and 2,000 captured. Theban losses were severe, including the annihilation of the elite 300-man Sacred Band. Thebes as an errant former ally of Macedonia was treated harshly: it lost control of the Boeotian cities and received a Macedonian garrison. Athens received more lenient treatment: though it was compelled to dissolve its maritime confederacy, it retained its formal autonomy and some overseas possessions and was given Oropus on the border between Attica and Boeotia. A league of Greek states was created, with its council meeting in Corinth; only Sparta remained aloof. Philip was now the undisputed master of Greece.

Hopes of freedom were raised by Philip's death in 336, but Alexander had little difficulty in establishing his control over Greece. Excited by a rumor of Alexander's death, Thebes revolted in 335. It was captured and destroyed by Alexander. The Spartans revolted in 331, while Alexander was campaigning in the east; the revolt was suppressed by Alexander's regent, Antipater. Athens played an active role in neither revolt. Not until Alexander's death in 323 did the Athenians judge that the right moment had come. Virtually the whole of northern Greece rose against Macedonia. This rebellion, too, was crushed (in 322), and the terms imposed on Athens this time were harsh, including the suppression of the democracy.

AESCHINES' LIFE

Our main sources for Aeschines' life are the speeches by himself and Demosthenes in 346/5, 343, and 330. Both orators adjust the facts, and neither can be taken as an objective source of truth. But between them they contrive to give us a reasonably clear view of Aeschines' career. He was born in 390.[3] Socially he came from a different class than did Demosthenes (who was the son of a wealthy manufacturer), as Demosthenes gleefully reminds him (18.265). His origins, while not disreputable, were humble. His father, Atrometus, was a teacher (Demosthenes 19.249, 18.129).[4] Aeschines in fact claims that his father had been a man of leisure but had lost his property during the Peloponnesian War (2.147). This is probably a fiction, and the fact that Aeschines sees fit to make the claim tells us more about Athenian prejudices than about Aeschines' background. Aeschines tells us little about his mother, Glaucothea. Demosthenes offers a lurid account of her career, from which the most we can conclude is that at some stage she probably acted as a priestess of some sort (19.199–200, 281; 18.130). Although Aeschines eventually married into a propertied family, it is generally doubted that his father could have afforded to provide him with an education in rhetoric, an invaluable preparation for a public career. On reaching adulthood, Aeschines fought with distinction in at least two campaigns (2.168–169).

Before turning to politics, Aeschines had two careers, which together served as an excellent preparation for political life. His first job was as a public clerk, and in this capacity he rose to become clerk to the Assembly. Demosthenes sneers at Aeschines' early employment (19.70, 200, 237, 314; 18.261). Certainly according to Athenian prejudices, working for pay was inferior to the self-sufficient ideal exemplified by the farmer. But the job later proved of enormous practical use to Aeschines. Apart from the opportunity to learn the related arts of politics and oratory by observation, this phase in his career introduced him to the public-record system of Athens. The impact of this acquaintance is visible throughout the corpus. It is explicit at 2.89 and 3.75, where he praises the Athenian public records; it is implicit in his extensive use of the records to provide factual support for his statements.

---

[3] See 1.49n.

[4] The claim at Demosthenes 18.129 that Aeschines' father's name was Tromes ("Trembler," where Atrometus would mean "Untrembling," i.e., "Fearless"), and that he was an ex-slave, is merely a gross fiction intended less to deceive the judges than to convert Aeschines into an object of ridicule.

One of his tasks as clerk to the Assembly was to read out documents. It was presumably while carrying out this function that he discovered and developed his fine voice, which in turn may have prompted the career move that took him into professional acting (Dem. 19.246, 337; 18.261–262). Aeschines attached himself to a distinguished troop of players (Dem. 19.246). The profession itself was respected. Demosthenes nowhere criticizes Aeschines for his choice of career, merely for being a failure as an actor. Like Ronald Reagan, Aeschines did not reach the top of his first profession. He remained "third actor," *tritagonistes*. As such he was not doomed to walk-on parts, but he would never get the bravura roles. However, the fact that Demosthenes feels the need to make the attack is revealing. The skills and qualities that had served Aeschines in the theatre were of equal value in the Assembly. There is abundant evidence that Aeschines had an impressive speaking voice (Demosthenes 19.126, 199, 206, 337; 18.127, 259), a fact that must particularly have unnerved Demosthenes, whose own vocal powers seem to have been limited. He will also have acquired the knack of delivery. Demosthenes in 343 sneers at Aeschines' appeal to the statue of Solon at Salamis during the trial of Timarchus in 346 (19.251–252).[5] In passing, he also gives us to understand that the consummate actor Aeschines mimicked the statue's posture at this point. Demosthenes' jibe is telling evidence for the impact of Aeschines' argument and delivery. Aeschines' abilities as a performer mean that the written text of his speeches cannot give us an adequate impression of the impact he made. These abilities must also be borne in mind when one considers the success of a seemingly flimsy case (in factual terms) like the prosecution of Timarchus. A lively and well-paced delivery will have enhanced the credibility of an already vivid narrative, while a resonant voice and authoritative manner will have reinforced the character effects sought.

Aeschines' political career, like that of many contemporary politicians, was defined by the burning question of relations with Macedonia. In 348, along with Eubulus, he had sought to unite the Greeks

---

[5] The reference is to Aeschines 1.25; see also 3.166n. Aeschines' use of stage skills in public debate is noted by Demosthenes at 18.15, 127, 287, 313, and 19.337, always with the implication that he is an actor playing a part.

against Philip. By 346 he was convinced that peace was necessary. He served on the various embassies to Philip in 346. On two of these embassies Demosthenes was among his colleagues. This may merely have been a marriage of convenience. Demosthenes almost certainly saw no long-term future in the peace. His support for the process was at best tactical, at worst self-serving.[6] Aeschines may have begun as an agnostic on the prospects for peace. What we can say is that from the outset of negotiations with Philip, he remained committed to peace with Macedonia. Although his readiness to claim credit for the peace diminished in direct proportion to its popularity,[7] he remained consistent in the belief that peace was the only sensible course for Athens.

In 346 Aeschines found himself targeted for prosecution by two politicians, Timarchus and Demosthenes, for his role in the negotiations. Politics is a rough trade, and rarely more so than in ancient Athens, where the structure of the democracy[8] meant that the only effective way to neutralize an opponent or deliver a significant setback to his group was to bring a serious political charge and inflict either a capital penalty or a crippling fine. Aeschines responded by prosecuting Timarchus and securing his conviction and disfranchisement; it was in this trial that the first speech in the corpus, *Against Timarchus,* was delivered. In 343 Demosthenes resumed the prosecution of Aeschines initiated in 346; the speeches *On the Embassy* by both Aeschines and Demosthenes were delivered at this trial (Aeschines 2; Demosthenes 19). By now public opinion was inclining firmly toward Demosthenes' hostile view of Macedonia. But Aeschines' personal credibility was still sufficient to secure his acquittal, though by a narrow margin.

The next serious clash between the two came in 339, when Demosthenes managed to reverse Aeschines' oratorical coup at Delphi by preventing Athens from joining the Amphictyonic campaign against

---

[6] If the peace proved a success, the political capital of its negotiators would be enormous.

[7] Contrast 1.174 with 2.12–20.

[8] Athenian direct democracy was based on continuing competition between individuals and informal groups for influence in the popular Assembly, unlike modern representative democracy, which is based on parties with an integrated program obtaining or losing a fixed-term mandate in regular elections. See further the Series Introduction.

Amphissa. The ultimate result was the defeat at Chaeronea. The Athenians evidently did not hold Demosthenes to blame, and he was chosen to give the funeral speech in praise of the war dead.

Aeschines now became less active in politics. However, he could not resist the opportunity for a final showdown with his old enemy. In 336 a political associate of Demosthenes, Ctesiphon, proposed an award for Demosthenes for his services in general, and specifically after Chaeronea. Such awards played an important role in Athenian politics, where, as in many systems, prestige and influence were no less important than financial reward. It was not uncommon for political opponents either of the proposer or of the honorand to bring a legal action against such decrees, and neither Demosthenes nor Ctesiphon will have been surprised by Aeschines' attack. The case was in part based on procedural irregularities in the manner of the proposed award, but the most important charge, to which the bulk of both the prosecution and the defense speeches is devoted, is that the grounds for the award proposed by Ctesiphon are false and that Demosthenes does not deserve any award. Since Demosthenes (as Aeschines could anticipate) appeared in person to answer the charges, technically as supporting speaker for Ctesiphon but in reality as presenter of the main defense case, the stage was set for a magnificent grudge-match when the case came to court in 330. In the event, Ctesiphon was acquitted by an overwhelming majority. Aeschines failed to get one-fifth of the votes cast. The result was both humiliation and (under the rules designed to prevent casual recourse to the courts) a fine of 1,000 drachmas and (probably) loss of the right to bring a similar action again. Since litigation was central to Athenian democratic politics, the latter was a severe blow. Aeschines left Athens and, according to one tradition, taught rhetoric on Rhodes.

Unlike Demosthenes, Aeschines never worked as a professional speechwriter for others. His total output was therefore devoted to his own political concerns. Probably the three surviving speeches represent his total published work.

The debate between Aeschines and Demosthenes continues. As the better writer, accepted by antiquity as the greatest of the Athenian orators, Demosthenes for a long time imposed his view on history. In the nineteenth century, scholarly opinion was firmly behind him. During the twentieth century, and especially in recent decades, scholars have become increasingly, sometimes passionately, critical of Demosthenes. With the benefit of hindsight, his commitment to an Athens rising again to lead the Greek world looks almost willfully unrealistic. Yet things must have looked very different to many of his contemporaries. Athens had shown itself to be remarkably resilient. It ended the fifth century without walls or armaments, a Spartan vassal. Yet within a decade it was playing a major role in international politics. The Athenian empire was dismantled at the close of the fifth century, yet within three decades Athens was at the head of a large maritime confederation. In contrast, experience showed both that Macedonian power was dependent on the person of its king (as the fate of Alexander's empire after his death confirmed) and that for members of the Macedonian royal family, life expectancy could be short. To anyone with a sense of history, it was anything but inevitable that Macedonia would triumph. Demosthenes' resistance to forces that threatened Athenian independence was in the tradition of the Greek yearning for autonomy, while his vision of Athenian destiny was one with which his audience had grown up and one with obvious appeal for many of his contemporaries. The revolts of 335 (Thebes) and 331 (Sparta) demonstrated how easily situations could be misread. Demosthenes was not alone in misjudging events, opponents, and opportunities.

Ultimately, however, his view of Athens' capacity, alone or in concert, to challenge Macedonia was misguided. Although due credit should be given to Philip's energy, psychological insight, and ruthless cunning, probably this was as much a matter of timing as anything else. The two powers began their struggle with widely different resources. Once Philip had consolidated his hold over Macedonia, he was master of enormous mineral wealth, while Athens began the struggle exhausted by the Social War. The loss of the more significant of its Aegean allies, subsequently compounded by the loss of Euboea in 348, left Athens without the additional resources to put Philip on the defensive. On the mainland itself, an anti-Macedonian coalition at an earlier stage might have achieved the critical mass needed to defeat Philip. But when finally Athenian politicians (largely, it is to be noted, those despised by Demosthenes) tried to put such a coalition in place, their efforts were rebuffed, and Philip was able continually to exploit the disunity of the old powers. If one can attribute specific errors to Demosthenes, probably one should look to the period after the Peace of Philocrates, when, along with others, he hastened to in-

crease the Athenian hostility toward Macedonia. Demosthenes himself realized that he had seriously underrated Philip in the 340s, as he
demonstrated by holding aloof from subsequent adventures in the period after Chaeronea. A more intelligent strategist might have been in
less of a hurry to undermine the peace. In his defense it should be
noted that even here, Athens was in a difficult position, since Philip's
influence continued to grow during the late 340s. Nonetheless, it is
difficult to resist the conclusion that Demosthenes was a better orator
and political operator than strategist.

The pragmatists who favored accommodation with Macedonia
were right in practical terms, in the limited sense that Athens would
inevitably be at a pronounced disadvantage in any conflict with Macedonia. The problem was that the pragmatists had no inspiring vision
to rival that of Demosthenes. Friendship with Macedonia in theory
offered the opportunity of a partnership, and much is sometimes
made of Philip's plans for Athens. But in any partnership Athens
would have been a junior partner. Given Athens' sense of its history,
this would have been a difficult role to accept. The collective psychological difficulty of accommodating the loss of major power status is a
phenomenon familiar to our own age. And even if such a policy could
have been sold to the Assembly, the fact remains that Aeschines was
badly let down by Philip. Aeschines expected great things from Philip,
and probably in 346 encouraged the Athenians to share his expectations, but the advantages never materialized. Though Philip's dealings
with Athens suggest respect for its past and even perhaps a degree of
affection, in broader policy terms Athens was of peripheral significance for him, and the concessions necessary to win its friendship were
unacceptable to him. The pragmatists were left with no gains to display from peace with Macedonia and no vision beyond peace as pref-
erable to destructive war. Popular opinion in the end preferred the
activism of Demosthenes, and even the defeat at Chaeronea was felt
to be a price worth paying in the attempt to retain autonomy and
influence.

NOTE ON THE TEXT

The present translation is based on the Teubner text of Aeschines
published by Mervin R. Dilts, *Aeschines: Orationes* (Leipzig, 1997).

Departures of any significance from his text are few and are signaled in the footnotes. Dilts' introduction includes a discussion (in Latin) of the relationship between the medieval manuscripts and a list both of these and of the copious papyrus fragments of the three speeches that have been unearthed in Egypt.

FURTHER READING

Aeschines has yet to receive the attention he deserves. The following works offer support for the English-speaking reader.

Adams, C. D. 1919. *The Speeches of Aeschines with an English Translation.* Cambridge, Mass. Greek text and fluent English translation, with introduction and sparse but helpful footnotes.

Cawkwell, G. 1978. *Philip of Macedon.* London. A brief but lucid account of the reign of Philip II, with some introductory material on his predecessors.

Davies, J. K. 1971. *Athenian Propertied Families, 600–300.* Oxford. An invaluable account of the wealthy Athenian families, arranged by stemma, containing a wealth of detail.

Dilts, Mervin R. *Aeschines: Orationes.* Leipzig, 1997.

Dover, K. J. 1974. *Greek Popular Morality in the Time of Plato and Aristotle.* Oxford. Though a quarter of a century old, this remains an invaluable guide to aspects of the value system of classical Athens, with copious source material.

———. 1978. *Greek Homosexuality.* Cambridge, Mass. An excellent general introduction to the subject of Greek homosexuality.

Ellis, J. R. 1976. *Philip II and Macedonian Imperialism.* London. An account of the career of Philip II, with a brief but useful account of his predecessors.

Errington, R. M. 1990. *A History of Macedonia.* Berkeley, Calif. A compact history of Macedonia.

Gwatkin, T., and E. S. Shuckburgh. 1890. *Aeschines in Ctesiphonta.* London and New York. A Greek text of Aeschines 3 with detailed commentary. Out of date on historical and textual issues, but still containing much useful information for the reader with some Greek.

Gwatkin, W. E. 1957. "The Legal Arguments in Aeschines' *Against Ctesiphon* and Demosthenes' *On the Crown.*" *Hesperia* 26: 129–141.

Halperin, D. 1990. *One Hundred Years of Homosexuality.* London and New York. A collection of essays dealing with aspects of sexuality in ancient Greece, devoted largely but not exclusively to homosexuality.

Hammond, N. G. L. 1989. *Alexander the Great.* 2d ed. Bristol.

Hammond, N. G. L., and G. T. Griffith. 1979. *A History of Macedonia.* Vol. 2. Oxford. The second volume of a monumentally detailed history of Macedonia, which includes the reign of Philip II.

Hammond, N. G. L., and F. W. Walbank. 1988. *A History of Macedonia.* Vol. 3. Oxford. Successor to the preceding, which begins with Alexander.

Harris, E. 1988. "The Date of Aeschines' Birth." *Classical Philology* 83: 211–214.

———. 1994. "Law and Oratory." In *Persuasion: Greek Rhetoric in Action.* Edited by I. Worthington. London. Discusses the legal validity of the charges brought by Aeschines in speech 3.

———. 1995. *Aeschines and Athenian Politics.* Oxford and New York. An account of Aeschines' life and political career, placed within the historical context, with appendices dealing with particular issues.

Harrison, A. R. W. 1968, 1971. *The Law of Athens.* 2 vols. Oxford. A scholarly and detailed treatment, with copious primary texts (in Greek).

Hornblower, S. 1983. *The Greek World, 479–323 B.C.* London. History of Greece from the end of the Persian Wars to the death of Alexander, useful both for the context of Aeschines' career and for fifth-century events mentioned in his speeches.

Lewis, D. M., et al. 1994. *The Cambridge Ancient History.* 2d ed. Vol. 6, *The Fourth Century B.C.* Cambridge. A vast and vastly expensive but also vastly informative overview of the fourth century, arranged by regions and themes.

Richardson, R. B. 1889. *Aeschines Against Ctesiphon (On the Crown).* Boston; reprinted New York, 1979. Cf. on Gwatkin and Shuckburgh above.

Tuttle, L. A., ed. 1997. *The Greek World in the Fourth Century: From the Fall of the Athenian Empire to the Successors of Alexander.* London and New York. A collection of broad discussions of the period, arranged partly by region, partly by period, partly by theme.

Usher, S. 1993. *Greek Orators.* Vol. 5, *Demosthenes On the Crown.* Warminster. Greek text and translation and commentary on Demosthenes 18, *On the Crown,* the defense speech delivered by Demosthenes in response to Aeschines 3.

Winkler, J. J. 1990. *The Constraints of Desire: The Anthropology of Sex and Gender in Ancient Greece.* London. A wide-ranging collection of essays dealing with aspects of gender and sexuality in ancient Greece, including homosexuality in classical Athens.

Wycherley, R. E. 1978. *The Stones of Athens.* Princeton, N.J. A valuable general account of the topography and material remains of ancient Athens.

See also the works by Edwards, Hansen, Kennedy, MacDowell, Sinclair, and Todd listed in the Series Introduction.

1. AGAINST TIMARCHUS

INTRODUCTION

Context

Although there was majority support for the conclusion of peace in 346, there remained elements in the city implacably and explicitly opposed either to the idea of peace with Macedonia or to the terms of the Peace of Philocrates. There were others, like Demosthenes, who saw the peace as a necessary but temporary arrangement. The opponents of the peace began working against it from the moment it was concluded. Aeschines was an early target. All Athenian officials had to submit to an examination on the expiry of their term of office. When Aeschines submitted to this process after the second embassy to Macedonia of 346, he was accused of misconduct by Timarchus, a minor politician of whose background we know no more than Aeschines tells us and on whose precise political affiliations we are badly informed,[1] and by Demosthenes. On the useful principle that attack is the best form of defense, Aeschines responded by launching a prosecution. He chose Timarchus, the weaker target. Demosthenes was both wealthy and, though not yet forty, a formidable political operator and public speaker. Neither his private life nor (at this stage) his political activity offered a secure base for prosecution. It is clear, however, from the present speech (and from Demosthenes' grudging admission at 19.284) that

---

[1] Though the inevitable conclusion from his attack on Aeschines that he favored a vigorous stance against Macedonia is confirmed by the testimony of Demosthenes (19.286–287) that he was the proposer of a decree making it illegal to export weapons or naval supplies to Philip.

Timarchus had had a scandalous youth. The speech can be dated to
346/5, though it is difficult to fix the date more precisely.

Despite the factual (though not rhetorical) weakness of the speech,
which is ultimately no more than a sustained attempt to throw sand
in the eyes of the jurors, Aeschines won the case and Timarchus was
disfranchised (Dem. 19.257, 284). Though Demosthenes was later (in
343) to treat Timarchus as an object of pity, the reader should bear in
mind that it was Timarchus who picked the fight. His mistake was
to underestimate his intended victim. By demonstrating his ferocity
and skill as a political fighter and his credibility with a judicial panel
of ordinary Athenians, Aeschines effectively checked his enemies' attempts to bring him to trial, and it was three years before Demosthenes felt able to return to the attack. The defeat stung Demosthenes,
who revisits the subject of Timarchus repeatedly in his speech *On the
Embassy* (Dem. 19), written for the prosecution of Aeschines in 343;
he also in that speech takes a certain grim pleasure in using against
Aeschines arguments used by Aeschines against Timarchus.

The Charge

The legal action used by Aeschines against Timarchus was *dokimasia tōn rhētorōn*, literally "scrutiny of public speakers."[2] The term
"public speaker" (*rhētōr*) was applied to individuals who regularly addressed the popular Assembly. Such people were professional politicians in the double sense that they devoted much of their time to
politics and they could hope to earn substantial sums from individuals
and groups keen to gain access to their political influence, though,
unlike modern democratic politicians, they received no income from
the state. The purpose of the *dokimasia tōn rhētorōn* was to test the
credentials of those who sought to direct public policy in the Assembly and to remove from influence those deemed unworthy. It was
open to any Athenian citizen to initiate it by publicly declaring his

[2] The date of the creation of this process is uncertain; it clearly reflects the
distinction, observable in the fifth but increased in the fourth century, between
the regular speaker (*rhētōr*) in the Assembly and formally appointed state officials
(especially the generals) and probably belongs to the period of the restoration of
the democracy in 403.

intention to subject a speaker to the process, which took the form of a trial before a jury. It is a strangely hybrid action. The process of initiation locates it within the public actions open to any volunteer prosecutor (*ho boulomenos*) against alleged infractions of the laws. But its title fixes it within the various processes of formal scrutiny (*dokimasia*) automatically imposed on the commencement of certain rights or responsibilities. Accordingly, as Todd (1993) has emphasized, the penalty is merely the confirmation of the formal restrictions automatically attaching (in most cases) to the activities it addresses.

Although Aeschines focuses specifically on one aspect of the *dokimasia,* it is clear from his account of the law in 28–32 that there was a list of acts that rendered a man ineligible to address the Assembly. The list, which may not be exhaustive, included violence toward or failure to support parents, military derelictions, prostitution, and squandering an inheritance. With the exception of the last item, these were all acts for which *atimia,* loss of citizen rights, was the prescribed penalty, and the penalty for an individual convicted on the *dokimasia tōn rhētorōn* was likewise *atimia.* Aeschines charges Timarchus specifically with having prostituted himself as a young man but also throws in for good measure the allegation that he squandered his inheritance (42, 94–101). Aeschines cannot formally accuse Timarchus of mistreating his father, who appears to have died when Timarchus was young, but he does draw on associated values by accusing him of mistreating an aged uncle (104).

Homosexuality and Male Prostitution

Greek homoeroticism is a complex subject that has attracted scholarly interest in recent years. The following summary of the subject is offered merely as a rough guide.

Though on occasion we find dissenting and condemnatory voices, many Greek sources from the archaic period onward take it for granted that grown men find males around the age of puberty sexually attractive. Although it was possible to be exclusively homosexual (as with Misgolas in this speech), there is no automatic assumption that homosexual tastes preclude heterosexual. Structurally, the practice of homosexuality differed from modern experience in that there is normally an age difference between the partners. As with sex in most societies, there appear to be elaborate proprieties. The roles of the partners are perceived as distinct, with the older man as pursuer, the younger as pursued, the older as achieving physical gratification, the younger as providing it.

Participation in such relationships was not in itself illegal, and prostitution, homosexual or heterosexual, was a legitimate profession for many noncitizens. But the sale of sexual favors was felt to be incompatible with citizen status and brought an automatic penalty of disfranchisement. No further penalties were imposed unless an individual so barred sought to exercise citizen rights. In addition to the *dokimasia tōn rhētorōn*, available against public speakers believed to have prostituted themselves, there was also a public action (the *graphē hetairēseōs*) that could be brought against any Athenian male who infringed the automatic bar consequent upon male prostitution, the penalty on conviction being death. Though this may look like a straightforward issue, in fact it was riddled with complications. Quite apart from the obvious difficulty of obtaining evidence about an activity carried out by two people in private, the common practice of giving gifts to a lover meant that the question of payment was necessarily a grey area.

The Speech

After an opening that stresses the orator's own moderation, an introductory section (4–6) stresses the importance of the laws. Aeschines then moves into an account of the laws dealing with decent conduct (6–36), arranged chronologically in order of the age of the individuals covered and culminating in those dealing with the morality of politicians and the conduct of the political process. Much of this section is at best only tangentially relevant to the main issue, though it does create a high moral tone and underline the importance of adherence to high standards of decency in public and private life.

After a transitional section (37–38) reasserting the moderate and decent character projected by the speaker, Aeschines proceeds to a narrative of Timarchus' sexual career (39–70) with testimony.

At this point Aeschines interrupts his narrative and turns to anticipation of the defense arguments, boldly tackling head-on the fact that he has not a shred of solid evidence against Timarchus (71–94). The essence of his answer, reiterated in a variety of ways, is that the members of the audience all know the truth and therefore have no need of further evidence. The last section of this refutation (94) acts as a springboard for the next section of narrative, which deals with the rest of Timarchus' career, his squandering of his inheritance (95–105), and his corruption and criminality in public office (106–116).

Aeschines now reverts to anticipation of defense arguments. First he deals with arguments anticipated from Demosthenes, who (Aeschines claims) will stress the absence of evidence from the officials who collect the prostitution tax and the unfairness of conviction on the basis of rumor (117–131). The first objection is met partly by righteous indignation, partly by insisting that the fact that Timarchus has not worked in a known brothel says nothing about the nature of his activities. The second is met by a magisterial appeal to the divine authority of Report, *Pheme,* a mystical force that promulgates the truth.

The next section of refutation (132–159) responds to an anticipated appeal to the traditions of Greek homosexuality. Aeschines will be presented by his opponents as inconsistent, as a pursuer of young men who attacks a young man who has had pursuers. It will also be claimed that homosexual relationships have long been sanctioned by tradition and have been the inspiration for noble deeds. Aeschines' response is to distinguish (without ever making explicit the basis for the distinction) between chaste homosexual love and the indecent conduct of people like Timarchus.

In 160–165 he returns to the problem of lack of evidence, to demolish the defense's demand that he produce a sexual contract between Timarchus and a client. In 166–169 he dismisses Demosthenes' anticipated attempts to use Macedonia as a means of exciting prejudice against Aeschines. After insisting that the jurors must not accept irrelevant pleas from the defense, he turns to an irrelevant character assassination of Demosthenes (170–176), finishing with a demand that the jurors keep Demosthenes to the point. In 177–187 he returns to the earlier theme of maintaining the laws, using both Sparta and the Athenian ancestors as examples.

At this point the speech accelerates, moving rapidly over an appeal to religion (188), the notoriety of Timarchus' life (189), and the wider implications of such conduct (190–191), before turning to the implications for Athens of the verdict in the present case (192–193) and a warning about the supporters of Timarchus (192–195). There is a brief conclusion (195).

Although it is possible to distinguish different sections within the speech, the boundaries are made fluid by a tendency on Aeschines' part to make use of narrative even in sections devoted to argument. Perhaps the most interesting aspect of the structure is the way narrative and proof (mainly refutation) are each divided and then interleaved. Part of the reason may be a desire for variety. But a more telling reason is the absence of solid proof. To impose on the speech a neat division of the sort recommended by rhetoricians, with separate long sections devoted to narrative and proof, would call attention to the factual weakness. As it is, the emotive power of the narrative is deployed to distract attention from this problem.

Given the difficulty of obtaining evidence, it strikes the modern reader as surprising that the prosecution succeeded. Probably we should conclude that Timarchus had a colorful past and was therefore a person against whom allegations such as these could plausibly be made. Moreover, we cannot tell how far the prosecution case was helped by the political climate, and Aeschines' own enhanced credibility as a result of his role in the negotiation of the peace. But we should also give due credit to the skill with which Aeschines presents the case. The prosecution is conducted throughout with dignity. The speaker projects a personality that is decent, moderate, and restrained, a character that invites trust. This mask enables him to turn the absence of incriminating detail to his advantage by attributing it to the salacious nature of the narrative and his consequent (laudable) reluctance to be explicit. He also undermines the moral authority of his opponents by tainting them, especially Demosthenes, with the crimes for which Timarchus is on trial and ably forces them to the defensive by making their *prima facie* powerful demand for evidence an evasion that is tantamount to an admission of guilt.

AGAINST TIMARCHUS

[1] Never before, men of Athens, have I brought an indictment (*graphē*)[3] against any man or persecuted him at his final audit;[4] no,

---

[3] Legal actions in Athens were divided into public and private. In private actions only the victim could sue, whereas in public actions anyone could prosecute. The *graphē* was the most common type of public action.

[4] All officials in Athens were subject to a final check (*euthyna*) on their conduct in office. This was in two phases, the first devoted to their financial accounts, the

I have in my opinion shown restraint in all such matters. But since I could see that the city was suffering serious damage from this man Timarchus, who addresses the Assembly illegally, and since I am personally the victim of his malicious prosecution[5] (just how, I shall explain later in my speech), [2] I concluded that it would be utterly disgraceful not to intervene in defense of the city as a whole, the laws, you, and myself. And in the knowledge that he is guilty of the charges that you heard the clerk read out just now, I declared this formal scrutiny[6] against him. It seems, men of Athens, that the claims usually made in public cases are not untrue: private enmities very often do put right public wrongs. [3] So you will see that Timarchus can put the blame for this whole prosecution not on the city or the laws or you or me but on himself. The laws warned him not to address the Assembly because of the disreputable life he has led; in my judgment, this was not a difficult command but a very easy one. And in my case he was free not to persecute me, if he had any sense. I hope, then, that my opening words on this matter have been reasonable.

[4] I am well aware, men of Athens, that you will certainly have

---

second to their general conduct; at the latter stage it was open to anyone to lodge a complaint. Given the role of litigation in Athenian politics, Aeschines' claim is surprising, but given his high profile at the time (which would make it difficult to lie about something so obvious), it may well be true. It could be (Harris 1995: 36) that he was constrained by his background, which left him without the network of influential supporters on which a wealthy Athenian could draw. The penalties for conspicuous failure in public actions (defined as failure to obtain 20% of the votes cast) included a fine of 1,000 drachmas, which might deter a man with limited resources. This does not mean that Aeschines had not been involved in any political litigation, since (as my colleague Lene Rubinstein notes) he could have acted as a supporting speaker.

[5] The Greek uses the verb *sykophantein,* derived from the noun *sykophantēs.* The word is so difficult to translate that it is frequently transliterated as "sykophant." It is used of individuals who exploit the legal system unfairly for advantage or profit, by bringing accusations where the law offered rewards, by bringing suits designed to extract damages, by blackmailing the innocent (or the guilty) with the threat of prosecution, or by hiring themselves out as prosecutors (for instance, to intimidate or discredit a man's enemy). The word is often thrown around rather vaguely in courtroom contexts.

[6] Greek *dokimasia;* for the *dokimasia tōn rhētorōn,* see Speech Introduction.

heard already from others what I am going to say at the outset; but I think it appropriate that I, too, should now make the same statement to you. It is agreed that there are three kinds of constitution in the whole world, dictatorship (*tyrannis*), oligarchy, and democracy,[7] and dictatorships and oligarchies are governed by the temperament of those in power, but democratic cities are governed by the established laws. [5] You are aware, men of Athens, that in a democracy the persons of citizens and the constitution are protected by the laws, while dictators and oligarchs are protected by distrust and armed guards. Oligarchs and all who run a constitution based on inequality must be on guard against people who attempt to overthrow the constitution by force; but you, and all who have a constitution based on equality and law, must watch out for people whose words and way of life contravene the laws. For your real strength is when you are ruled by law and are not subverted by men who break them. [6] My own belief is that whenever we pass laws, our concern should be how to make laws that are good and advantageous for our constitution, and once we have passed them, we should obey the laws in existence and punish those who disobey, if the city is to flourish.

Consider, men of Athens, how great a concern for decency was shown by that ancient legislator Solon,[8] and Draco, and the other legislators of that period. [7] First of all they legislated for the decency of our children, and they laid down explicitly how the freeborn boy should live and how he should be brought up, then secondly

---

[7] For the (commonplace) tripartite division of constitutions, cf. e.g., Herodotus 3.80–82; Plato *Republic* books 8–9; it is found as early as Pindar in the 470s (*Pyth.* 2.85–86).

[8] At the turn of the sixth century B.C., Athens was approaching a crisis, as aristocratic abuses led to conflict between rich and poor. Solon was chosen to mediate. Since his legal and constitutional changes were the first of a prolonged series of adjustments to the political power ratio that culminated in the full democracy of the fifth and fourth centuries, he was regarded as the father of Athenian democracy. Draco was the first to codify the Athenian laws late in the seventh century. His law code was superseded by that of Solon, who allegedly retained only the homicide laws of Draco; later sources (on uncertain authority) treat the Draconian code as notorious for its cruelty, whence the term "draconian." Cf. Series Introduction, pp. xxv–xxvi.

for young men and thirdly for the other age groups in succession, not only for private citizens but also for public speakers. They wrote these laws down and entrusted them to your care, making you their guardians.

[8] What I want to do now is to use the same order in my own speech to you as the legislator uses in the law. First of all I shall describe the laws that are laid down for the good conduct of your children, then secondly those for the young men, and thirdly in succession the laws for the other age groups, not only for private citizens but also for public speakers. In this way, I think, my argument will be easiest to grasp. At the same time, men of Athens, I also want first to give you a preliminary account of the city's laws, and then after that to examine Timarchus' character; for you will find that his way of life has been contrary to all the laws.

[9] To start with, in the case of teachers,[9] into whose care of necessity we hand our children, for whom decency means a livelihood and the opposite means poverty, even so the legislator was clearly suspicious, and he lays down explicitly the time of day when a free boy should go to school, then how many other children should go there with him,[10] and the time he should leave. [10] He forbids the teachers to open the schools and the athletic trainers to open the wrestling schools before the sun is up and instructs them to shut them before sunset. He holds seclusion and darkness in particular suspicion. As to the young pupils, he prescribes who they should be and what ages, and the official who is to be responsible for them, and provides for the oversight of slave attendants (*paidagogoi*)[11] and the celebration of the festival of the Muses in the schools and of Hermes in the wrestling schools, and finally for the company kept by the boys at school and

---

[9] It is to be borne in mind that there was no state provision for schooling in Athens; the state merely set rules within which such establishments must operate.

[10] If Aeschines is presenting the legal situation accurately, presumably the aim is to ensure that numbers (which the teachers have a financial incentive to maximize) are kept to a level at which pupils can be properly supervised.

[11] Any Athenian boy whose parents could afford it would be accompanied everywhere by a slave attendant (*paidagogos*), who would provide physical protection and prevent admirers from becoming a nuisance or compromising the boy's reputation.

the circular dances.¹² [11] For he instructs that the chorus producer,¹³ who will be spending his own money for you, should be over forty years of age when he undertakes this task, so that he is already at the age of greatest self-control when he is in the company of your sons.

Now the clerk will read out these laws to you, to show you that the legislator believed that a boy who had been brought up properly would be a useful citizen when he reached manhood. But when the individual's nature at the outset gets a corrupt start in its education, he thought that badly brought up boys would become the sort of citizens that Timarchus here is. Read these laws to them.

[12] [LAWS] *The teachers of the boys are not to open the schools before sunrise and are to close them before sunset. People older than the boys are not to enter while the boys are inside, except for the teacher's son or brother or daughter's husband. If anyone enters in defiance of this rule, he is to be punished with death. And the gymnasium masters are not to allow anyone who has reached manhood to participate in the Hermaea with them. If he so permits and does not exclude them from the gymnasium, the gymnasium master is to be liable under the law dealing with the corruption of the freeborn. The chorus producers appointed by the people are to be over forty years of age.*¹⁴

---

¹²The *kyklios choros* or circular dance was the dithyramb in honor of Dionysus. There were dithyrambic contests (organized on a tribal basis) both for men and for boys at a number of Athenian festivals.

¹³Greek *chorēgos*. The role of *chorēgos* was part of the liturgy (*leitourgia*) system imposed on rich Athenians. Except for war levies, the Athenians avoided direct taxation; under the liturgy system, property taxation involved a combination of expenditure and service. The role of *chorēgos* involved organizing and paying for the training of a chorus either for the dithyrambic contests (as here) or for the dramatic competitions. See further Series Introduction, p. xxiii.

¹⁴This is the only speech by Aeschines for which the manuscripts preserve what purport to be the documents cited in the trial. Unfortunately, all are later forgeries (as often, though not invariably, in the texts of the orators); they were probably intended not to deceive but to give an impression of what the original might have looked like. In the present case, though Aeschines asks the clerk of the court (1.11) to read out several laws, the composer has cobbled together a single law combining provisions from different areas (schools, choral training), relying wherever possible on the author's own words in the context.

[13] Now after this, men of Athens, he legislates for offenses that, though they are grave, still (I think) occur in the city. For it was the fact that some unseemly acts actually took place that led the men of old to lay down the laws. Anyway, the law states explicitly that if any father or brother or uncle or anyone at all in the position of guardian hires a boy out as a prostitute—it does not allow an indictment (*graphē*) to be brought against the boy in person but against the man who hired him out and the man who paid for him, the former because he hired him out and the latter, it says, because he hired him. And it has made the penalties the same for each of them, and it adds that any boy who has been hired out for prostitution is not obliged on reaching maturity to keep his father or provide him with a home, though on the father's death he is to bury him and to carry out the other customary rites. [14] Observe how fair this is, men of Athens. In life the law deprives him of the advantages of parenthood, as he deprived his son of the right of free speech,[15] while after death, when the recipient cannot perceive the benefit conferred on him but it is the law and religion that receive the honor, finally it instructs the son to bury his father and to perform the other customary rites.

What other law did he lay down to protect your children? The law against procuring, to which he attached the most severe penalties, if anyone procures for prostitution a free boy or woman.

[15] What other law? The law of outrage (*hybris*),[16] which sums up in a single statement all such acts. In this law is written explicitly that if anyone commits outrage against a boy (and anyone who hires him commits outrage, I imagine) or man or woman, whether free or slave, or if he does anything contrary to law to any of these, it has allowed

---

[15] I.e., the right to address the Assembly, the Council, or the courts.

[16] The Athenian law of *hybris* has generated much debate in the recent past. The word itself is difficult to pin down but seems to designate both a state of mind combining overconfidence and arrogance, and conduct (often but not necessarily violent) either designed to humiliate others or showing reckless contempt for the rights and status of others. As an offense under the laws, *hybris* overlaps with crimes of violence (assault, rape), but scholars are not agreed on the degree to which the law might be applied to nonviolent conduct. Aeschines argues that hiring a free boy is *hybris,* but the addition of "I imagine" betrays an attempt at persuasive definition.

for an indictment (*graphē*) for outrage and prescribed assessment[17] of the penalty he is to suffer or pay. Read out the law.[18]

[16] [LAW] *If any Athenian commits outrage against a free boy, the boy's guardian is to bring an indictment before the Thesmothetae, on which he is to specify the penalty assessed. Anyone convicted by the court is to be handed over to the Eleven and put to death the same day. If anyone is condemned to pay a fine, he is to pay it within eleven days of the trial, if he is unable to pay it immediately. He is to be imprisoned until he has paid. Those who commit offenses against the persons of slaves are also to be liable to these charges.*

[17] It may be that someone at first hearing might wonder why on earth this term, slaves, was added in the law of outrage.[19] But if you consider it, men of Athens, you will find that it is the best provision of all. For the legislator was not concerned about slaves; but because he wanted to accustom you to keep far away from outrage on free persons, he added the prohibition against committing outrage even against slaves. Quite simply, he thought that in a democracy, the man who commits outrage against anyone at all was not fit to share the rights of citizenship. [18] Please remember this, too, men of Athens, that at this point the legislator is not yet addressing the boy in person

---

[17] For some offenses Athenian laws laid down specific penalties (the term for such a case was *agōn atimētos*, "non-assessed action"). In other cases the penalty was decided by the jurors (this type was termed *agōn timētos*, "assessed action"). In such cases each party proposed a penalty, and it was for the jurors to choose between the competing proposals. We have a surviving (and notorious) example in Plato's *Apology* 35e–42.

[18] Again the document is spurious; it contains garbled details (such as the boy's guardian as prosecutor in a public action where the prosecution should be explicitly open to anyone, the fluctuation in the conception of the penalty) and conflicts with the (more plausible) text of the law offered at Demosthenes 21.47 (though the authenticity of this, too, is contested).

[19] Demosthenes (21.48–49) also stresses the paradoxical inclusion of slaves under *hybris* law. Since the concept of *hybris* is closely connected with Athenian views on status and honor, this provision is surprising. Todd (1993) explains this element as reflecting a degree of residual status for slaves. More probably it is a protection of owners' rights.

but those connected with the boy—father, brother, guardian, teachers, in sum those responsible for him. But once he is entered in the deme register[20] and knows the city's laws and is now able to determine right and wrong, the legislator from now on addresses nobody else but at this point the individual himself, Timarchus. [19] And what does he say? If any Athenian (he says) prostitutes himself, he is not to have the right to serve as one of the nine archons (the reason being, I think, that these officials wear a sacred wreath), nor to undertake any priesthood, since his body is quite unclean; and let him not serve (he says) as advocate[21] for the state or hold any office ever, whether at home or abroad, whether selected by lot or elected by a vote;[22] [20] let him not serve as herald, nor as envoy (nor let him bring to trial people that have served as envoys, nor let him act as a sykophant[23] for pay), nor let him voice any opinion in the Council or the Assembly (not even if he is the cleverest speaker in Athens). If anyone acts against these provisions, he has allowed for indictments (*graphai*) for prostitution and imposed the most severe penalties. Read this law out to them as well, to make you aware of the noble and decent character of the established laws, against which Timarchus has dared to address the Assembly, a man whose way of life is known to you all.

---

[20] The deme (which might be either a village or a town district) was the smallest political unit in Attica. Membership in the deme was hereditary on the male side, but in the classical period it need not coincide with residence. At the age of eighteen an Athenian male obtained full citizen rights. He was subjected to a scrutiny (*dokimasia*) by the deme to check his age and birth qualifications, and once he had passed his name was inscribed on the deme register (*lēxiarchikon grammateion*).

[21] Greek *syndikein,* from *syndikos,* literally "supporter in a suit." The term here refers to individuals elected to present the prosecution in certain political cases.

[22] Offices that were held to be within the competence of an intelligent adult male were filled by lot. In the case of offices for which specific skills or experience were required, election was by show of hands (not secret ballot, which was rare in the Assembly).

[23] For the *sykophantēs,* see 1.1n. Aeschines' use of documents (perhaps influenced by his years as a public clerk reading out documents) is astute and would merit further study. Here he mixes quotation from the law with (pejorative) addition and interpretation.

[21] [LAW] *If any Athenian has prostituted himself, he is not to have the right to become one of the nine archons or to undertake any priesthood or to serve as advocate for the people or to hold any office whatsoever, whether at home or abroad, whether selected by lot or elected by vote; nor is he to be sent out as herald, or to voice an opinion, or to enter the public temples or to wear a garland when the citizens collectively are wearing garlands, or to enter within the purified area of the Agora.*[24] *If anyone acts in defiance of these restrictions when convicted of prostitution, he is to be punished with death.*[25]

[22] This was the law he passed to deal with young men who commit reckless offenses against their own bodies, while the ones he read to you a little earlier deal with boys; and the ones I am now about to describe deal with the rest of the Athenians. Having finished with the previous laws, the legislator turned his attention[26] to the way in which we should deliberate collectively in the Assembly about matters of the greatest importance. Where, then, does he begin? "The laws on discipline," he says. He began with morality, in the belief that the best-governed city will be the one with the most orderly conduct. [23] So how does he instruct the Chairmen (*proedroi*)[27] to conduct business? When the purifying victim[28] has been carried around and the herald

---

[24] The Greek says literally "pass within the containers of sprinkling water (perirrhanteria)," i.e., the area demarcated by the containers of lustral water for purification purposes situated (according to the ancient commentators) at the entrance to the Agora, which was the political and religious center of the city.

[25] The document contains no detail independent of the preceding text (it is also silent on the important issue of legal procedure) and is probably a forgery.

[26] Aeschines presents as a single coordinated process a whole range of laws that were probably the products of different periods.

[27] The business of the popular Assembly was managed by the Council of Five Hundred (*boulē*). For much of the fourth century, meetings both of the Council and of the Assembly were chaired by a body of nine *proedroi* selected on the day of the meeting from within the Council (Aristotle *Constitution of Athens* 44.2), one from each tribal contingent, except the one serving as *prytaneis* (see 2.53n).

[28] Pollution and purification played a major role in Greek religion. Ritual pollution could be acquired in a whole range of ways, varying from the criminal (such as homicide) to unavoidable contact with contaminating agents (such as the dead or childbirth) that are neither criminal nor immoral in themselves. Pollution was

has pronounced the traditional prayers, the legislator instructs the Chairmen to deal first with voting on matters of traditional religion, heralds, embassies, and secular matters, and then the herald puts the question: "Who wishes to speak, of those who are over the age of fifty?" And only when these have all spoken does he invite any other Athenian who wishes, and has the right,[29] to speak. [24] Observe how fair this is, men of Athens. The legislator was not unaware, I think, that older men are at the peak of their powers of reasoning, and their daring has already begun to diminish because of their experience of the world. Because he wanted to make it a habitual and compulsory practice for the men with the best judgment to speak on public business, since he could not address each one of them by name, he includes them under the title of the whole age group and invites them to the platform and encourages them to address the people. At the same time, he teaches the younger men to show respect for their elders and to take second place to them in all matters, and to honor the age to which all of us will come, if we are spared. [25] And those public speakers of old, Pericles and Themistocles and Aristides (who bore a title quite unlike that of this man Timarchus—he was known as "the just"[30]) were so decent that in their day this habit that we all practice

---

contagious, and ritual uncleanness could adversely affect the outcome of both religious and secular activity. Accordingly, public meetings were preceded by a purification involving the sacrifice of a victim and the sprinkling of the periphery with its blood.

[29] This would exclude people who qualified for Athenian citizenship by birth but had been deprived of their citizen rights; the term for such a person was *atimos,* literally "without honor(s)."

[30] The nineteenth-century scholar Scheibe deleted "he was known as 'the just'"; the words "who bore . . . 'the just'" occur in a different order at 3.181, and the phrase "[who was] known as 'the just'" at 2.23. The phrase at 2.23 looks like an intrusive explanatory note, and I have deleted accordingly. I have tentatively left the text unchanged at 1.25 and 3.181. Though the style in both cases would become more terse if the phrase were deleted, Aeschines is not always the most elegant of stylists. The repetition need cause no anxiety, in view of Aeschines' tendency to repeat not only ideas but also wording. Aristides was prominent enough in the 480s to be ostracized (exiled for ten years) in 482. He was recalled in the shadow of the Persian invasion of 480 and served with distinction at Salamis in 479. In 478/7 Athens took the lead in forming the Delian League, a confedera-

nowadays, of speaking with the hand outside the clothing, was considered something brash, and they avoided doing it. And I think I can offer you convincing and solid evidence of this fact. I am certain that you have all sailed to Salamis and have viewed the statue of Solon,[31] and you yourselves could bear witness that Solon stands in the Agora on Salamis with his hand inside his robe. This, men of Athens, is a representation and a reminder of the posture that Solon in person used to adopt when he spoke to the Athenian people.

[26] Now observe, men of Athens, the enormous difference between Solon and those great men whom I mentioned a little earlier in my speech and Timarchus. While they for their part thought it shameful to speak with their hand outside their robe, this man here, not some time ago but just the other day, threw off his robe and cavorted like a pancratiast[32] in the Assembly, stripped, in such a vile and shameful physical condition on account of drunkenness and other abuses that decent men covered their faces out of shame for the city, that we take advice from people like this. [27] With this in mind, the legislator explicitly declared who should address the people and who should not speak in the Assembly. He does not expel a man from the platform if his ancestors have not served as generals, nor if he works at some trade to provide for the necessities of life; indeed, he especially welcomes these men, and this is why he repeatedly asks: "Who wishes to speak?"

[28] Which men, then, did he think should not speak? People who have lived a life of shame—these are the ones he does not allow to address the people. And where does he state this? When he says: "The scrutiny of public speakers: if anyone who beats his father or mother

---

tion of Greek states, to pursue the war against Persia and free the Greek cities under Persian rule. Aristides was responsible for fixing the tribute for the various states; his sobriquet reflects the fairness with which he carried out the task.

[31] Demosthenes sneeringly replies in 343 that the statue was a modern one and had no bearing on the actual posture of Solon (19.251–252). From Demosthenes' account, it is clear that Aeschines acted out the posture of the statue (cf. 3.166n). The same charge of breaking with traditions of restraint in public speaking lodged here was already made 80 years earlier against the fifth-century politician Cleon and reflects less actual developments than the tendency to idealize (and exploit) the past.

[32] Cf. 1.33n.

or does not keep them or provide a home³³ speaks in the Assembly"; this man he does not allow to speak. A fine rule, by Zeus, in my personal opinion. Why? Because if anyone mistreats the ones he should honor on a level with the gods, what sort of treatment, says the legislator, will people unconnected with him, and indeed the city as a whole, receive from him? [29] And who are the next ones he forbids to speak? "Or anyone," he says, "who has not performed all the military service he is ordered to, or has thrown away his shield,"³⁴ and rightly. Why exactly? Mister, when you do not take up arms for the city or because of cowardice cannot protect it, do not presume to give it advice. Who are the third group he addresses? "Or anyone who has been a prostitute," he says, "or has sold himself."³⁵ For the man who has willfully sold his own body would, he thought, casually sell out the interests of the city. [30] Who are the fourth group he addresses? "Or anyone who has squandered his paternal estate," he says, "or any other property he has inherited."³⁶ For he considered that the man who has mismanaged his private household would treat the city's interests in much the same way; and the legislator could not conceive

---

³³Athenian laws gave parents the right to nurture in old age and protection from violence at the hands of their children. The rights were covered by a public action so that anyone could intervene; the penalty for the convicted offspring was loss of citizen rights.

³⁴The penalty for failure to serve or desertion in battle was loss of citizen rights. The offense was covered by a public action (*graphē*), and the case was judged by soldiers who had served on the campaign, with the military officers presiding.

³⁵The Greek uses two distinct verbs, *porneuesthai,* "to work as a prostitute" (from *pornos/pornē,* "male/female prostitute"), and *hetairein,* literally "be companion (to)." The distinction suggested below (1.51) between the former as promiscuous sex for pay and the latter as denoting the position of a financially dependent passive homosexual partner is supported by other sources, though the difference appears to have had no juridical significance.

³⁶That is, from any other branch of the family. The hostility toward the squandering of inherited property reflects the recognition (attenuated but persisting in the classical period) of the solidarity of the family, that is, the family as a unit that subsumes and transcends its individual members. Thus there were limits on disposing of property by will and disinheriting legitimate sons. There is evidence that a man had more freedom to dispose of acquired wealth.

that the same individual could be worthless in private life and useful to the public good, nor did he believe that a public speaker should come to the platform fully prepared in his words and not in his life. [31] He believed that statements from a good and decent man, even when expressed in a clumsy or simple way, would be of advantage to the hearers, while those from an unprincipled man who had treated his own body with contempt and disgracefully squandered his ancestral property would not benefit the hearers even when expressed with great eloquence. [32] These, then, are the men he bars from the platform; these are the ones he forbids to address the people. And if anyone in defiance of these rules does not just speak but plays the sykophant and behaves unscrupulously, and the city can no longer tolerate such a man, "Let any Athenian who wishes and has the right," he says, "declare a scrutiny," and at that point he bids you to decide the case in court. And it is under this law that I have now come before you.

[33] Now these regulations have long been law. But you added another new law after the splendid pancratium[37] this man staged in the Assembly, in utter shame at the incident: that at each Assembly a tribe[38] should be selected by lot to preside over the platform.[39] And what did the proposer of the law order? He instructs the members of the tribe to sit as protectors of the law and the democratic constitution on the ground that, unless we summon help from some source against men who have lived like this, we shall not be able to debate even the most serious matters. [34] It is useless, men of Athens, to attempt to drive people of this sort from the platform by shouting them down; they are without shame. We must use punishments to change their ways; this is the only way to make them bearable.

Now he will read out to you the laws established to ensure the orderly conduct of public speakers. For the law on the presiding role

---

[37] The pancratium was a particularly brutal mixture of boxing and wrestling. The association of the law with Timarchus' (alleged) conduct is not demonstrated.

[38] In the classical period there were ten Athenian tribes, each made up of demes (1.18n) from different parts of Attica; they were created by Cleisthenes at the close of the sixth century to replace the old four tribes that Athens shared with the other Ionian Greeks.

[39] That is, the speaker's platform on the Pnyx where the Assembly met.

of the tribes has been indicted as inexpedient[40] by a coalition consisting of this Timarchus and other speakers of the same sort, to free them to live and speak just as they choose.

[35] [LAWS] *If any public speaker addresses the Council or the Assembly other than on the subject that is under discussion, or does not speak on each issue separately, or speaks twice on the same subject on the same day, or speaks abusively or slanders anyone, or heckles, or stands up when business is being conducted and speaks on a subject that is not part of the proceedings, or urges on others, or assaults the Chairman, once the Assembly or Council is adjourned, the Chairmen (proedroi) are empowered to register a fine of up to fifty drachmas for each offense and pass the record to the Collectors. If he deserves a more severe punishment, they are to impose a fine of up to fifty drachmas and refer the matter to the Council or the next Assembly. When the summonses are lodged, the relevant body is to judge the case, and if he is convicted by secret ballot, the Chairmen are to record his name for the Collectors.*[41]

[36] You have heard the laws, men of Athens, and I have no doubt that you consider them sound. But whether these laws are to be of use or not depends on you. If you punish the guilty, your laws will be sound and valid, but if you let them go, the laws will still be sound but no longer valid.

[37] But as I proposed at the beginning of my speech, now that I have spoken about the laws, I want to turn to the examination of Timarchus' way of life, so you will realize how much it differs from

---

[40] In the fourth century, there were two legal procedures for attacking measures placed before the Assembly. Decrees were exposed to the *graphē paranomōn*, "indictment for illegality/illegal legislation" (on the ground that in form or content they breached an existing law), laws to the *graphē nomon mē epitēdeion theinai*, "indictment for having made an inexpedient/disadvantageous law." If the action was brought within a year, the target was the proposer of the suspect legislation; after that period, the legislation could be indicted and repealed, but the proposer was no longer personally liable. As we can see from 3.4, the law survived this attack.

[41] The content of this law is more plausible than the rest of the documents inserted in the speech. It may simply be a more felicitous forgery, though it may conceivably contain details derived from a reliable source.

your laws. And I ask you, men of Athens, to pardon me if, when forced to speak about activities that by their nature are distasteful but have actually been practiced by this man, I am induced to use any expression that resembles Timarchus' actions. [38] It would not be fair for you to criticize me, if in my desire to inform you I were to use rather plain language, but rather criticize this man, if he has actually led such a life that anyone describing his behavior is unable to say what he wants to say without using expressions of this sort. But I shall avoid doing so to the very best of my ability.[42]

[39] Observe, men of Athens, how reasonable I shall be in dealing with this man Timarchus. Any abuses he committed against his own body while still a boy I leave out of account. Let it be void, like events under the Thirty[43] or before Euclides,[44] or any other official time limit of this sort that has been laid down. But the acts he has committed since reaching the age of reason and as a young man and in full knowledge of the laws, these I shall make the subject of my accusations, and I urge you to take them seriously.

[40] Now this man first of all, as soon as he ceased to be a child, settled in the Piraeus in the establishment of the doctor Euthydicus, ostensibly to learn the profession but in reality because he had determined to sell himself, as events themselves showed. I pass over voluntarily all the merchants or other foreigners or our fellow citizens who had the use of his body during that period, so that nobody can say

---

[42] Aeschines established at the outset a persona based on moderation and decency that operates throughout the speech (cf., e.g., 1.39). Here and elsewhere the speaker both dissociates himself from the salacious material he has (of his own volition) decided to narrate and frees himself from the need to provide detail.

[43] In the wake of the Athenian defeat of 404 in the Peloponnesian War, an oligarchic regime run by thirty men was set up in Athens with Spartan support. After a promising start, it rapidly degenerated into venality and brutality. In the following year, a group of exiles seized Phyle on the border between Attica and Boeotia as a base and, after taking the Piraeus, overthrew the oligarchy. The restored democracy declared a general amnesty (with specific exceptions) for acts committed under the oligarchy.

[44] A revision of the law code was begun in the last decade of the fifth century and was completed after the restoration of the democracy (preceding note). The revised code came into effect in the archonship of Euclides (403/2) and in the case of new provisions was not retroactive.

that I am dwelling excessively on every detail. I shall confine my account to the men in whose house he has lived, bringing shame on his own body and the city, earning a living from the very practice that the law forbids a man to engage in, or forfeit the right to address the people.

[41] There is a man named Misgolas son of Naucrates of Collytus,[45] men of Athens, a man who in other respects is decent and above criticism but who has a phenomenal passion for this activity and is always in the habit of having male singers and lyre-players[46] in his company. I say this not to indulge in low gossip but so you will recognize who he is.[47] This man, perceiving the reason for Timarchus' spending his time at the doctor's house, paid a sum of money in advance and moved Timarchus and set him up in his own house, a fine figure of a man, young and unprincipled and ready for the acts that Misgolas was eager to perform, and Timarchus to have done to him. [42] Timarchus had no inhibition but submitted to it, though he did not lack the resources for all reasonable needs. For his father had left him a very large estate, which he had squandered, as I shall show later in my speech. No, he did all this as a slave to the most disgraceful pleasures, gluttony and expensive eating and flute-girls and courtesans[48] and dice and the other activities that should never have control of a

---

[45] The formal nomenclature of an Athenian citizen was given name, patronymic, and deme (here Collytus). Misgolas' passion for handsome young men and particularly his predilection for lyre-players were sufficiently notorious to make him a frequent target for comic ridicule (Athenaeus 8.339a–c, citing the comic poets Alexis, Antiphanes, and Timocles).

[46] Presumably Aeschines has in mind entertainers who performed at symposia; certainly in the case of females in this category, the borderline between musician and prostitute was fluid.

[47] Less probably "what he's like." The point is disingenuous.

[48] The Greek term *hetaira* is difficult to render. It is used of the common prostitute (for which the more usual term was *pornē*) but also of the cultivated and expensive females whose skills encompassed far more than sex (for which the now outmoded word "courtesan" is the nearest modern equivalent). The objection to spending money on courtesans derives less from disapproval of extramarital sex by males than from hostility toward squandering money and its consequences. The combination of homosexual and heterosexual activity strikes the modern reader as surprising but is not unusual for classical Greece.

decent and freeborn man. But this vile man felt no shame in abandoning his father's house and living with Misgolas, a man who was not a friend of his father nor one of his own age group nor a guardian, no, a man who was unconnected and older than himself, a man without restraint in such activity, when he himself was young and handsome.

[43] Of the many ridiculous acts of Timarchus in that period, there is one that I want to recount to you. It was during the procession for the City Dionysia, and Misgolas, the man who had taken him up, and Phaedrus[49] son of Callias of Sphettus were both taking part in the procession. This man Timarchus had agreed with them that he would join them in the procession, and they were busy with their preparations; but Timarchus had not returned. Angry at this, Misgolas went in search of him with Phaedrus; acting on information received, they found him dining in a lodging house with some foreign guests. Misgolas and Phaedrus threatened the foreigners and ordered them to come with them at once to the prison for corrupting a free youth; the foreigners took fright and ran off, leaving everything behind.[50]

[44] The truth of this story is known to everyone who was familiar with Misgolas and Timarchus at that time. And I find it very gratifying that my dispute is with a man who is not unknown to you, and is known for precisely the practice on which you will be casting your vote. For in a case that concerns unknown individuals, it is perhaps incumbent on the prosecutor to offer explicit proof, but where the facts are generally agreed, it is no great task in my view to act as prosecutor; for he needs only to remind his hearers. [45] Now although the matter is generally agreed, since we are in a lawcourt, what I have done is draft a deposition for Misgolas,[51] one that is accurate but not gross,

---

[49] A member of a propertied family and an active politician and general. He served as general in 347/6, in the late 330s, and finally in the Lamian War in 323, over two decades after the present trial.

[50] The allegation is never proved, since Aeschines evidently anticipates that Misgolas will refuse to testify.

[51] In the fifth century, witnesses deposed in person. Early in the fourth century, a system of written depositions was introduced. The litigant drafted the deposition for the witnesses, who merely affirmed that they accepted responsibility for the content of the statement (see 1.46n) after it was read out by the clerk of the court.

or so I believe. The actual terms for the acts he committed on this man are not included, nor have I written down anything that renders a witness admitting the truth subject to punishment under the laws;[52] what I have written is recognizable to you but without risk to the witness or disgrace.

[46] Now if Misgolas is prepared to come forward here and testify to the truth, he will be doing what is right. But if he would rather ignore the summons[53] than testify to the truth, then you can see the whole business plainly. For if the active partner is to feel ashamed and prefer to pay 1,000 drachmas to the Treasury to avoid showing his face to you, while the passive partner is to speak in the Assembly, it was a wise legislator who barred people as vile as this from the platform.[54] [47] But if he obeys the formal summons but takes the most shameless course, which is to deny the truth on oath, with the intention of showing his gratitude to Timarchus and at the same time demonstrating to others that he knows how to keep such activities secret, firstly he will be harming himself, and secondly he will achieve nothing.[55] I have drafted another deposition for the people who know that this man Timarchus abandoned his father's house and lived with Misgolas, though the task I am attempting is, I think, a difficult one. For I must offer as witnesses neither my own friends nor their enemies, nor

---

[52] The statement is based on Aeschines' earlier tendentious definition of *hybris* (1.15).

[53] A witness had only limited freedom of action; he could either affirm the testimony, or, if he objected to the deposition attributed to him, he could take an oath of disclaimer (*exōmosia*) to the effect that he had not been present at the incident in question or did not know that the facts were as stated. If he refused to do either, he was subject to a procedure called *klēteusis* (here "summons"), which appears to have involved formal summons to testify by a herald, with a penalty of 1,000 drachmas for failure to respond.

[54] Aeschines astutely compensates for his lack of testimony by making Misgolas' refusal to confirm his account a tacit confirmation. Cf. 1.71–73, which make clear that the lack of evidence will be seized on by the defense, and where again Aeschines blusters.

[55] The passage shows that there was no formal penalty attaching to the (alleged) false oath of disclaimer, unlike false testimony, for which a litigant could sue his opponent's witnesses.

people who know neither of us, but their friends.[56] [48] But if it transpires that they dissuade these witnesses from testifying (I don't think they will, not all of them anyway), this at least they will never be able to do, eradicate the truth, nor the general report in the city about Timarchus; I did not create this for him, he did it for himself. For the decent man's life should be so clean that it does not allow even the suspicion of blameworthy conduct.

[49] I want to say something else in advance, in case Misgolas obeys the laws and your authority. There are men who by their nature differ from others in their physical appearance as far as age is concerned. There are some men who, though young, appear mature and older, while others, though old when one counts the years, seem positively young. Misgolas is one of these. He is in fact a contemporary of mine and was an ephebe[57] with me; we are both in our forty-fifth year.[58]

---

[56] Witnesses tended to be friends of the litigant (it was normal for anyone approaching matters that might involve subsequent litigation to take friends as witnesses) or neutral observers; in extreme cases (as here and Dem. 57.14), a litigant might have to rely on hostile witnesses. Witnesses in Athens were often as much supporters as testifiers to fact. One modern view, not shared by the present writer, would place the emphasis solely or predominantly on the role as supporter.

[57] The *ephebeia,* consisting of two years' military service from the age of eighteen, was probably an old institution. It seems to have been fairly loosely administered until it was reorganized along more rigid lines in the wake of the defeat at Chaeronea in 338.

[58] The manuscript text presents a problem. Misgolas is by implication older than Timarchus (he is financially independent and controls his own household, into which he brings the young Timarchus). Yet the statement at 1.109 that Timarchus was on the Council in 361/0, a post for which the minimum age was 30, indicates that he was born in 391/0 at the latest, which would make him a contemporary of Aeschines and therefore Misgolas. The emendation "fifty-fourth year" (*tetarton kai pentēkoston* for *pempton kai tettarakoston*) has been proposed. The manuscript text can be retained if we assume that Aeschines is lying about the relationship between Misgolas and Timarchus (see Harris 1988): 211–214). Certainly his advance warning here indicates that he anticipates audience skepticism that Misgolas can really be older than Timarchus. The interval between this statement and 1.109 would prevent Aeschines' arithmetic coming under undesirable scrutiny. Misgolas' notoriety (see 1.41n) made him a useful element in Aeschines' narrative, since his presence would both enhance the plausibility of Aeschines'

And I myself have all these grey hairs that you see, but he doesn't. Why do I give this advance warning? So that when you suddenly see him you will not be surprised and mentally respond: "Heracles! He is not much older than Timarchus!" For it is a fact both that his appearance is naturally like this and that Timarchus was already a youth when Misgolas had relations with him.

[50] But to delay no longer, first of all call the witnesses who know that this man Timarchus lived in Misgolas' house, then read out the deposition of Phaedrus, and finally take the deposition for Misgolas himself, just in case he agrees to attest the truth out of fear of the gods and shame in front of the people who know the facts, the rest of the citizen body and you the jurors.

[DEPOSITIONS] *Misgolas son of Nikias of Piraeus testifies as follows. Timarchus, who once stayed at the establishment of the doctor Euthydicus, was associated with me, and from my earlier acquaintance with him to the present I have not ceased to hold him in high regard.*[59]

[51] Now, men of Athens, if this man Timarchus had stayed with Misgolas and had not gone to live with anyone else, his conduct would have been more decent, if indeed there is any decency in such behavior, and I would have hesitated to charge him with anything beyond the frank term used by the legislator, that is, only with having been a kept lover. For I think that this is exactly the charge for anyone who engages in this activity with a single partner but does so for pay. [52] But if, ignoring these wild men, Cedonides and Autoclides and Thersander, into whose houses he has been taken to live, I remind you of the facts and demonstrate that he has earned his living with his body not only at the home of Misgolas but also in the house of another and then another, and that he went from this one to yet another, then it will be clear that he has not only been a kept lover but (and by Dionysus!—I don't think I can evade the issue all day) has actually

---

account and taint Timarchus by association; the need to finesse the age problem was evidently a price worth paying.

[59] Forgery is betrayed by the presence of a single deposition where the speech calls for several, by the false demotic and patronymic, and by the garbled format; written depositions in Athenian courts were made in the third person ("X attests/XX attest that, etc.").

prostituted himself. For I think that this is exactly the charge for anyone who engages in this activity casually with many partners for pay.

[53] Now when Misgolas tired of the expense and dismissed Timarchus from his house, Anticles[60] the son of Callias of Euonymon
next took him up. Anticles is away in Samos as one of the colonists;[61]
but I shall tell you what happened after that. When this Timarchus
left Anticles and Misgolas, he did not reflect on his conduct or turn
to better ways but spent his days at the gaming house where the gambling board is set up and people engage in cock fighting and dice
playing. I imagine that some of you have already seen the place or, if
not, have at least heard of it. [54] One of the people who pass their
time there is a man called Pittalacus; this person is a public slave of
the city.[62] Now Pittalacus, who was financially well-off and had seen
Timarchus passing his time there, took him up and kept him at his
house. And this vile creature was not bothered even by this, that he
was about to shame himself with a person who was a public slave of
the city; no, his only concern was to get a backer (*chorēgos*)[63] to finance his vile habits, while to questions of decency or disgrace he gave
not a moment's thought. [55] Now the abuses and outrages that I have
heard were committed on the person of Timarchus by this individual

---

[60] Presumably son of the Callias of Euonymon attested by an inscription as a
treasurer of the Athenian empire in 410/9.

[61] In 365 Timotheus captured Samos from Persia. The island was treated not
as an Athenian ally but as an Athenian possession, and Athenian colonists ("cler-
uchs," *klērouchoi*) were sent out. Anticles' absence is convenient for Aeschines,
since it provides an excuse for his lack of evidence for this stage in Timarchus'
career.

[62] If Aeschines is telling the truth about Pittalacus' status, this incident is very
revealing for the role, economic potential, and status of public slaves. Since they
were themselves property, slaves technically had no possessions (though see 1.97n);
Pittalacus appears to be wealthy and to associate freely with wellborn Athenians.
He is also represented as bringing a suit (1.62); slaves lacked legal personality and
were unable either to bring a suit or to address a court. It has been suggested
plausibly that Aeschines misleads us and that Pittalacus was a freedman (i.e., ex-
slave); the fiction would enable the prosecutor to stir up prejudice against a defendant who was allegedly ready to sell himself even to a slave.

[63] For the *chorēgos* (here metaphorical), see 1.11n.

were such that—in the name of Olympian Zeus!—I could not bring myself to describe them to you. The acts that this man felt no shame to commit in practice are ones that I would rather die than describe clearly in words among you.

But about the same time that this man was living with Pittalacus, Hegesander [64] sailed back to Athens from the Hellespont. I am aware that you have been puzzled for some time at my failure to mention him, so notorious are the events I am about to narrate.

[56] This Hegesander, whom you know better than I, arrived. As it happened, he had at that time sailed to the Hellespont as treasurer to Timomachus of Acharnae, [65] who served as general, and he returned to Athens the beneficiary, it is said, of Timomachus' gullibility, in possession of not less than eighty minas of silver; [66] and in a way he was not the least to blame for Timomachus' ruin. [57] Well-off as he was, and as a regular visitor to the house of Pittalacus, who was a gambling partner of his, he saw Timarchus there for the first time. He was impressed, and his passion was aroused, and he wanted to take him into his own house; he thought, I imagine, that Timarchus' nature closely resembled his own. First of all he spoke to Pittalacus, urging him to let him have Timarchus; and when he could not persuade Pittalacus, he assailed Timarchus here in person. It did not take much argument; he persuaded him instantly. Indeed, when it comes to the actual business, his candor and openness to persuasion [67] are remarkable; for this very reason he should properly be an object of hatred.

[58] After he had left Pittalacus and been taken in by Hegesander, Pittalacus was, I think, distressed at having spent so much money (as

---

[64] A minor politician from a propertied family. For his brother Crobylus, see 1.64n.

[65] Timomachus was one of a number of Athenian commanders of the fleet in the north Aegean who suffered for their failure to contain the Thracian king Cotys in the 360s. He was exiled in 361.

[66] A substantial sum of money (1⅓ talents in a society where three to four talents made a man liable to the liturgy system, for which see 1.11n).

[67] Manuscripts are divided. I have with great deliberation adopted the reading *he akakia kai eupeistia.* The words are said with contempt and refer to Timarchus' readiness to do business frankly and consider all offers. Dilts accepts the alternative *he kakia kai apistia,* "wickedness and infidelity."

he saw it) to no purpose and jealous of what was going on. And he
kept going to the house. And because he was annoying them, observe
the great feat of Hegesander and Timarchus! At one point they and
some others whose names I prefer not to mention got drunk and
[59] burst at night into the house where Pittalacus was living. First of
all they broke his equipment and threw it into the street (throwing
dice and dice cups and other gaming items), and they killed the quails
and cocks[68] on which the wretched man doted, and finally they tied
Pittalacus himself to a pillar and inflicted on him the worst whipping
imaginable for so long that even the neighbors heard the commotion.
[60] Next day, Pittalacus, enraged at the treatment, went robeless into
the Agora and sat as suppliant at the altar of the Mother of the Gods.[69]
A crowd assembled, as usually happens, and Hegesander and Timarchus, in panic that their vile behavior might be announced to the
whole city (the Assembly was about to meet), ran up to the altar,
accompanied by some of their dicing partners. [61] They clustered
around Pittalacus and begged him to leave the altar, maintaining that
the whole incident had been a drunken prank. Timarchus himself
(who was not yet as ugly-looking as nowadays—heavens, no—but
still serviceable) touched the fellow's chin in supplication and said he
would comply with all his wishes. Eventually they induced the fellow
to quit the altar on the understanding that he would receive some
sort of justice. But once he left the Agora they took no further notice
of him. [62] And Pittalacus, angered at the outrageous treatment,
brought a suit against each of them.[70]

When he was bringing these suits, observe the great feat of Hegesander! This fellow had done him no wrong but, quite the reverse, had
been wronged by him; he had no connection with him but was the
public slave of the city. Yet Hegesander seized him as a slave, claiming

---

[68] The reference is to quails and cocks kept for fighting (with attendant
gambling).

[69] The shrine of the Mother of the Gods was on the west side of the Agora,
and the altar referred to here was in front of the shrine. Many people going to the
Pnyx for an Assembly would go through the Agora (either because it was on their
way or to shop en route) and pass the shrine, hence the parenthesis in the next
sentence.

[70] For the slave bringing a suit, see 1.54n.

he was his property. In his wretched situation, Pittalacus encountered a real man and a truly good one. There is a man named Glaucon[71] of Cholarge. This man asserted Pittalacus' freedom.[72] [63] Lawsuits now began. After a period of time they[73] entrusted the decision[74] of the dispute to Diopeithes of Sunium,[75] a member of Hegesander's deme who had already in fact had dealings[76] with him when he was young. On taking over the case, Diopeithes caused delay after delay as a favor to these people. [64] And when Hegesander began to appear as a speaker at your platform, at the time when he was also engaged in a feud with Aristophon of Azenia,[77] before the latter threatened him in

---

[71] Otherwise unknown.

[72] When one individual seized another as his (alleged) slave, it was open to a third party to challenge the seizure (the Greek term is *aphaireisthai eis eleutherian,* literally "remove to freedom"). The intervening party had to provide sureties for the alleged slave pending a hearing to determine status. If Aeschines is telling the truth about Pittalacus' status in 1.54, either public slaves enjoyed an ambiguous status or Glaucon used the intervention process to challenge Hegesander's ownership rather than to make an absolute statement about Pittalacus' status. See, however, 1.54n.

[73] I.e., the parties to the suits.

[74] Arbitration in Athens took two forms, public and private. For most private cases, the first stage after suit was served was automatic referral to a state-appointed arbitrator as an attempt at resolution without involving the courts. But before reaching this stage, and in cases where there was no such automatic referral, it was possible for parties to select mutually acceptable individuals to resolve the dispute; the decision of privately chosen (unlike state-appointed) arbitrators was final.

[75] Diopeithes was a member of a propertied family and was himself active in public life. We later find him fighting in the Thracian Chersonnese (Gallipoli) on behalf of the Athenian colonists in 343/2 as general of a band of mercenaries, contributing to the friction between Athens and Macedonia. It is not surprising to find him associated with Timarchus and regarded with hostility by Aeschines.

[76] Greek *chrēsthai,* an ambiguous term that can mean "associate with," etc., socially, but whose primary meaning is "use," which can include sexual use.

[77] Aristophon of Azenia was one of the most durable politicians of fourth-century Athens. He first appears on the political scene at the time of the restoration of the democracy at the close of the fifth century, and his career lasted into

the Assembly with exactly the declaration of formal scrutiny[78] that I have made against Timarchus, and when Hegesander's brother Crobylus[79] was a regular speaker in the Assembly and these people had the nerve to advise you on the politics of Greece, at that point Pittalacus lost confidence in himself. He reflected on who he was and who his enemies were and (the truth must be said) reached a sensible decision: he kept quiet and was grateful to receive no fresh abuse. At this point, having won this glorious victory with ease, Hegesander kept Timarchus here in his house. [65] You all know the truth of my account. Which of you has been to the food stalls and not observed the extravagance of these people? Which of you has come upon their carousing and brawls and not felt resentment for the city's sake? Still, since we are in a lawcourt, please call Glaucon of Cholarge, the man who asserted Pittalacus' freedom, and read out the other depositions.

[66] [DEPOSITIONS] *Glaucon son of Timaeus of Cholarge testifies. I asserted the freedom of Pittalacus when he was being seized as a slave by Hegesander. Subsequently Pittalacus came to me and said that he wanted to send to Hegesander and resolve his dispute with him on the*

---

the middle of the fourth. Even in old age he was an able political fighter. He was one of the prosecutors of the general Timotheus in the mid-350s and secured his conviction with a crushing fine of 100 talents. Demosthenes (18.162, 19.291) makes Aeschines earlier in his career an associate of Aristophon. Harris (1995: 155) is skeptical. Certainly Aeschines is critical of Aristophon at 3.194. However, Aristophon fiercely opposed the terms of the peace with Macedonia in 346 (see 2.74n), and it may be that policy differences over Macedonia led to a rupture between the two.

[78] That is, the *dokimasia tōn rhētorōn* (see Speech Introduction). This action could be brought on a number of grounds (1.28–30), and we are not explicitly told which formed the basis of Aristophon's threat, though the text implies that the charge was the same as that against Timarchus. The statement is never substantiated.

[79] Given name Hegesippus; Crobylus ("Topknot," an antiquated hairstyle) was a nickname. Politically active for thirty years from the mid-360s, he was stridently opposed to peace with Philip and, like Demosthenes, worked to subvert it. Some critics in antiquity (probably correctly) credited him with the speech *On Halonnesus,* the seventh in modern printed editions of Demosthenes.

basis of the withdrawal of his suit against Hegesander and Hegesan-
der's action for slavery against him. And they resolved the dispute.[80]

Likewise Amphisthenes testifies. I asserted the freedom of Pittalacus
when he was being seized as a slave by Hegesander and so forth.

[67] So then, I shall call Hegesander in person for you. I have
drafted for him a deposition more decent than his character but a little
more explicit than the one for Misgolas. I am aware that he will swear
the disclaimer and lie on oath. Why, then, do I call him to give the
testimony? To show you the way this practice affects the characters
of men, how contemptuous of the gods they become, how disrespect-
ful of the laws, how indifferent to every source of shame. Please call
Hegesander.

[68] [DEPOSITION] *Hegesander son of Diphilus of Steiria testifies.*
When I sailed back from the Hellespont, I found Timarchus son of
Arizelus living at the house of Pittalacus the gambler, and as a result
of that acquaintance I consorted with Timarchus and used him for the
same activity as I had used Leodamas previously.[81]

[69] I was not unaware that he would show no respect for the oath,
men of Athens; I warned you in advance. And one thing is certainly
clear, that since he now refuses to give evidence, he will shortly appear
for the defense. And by Zeus it is no wonder. He will mount this
platform, I expect, with confidence in his way of life, an upright man,

---

[80] Forgery is indicated principally by the use of the first person in these depositions (see 1.50n), also by the discrepancy between the number of depositions
called for by Aeschines and the number preserved in the text. One would like
to know how much of the narrative was confirmed here. Glaucon will presumably confirm that Hegesander claimed Pittalacus as his slave and that he intervened. He and the other witnesses will confirm that Pittalacus instituted and then
dropped proceedings against Hegesander. But the narrative background, including the role of Timarchus, may not have figured in the depositions.

[81] Forgery is indicated by the formal flaws (use of the first person; see 1.50n)
and factual errors (the deposition inverts the relationship between Hegesander
and Leodamas, which is given in 1.111 below).

enemy of wickedness, who doesn't even know who Leodamas⁸² was, Leodamas at whose name you all yelled when the deposition was being read out. [70] Shall I bring myself to speak a little more frankly than is my nature? Tell me, in the name of Zeus and the other gods, men of Athens, when a man has shamed himself with Hegesander, don't you think he has played whore to a whore? What excesses of vile behavior do we suppose they did not practice when drunk and on their own? Don't you think that Hegesander, trying to compensate for his notorious activities for Leodamas, of which you all know, made arrogant demands in the belief that his own past behavior would seem moderate in comparison with the extremes of Timarchus?

[71] Nonetheless, you will see that Hegesander himself and his brother Crobylus will leap up here shortly and, with considerable deviousness and rhetorical skill, will claim that my case is one of downright stupidity. They will demand that I present witnesses who testify explicitly where he carried out the acts and who saw and what kind of act. This I think is a scandalous demand. [72] I don't consider you so forgetful that you do not recall the laws you heard read out a little earlier, in which it is written that anyone who hires an Athenian for this activity or anyone who hires himself out is liable to the most severe penalties, the same in both cases. What man is so witless that he would agree to give explicit testimony of this sort, by which it is certain, if he attests the truth, that he proves himself liable to the most extreme penalties? [73] So, then, all that is left is for the passive partner to admit the facts himself. But this is why he is on trial, because after engaging in this activity he addressed the Assembly in defiance of the laws. So do you want us to abandon the whole issue and not investigate? By Poseidon, we shall really manage the city well, if when we know that acts are taking place, we are to ignore them simply because someone does not come forward in court and testify explicitly without shame.

[74] Consider the issue on the basis of parallels; and I suppose the

---

⁸²Politically active from the 370s, Leodamas is located by Aeschines at 3.139 among the proponents of alliance with Thebes. His eloquence is praised by Aeschines there and by Demosthenes (20.146).

parallels will have to resemble Timarchus' practices. You see these men who sit in the brothels, the ones who on their own admission practice this activity. Yet these men, when they are required to engage in the act, still throw a cloak over their shame and lock the doors. Now if someone were to ask you, the men passing by in the street: "What is this person doing at this moment?" you would immediately give the name of the act, without seeing who had gone in; no, once you know the chosen profession of the individual, you also recognize the act. [75] So you should investigate Timarchus in the same way and ask not whether anyone saw him but if this man has engaged in the practice. For by the gods, what is one to say, Timarchus? What would you yourself say about another person who was being tried on this charge? What is one to say when a young lad leaves his father's house and spends his nights in the homes of others, a lad of unusual beauty, and enjoys lavish dinners without making any contribution, and keeps flute-players and the most expensive courtesans, and plays at dice, while he pays out nothing himself but another man pays for him? [76] Does one need to be clairvoyant? Isn't it obvious that the man who makes such enormous demands of others must himself inevitably provide certain pleasures in return to the men who pay out the money in advance? By Olympian Zeus, I can find no more decorous way of referring to the grotesque acts that you have practiced.

[77] Consider the matter, if you would, on the basis of parallels from political affairs, too, and especially matters with which you are currently dealing. Ballots[83] have taken place in the demes, and each of you has submitted himself to the vote, to see who is truly Athenian and who is not. And when I personally find myself in the courtroom and listen to the litigants, I see that the same factor is always influential with you. [78] Whenever the accuser says: "Jurors, the demesmen with their vote rejected this man on oath, though nobody in the world accused him or bore witness against him; they voted on the basis of

---

[83] Greek *diapsēphisis,* literally "voting among/between." In 346/5 the politician Demophilus carried a decree requiring all demes to assemble and vote collectively on each member in turn to determine their entitlement to citizen rights. Those rejected by the deme could appeal to the courts; if successful, they were reinstated, if unsuccessful, they were (probably) enslaved. Demosthenes 57 was written for an appellant rejected by his deme, Halimus.

their own knowledge," without hesitation, I think, you make a commotion, convinced that the man on trial has no claim to citizen rights.
For your view, I think, is that you need no further discussion or testimony in matters that a man knows himself for certain. [79] Come
now, in the name of Zeus, if Timarchus had been compelled to submit to a vote on this way of life of his like that on birth qualifications,
to determine whether he is guilty or not, and the issue was being decided in court, and was being brought before you as now, but it was
forbidden by some law or decree either for me to make an accusation
or for Timarchus to offer a defense; and the herald here standing
near me put to you the proclamation in the law: "Of the voting counters, the hollowed one for whoever believes Timarchus has prostituted
himself, the solid one for whoever believes he has not,"[84] how would
you have voted? I know full well that you would have convicted him.
[80] And if any of you were to ask me: "How do you know whether
we would have convicted him?" I should reply: "Because you have
spoken frankly and told me." When and where each of you did so I
shall now remind you: whenever this man steps up in the Assembly,
and last year when he was a member of the Council.[85] Whenever he
mentioned work on walls or a tower or said that someone had been
taken off somewhere, you would yell out at once and laugh and
yourselves utter the terms for the acts of his you know about.[86] [81]
I shall leave out most of these occasions that occurred some time
ago; but I do want to remind you of what happened in the actual
Assembly when I made formal declaration of this scrutiny against
Timarchus.

---

[84] As the text indicates, each member of the panel of jurors in court was issued
two disc-shaped votes: one had a short hollow bar through the center, the other a
short solid bar. There were two voting urns, one for the vote reflecting the juror's
positive verdict, the other for the voided vote. The system of having every juror
cast two votes guaranteed anonymity.

[85] Timarchus will no doubt have replied that he had passed a *dokimasia* (preliminary scrutiny) for the Council in which his citizenship qualifications were
tested and an opportunity was offered to anyone to query them.

[86] The passage is full of sexual double meanings that are lost on the modern
reader. The comic playwrights of the fifth and early fourth centuries indicate that
the stock of Greek colloquial sexual metaphor was very rich.

The Council of the Areopagus[87] was appearing before the Assembly in accordance with the decree that this man had proposed on the subject of the houses on the Pnyx.[88] The man who was speaking for the Areopagites was Autolycus,[89] a man who has lived an honorable life, by Olympian Zeus and Apollo, with dignity and in a manner worthy of that body. [82] And when in the course of his speech he said that the Areopagus disapproved of Timarchus' proposal, "and on the matter of this deserted locality and the area of the Pnyx, do not be surprised, men of Athens, if Timarchus is more familiar with it than the Council of the Areopagus,"[90] at that point there was uproar, and you said that what Autolycus said was true, that this man was familiar with the place. [83] And Autolycus, not understanding the reason for your uproar, scowled fiercely and, after a pause, said: "Men of Athens, we members of the Areopagus neither accuse nor defend (it is not our traditional practice), but we have some sympathy for Timarchus for the following reason; he perhaps," he said, "thought that while things were so peaceful, the outlay for each of you was small."[91] Once more

---

[87] The Areopagus, a council made up of ex-archons, had originally been the most influential political body in Athens. It was stripped of its authority in the mid-fifth century by the democratic reformers and left with a largely religious role, in particular the judgment of homicide cases. The second half of the fourth century saw a growth in its political influence.

[88] Evidently Timarchus had proposed a measure for clearing the area around the Pnyx. Harris (1995: 104) suggests that the Areopagus had been instructed by the Assembly to report on the proposal; it may be that some of the buildings in the area were shrines. (For the role of the Areopagus in religion, see the preceding note.) The Pnyx, adjacent to the Areopagus, was the hill on which the Assembly met.

[89] Of Autolycus' earlier career nothing is known; after Chaeronea in 338 (according to Lycurgus *Leocrates* 53 and the lexicographer Harpocration's entry under *Autolykos*), he was tried and punished for secretly spiriting away his family from the city, though he himself stayed on (for attitudes toward such conduct, cf. 3.252).

[90] Autolycus presumably means that as an active politician frequenting the Pnyx, Timarchus would know the area well; his audience takes this as a reference to grubby sexual encounters in deserted places.

[91] Another unintentional double meaning. Autolycus means presumably that Timarchus feels that at a time of peace the financial burden of the clearance project would be small; his audience takes this as a reference to the low cost of sex with Timarchus in a quiet place.

at the mention of quiet and small outlay he met with still greater commotion and laughter from you. [84] When he mentioned foundations and cisterns, you just couldn't contain yourselves.[92] At this point Pyrrhander[93] came forward to reproach you and asked the Assembly if they were not ashamed to be laughing when the Council of the Areopagus was present. But you shouted him from the platform and replied: "Pyrrhander, we know that we should not be laughing in their presence. But so strong is the truth that it overcomes all human logic." [85] This I take to be the testimony offered to you by the Athenian people, who cannot properly be convicted of false witness. Isn't it bizarre, men of Athens, if without a word from me, you yourselves shout out the name of the acts you know he has committed, but when I state them you forget? Or if he was convicted when the issue did not come to trial but he is to be acquitted now that it has been proved?

[86] Since I have mentioned the deme ballots and the policies of Demophilus,[94] I want to offer another example in this connection. For this same man made a similar maneuver before. He alleged that there were individuals who were trying to bribe the Assembly and the lawcourts as well, an allegation also made by Nicostratus recently. Some of the trials on these charges took place a while ago, and others are still pending. [87] Well then, by Zeus and the gods, if those involved had resorted to the same defense used now by Timarchus and his supporting speakers, and insisted that either there should be explicit testimony on the charge or the jurors should disbelieve it, then it would certainly be necessary following this logic for the one man to attest that he offered a bribe and the other that he took it, when there is a penalty of death laid down in law for each, just as on the present matter if someone hires out an Athenian for abuse, and again if any Athenian willingly takes money for the shameful use of his body. [88] Is there a man alive who would have given evidence, or any accuser who would have attempted to prove the case on this basis? Certainly not. So what happened? Were the accused acquitted? No, by

---

[92] As in 1.80, we have words whose metaphorical meanings carry sexual connotations. Presumably "cistern" would refer to the anus and "foundation" to either the buttocks or the anus.

[93] For Pyrrhander, see 3.139n.

[94] For Demophilus, see 1.77n.

Zeus; they were condemned to death, when they had committed a much less serious offense—by Zeus and Apollo!—than this person here. In the case of those unfortunate men, they met with this catastrophe because they were unable to protect themselves against old age and poverty together, the worst evils in human life, in Timarchus' case because he could not restrain his own vile nature.

[89] Now if this trial were taking place in another city that had been called to adjudicate, I should have expected you to be my witnesses, as the ones who know best that I am telling the truth. But since the trial is in Athens and you are at the same time judges and witnesses to my account, my task is to remind you and yours not to doubt me. For in my opinion, men of Athens, Timarchus here is concerned not only for himself but also for all the rest who have practiced the same profession. [90] If this practice is to take place, as is usually the case, secretly and in isolated spots and private houses, and the man who possesses the fullest knowledge, but has shamed a citizen, is to be liable to the most severe penalties if he testifies to the truth; while the man on trial, against whom his own life and the truth have given evidence, is to insist on being judged on the basis not of what is known but of the depositions, the law and the truth are destroyed and a clear route has been revealed for those guilty of the worst felonies to be acquitted. [91] For what mugger or thief or seducer or homicide, or anyone else who commits the gravest offenses but does so in secret,[95] will be punished? For in fact, those of them who are caught with their guilt manifest are executed at once if they confess, but those who go undetected and deny their guilt are tried in the courts, and the truth is discovered on the basis of likelihood.

---

[95] Muggers (*lōpodytai,* literally "clothes-strippers") and thieves belonged to a class of criminal called *kakourgoi* (literally "evildoers"), who were liable to summary arrest (*apagōgē*) if caught in circumstances that pointed to guilt (*ep' autophorōi*). They could be hauled before the officials called the Eleven, and if they confessed, they were executed without trial; if they denied guilt, they were tried, and executed if convicted. Homicides, too, could in certain circumstances be subjected to summary arrest, though (despite the next sentence) they could be executed without trial only if they were previously convicted homicides returning from exile without permission. Homicide law exempted from punishment an aggrieved male who killed a seducer (*moichos;* see 1.183n) caught with certain female relatives. Scholars dispute whether seducers could be classed as *kakourgoi.*

[92] Now take as an example the Council of the Areopagus, the most exact body in the city. I have often at meetings of that council seen men who spoke well and provided witnesses convicted; and before now I know of some men who spoke very badly and had no witnesses for their case but succeeded. For they vote not just in response to the speech nor to the witnesses but on what they themselves know and have investigated. And so that body continues to enjoy respect in the city. [93] Now, men of Athens, you, too, should judge this case in the same way. First of all, nothing should have greater credence with you than your own knowledge and conviction concerning Timarchus here, and secondly, you should consider the issue not in relation to the present but in relation to the past. For the statements that were made in the past about Timarchus and his way of life were said because of their truth, but those that will be made on this day will be said because of the trial in order to deceive you. Cast your vote, then, in favor of the longer period, the truth, and your own knowledge.

[94] Yet a speechwriter,[96] the one who has devised his defense, claims that I contradict myself.[97] He says that in his view it is impossible for the same man to have prostituted himself and squandered his inheritance; to have misused one's body is the conduct of a child,

---

[96] I.e., Demosthenes. Demosthenes' inheritance was plundered by his guardians, whom he successfully sued on coming of age (see Dem. 27–30). It was probably a combination of the need to restore his family finances, the celebrity brought by this success, and his political ambitions that induced him to become a "logographos," a professional writer of speeches for delivery in court, the nearest the Athenian system ever came to the profession of lawyer (see further Series Introduction, p. xv). There is independent testimony that speechwriters were regarded, overtly at least, with hostility and distrust, though their services were evidently much in demand.

[97] The anticipation of defense arguments not surprisingly was a standard feature of prosecution speeches. In those cases which went to public arbitration (see 1.63n), litigants would have had a very good idea of the opponent's case because no new evidence could be introduced after arbitration. Where there was no arbitration (this included all public actions), the litigant would have to rely partly on such information as he could glean from common gossip, direct approaches from the opponent's enemies, and common sense. Since we rarely have both sides of a dispute, it is often difficult to determine whether we are offered solid information, guesswork, or invention.

while to have squandered one's inheritance is the conduct of a man. Furthermore, he claims that men who shame themselves charge fees for the practice. So he is going around the Agora expressing surprise and wonderment that the same man has prostituted himself and squandered his inheritance. [95] But if anyone does not realize how the matter stands, I shall attempt to lay it out more clearly in my account. While the estate of the heiress whom Hegesander, Timarchus' husband, had married, and the money that he brought back from his period abroad with Timomachus lasted, they indulged in enormous excess and extravagance. But when it was all gone, wasted on dicing and lavish dinners, and Timarchus had passed his prime, as one would expect, nobody would pay money any more, while his vile and unholy nature still longed for the same pleasures, and in its extreme dissipation made continuing demands on him, and he was drawn back to his daily habits; [96] at that point he turned to eating up his inheritance. And he not only ate it up, but—if one can say this—drank it up as well! And indeed, he sold off each of his possessions, and not even at its true value; he could not wait for a profit or a good price but sold it for what it would realize immediately. So compelling was his haste to enjoy his pleasures.

[97] For his father left him an estate from which another man would actually have performed public services,[98] but this man proved unable even to preserve it for his own use. There was a house behind the Acropolis, a country property at Sphettus, another farm in Alopece,[99] and in addition nine or ten slave craftsmen who made shoes,[100] each of whom paid him a commission[101] of two obols a day, while the foreman of the workshop paid three, and besides, a woman skilled in working linen, who took her work to the market, and a male embroiderer, and debtors owing him money and furniture.

---

[98] Greek *leitourgiai*. See 1.11n.

[99] Sphettus was a rural deme east of Mount Hymettus, Alopece a deme just outside the city, to the southwest.

[100] Manufacturing in ancient Greece was based on slave labor.

[101] Some slaves lived apart from their masters and carried out a trade independently, paying a commission (*apophora*) to the master. They were termed *chōris oikountes* (literally "living apart").

[98] To prove I am telling the truth in this, I shall now, by Zeus, provide you with clear and explicit testimony from the witnesses. For unlike before, there is no danger or disgrace facing anyone attesting the truth. The house in the city he sold to Nausicrates the comic poet, and Cleaenetus [102] the chorus-trainer subsequently bought it from Nausicrates for twenty minas. The country estate was bought from him by Mnesitheus [103] of Myrrinus; it was a substantial property but had been left by Timarchus to run wild to an appalling degree. [99] The farm at Alopece was eleven or twelve stades [104] from the city wall; his mother had begged and pleaded with him, so I am told, [105] to leave this, if nothing else, unsold and to leave this plot at least for her to be buried in. But he did not hesitate; he sold this, too, for 2,000 drachmas. And he left none of the male and female slaves but has sold them all. And to prove I am telling the truth, I for my part will provide witnesses to the fact that his father left them to him; let him, if he claims that he has not sold them, provide the slaves visibly in person. [100] And to prove that his father had also lent out money to some people, which Timarchus spent when it was repaid, I shall present Metagenes [106] of Sphettus, who had owed the father more than thirty minas and repaid to Timarchus here seven minas, the amount outstanding when his father died. Please call Metagenes of Sphettus. But first of all read out the deposition of Nausicrates, the man who bought his house. And take all the other depositions on the points I have made on the same subject.

---

[102] The manuscripts are divided between "comic poet" and "comic actor." Nausicrates is known from an inscription (giving the name of victors at the Lenaea) as the name of both a comic poet and a comic actor, though it has been suggested that the two are in fact one. I have followed Dilts in opting for "poet," but without confidence. Cleaenetus is otherwise unknown.

[103] An inscription of the late 340s places Mnesitheus in the liturgical class (see 1.11n), confirming the implication of the text that he was a wealthy man.

[104] The stade was approximately 200 yards (185 meters), giving a distance of a mile and a quarter or a mile and a third.

[105] Unsubstantiated but effective, adding the force of Athenian attitudes on duties to parents to their hostility to profligacy.

[106] Possibly the same as the witness at 2.134.

[DEPOSITIONS]

[101] Now I shall prove to you that his father had no small sum of money, which this man has squandered. For in his fear of liability for public services (*leitourgiai*), he had sold off his properties,[107] apart from the ones already mentioned; these were a farm at Cephisia, another at Amphitrope,[108] and two processing plants[109] in the region of the silver mines, one at Aulon and the other at Thrasymus.[110]

[102] How he acquired these I shall tell you. There were three brothers, Eupolemus the trainer, and Arizelus, Timarchus' father, and Arignotus,[111] who is still alive today, though old and without his sight. Eupolemus was the first of them to die, while the estate was still undivided; next was Arizelus, Timarchus' father. While he was alive, he managed the whole property because of Arignotus' frailty and his unfortunate loss of sight, and because Eupolemus was dead, and he gave Arignotus an agreed sum for his support. [103] When Arizelus, the father of Timarchus here, also died, in the early period, while Timarchus was still a boy, Arignotus received all that was reasonably due to him from the guardians of the estate. But when Timarchus here was enrolled in the deme register and gained control of the estate, he pushed aside an old and unfortunate man, his own uncle, and squandered the property; he saw to none of Arignotus' needs; no, after such

---

[107] I.e., to conceal the extent of his property in order to assess it below the threshold for liturgies (1.11n).

[108] Cephisia was a deme in north central Attica, Amphitrope a deme in southwest Attica. Timarchus' father had a collection of properties scattered all over Attica (cf. 1.97).

[109] The silver mines under Attica were the property of the state, but the ore was extracted by private individuals who leased concessions from the state. The plants in question were for processing the silver ore.

[110] Manuscripts have "at Thrasyllus" (with minor variations); the phrase, which occurs elsewhere in the orators, was explained by lexicographers in antiquity as "at (the monument/tomb of) Thrasyllus." Inscriptions indicate that the location was really called Thrasymus, in the mining region of Maronea in southern Attica. Aulon likewise was in the mining area.

[111] Aeschines is our sole source for Timarchus' family.

wealth, he left him to collect the disability dole.[112] **[104]** Finally, and
most outrageous, when the old man had been missed from the list for
consideration and had made formal supplication before the Council
for the dole,[113] though Timarchus was serving on the Council and was
presiding on that day, he did not see fit to speak in his support, but
stood by while Arignotus lost the allocation for that prytany (*prytaneia*).[114] To prove the truth of this statement, please call Arignotus of
Sphettus and read out the deposition.

[DEPOSITION]

[105] It might be suggested that after selling his inherited estate, he
acquired other property elsewhere in the city, and that instead of the
country estate and the farm at Alopece and the slave craftsmen, he
invested in the silver mines like his father before him. But he has
nothing left, no house, no apartment, no farm, no slaves, no money
out on loan, none of the other sources of income for men who aren't
felons. Instead of his ancestral property, what he has left is vileness,
sykophancy, rashness, self-indulgence, cowardice, unscrupulousness,
and an inability to blush at what is shameful, things that produce the
most immoral and useless citizen.

[106] Now he has devoured not only his inherited property, but in
addition all of your public property that he has had in his control. For
at the young age that you see, there is no office he has not held, and

---

[112] The disability dole consisted of one obol per day at the beginning of the
fourth century, but by the 320s (Aristotle *Constitution of Athens* 49.4) it had been
raised to two obols. It was means-tested (subject to a property limit of three minas) and available to those who were physically incapable of working. Recipients
were vetted by the Council to determine eligibility (Lysias 24 was written for a
rejected candidate).

[113] For formal supplication, see 2.15n.

[114] A little over one month's pay. The Athenian administrative year was divided
into ten *prytaneiai*. The presence of a deposition from Arignotus seems to confirm
the loss of pay, though as Harris (1995: 104) notes, we do not know if it confirmed
Timarchus' responsibility for his financial circumstances (indeed, since the Athenians were alert to the possibility of benefit fraud, and this family was skilled at
concealing assets, even the extent of the uncle's poverty remains uncertain).

he acquired none of them by selection by lot or election but bought every one illegally. The majority of them I shall ignore and just mention two or three. [107] He became auditor (*logistēs*)[115] and did enormous damage to the city by receiving bribes from people guilty of malpractice in office, though his favorite practice was to persecute[116] innocent men undergoing their final audit. He was magistrate at Andros,[117] an office he bought for thirty minas, money he borrowed at a rate of eighteen percent,[118] using your allies as a means of funding his vile habits. And he displayed appetite on a scale never before seen from anyone in his treatment of the wives of free men. I present none of the men here to testify in public to the personal misfortune that he chose to conceal; I leave it to you to investigate. [108] But what do you expect? When the same man committed outrages (*hybris*) not only on others but also on his own person while here in Athens, under the rule of law, with you watching and his enemies nearby, who could imagine that once he obtained impunity,[119] opportunity, and public office, he would leave undone any act of the most extreme wantonness? Many times before now, by Zeus and Apollo, I have reflected on the good luck of our city, not least among many reasons for the fact that in that period no buyer could be found for the city of Andros![120]

[109] But perhaps one could argue that he was unprincipled when

---

[115] The board of ten auditors (*logistai*) examined the accounts of all outgoing magistrates as the first stage of the process of *euthyna*, for which see 1.1.

[116] *Sykophantein;* see 1.1n.

[117] Athenian magistrates (that is, direct control of an allied state from Athens) are attested for Andros and Amorgos; we cannot be sure how widespread the practice was. Since (as far as we can see) Aeschines follows his usual preference for chronological narrative, the date is presumably in the 360s.

[118] A high rate of interest for a non-maritime loan. The normal rate was 12% per annum.

[119] Not literally true. Though he was not immediately visible to the Athenians, the allies could complain to Athens; he had to face *euthyna* (1.1n) on his return. No evidence is ever adduced to prove the allegation; so presumably no formal charge was ever brought. Aeschines tacitly meets this objection by offering a reason why victims might keep quiet.

[120] The Athenian confederacy of the fourth century was created on the basis of assurances that the imperialism of the fifth century would not recur. Athens' treatment of the allies eventually led to a revolt (the Social War of 357–355). Aeschines associates Timarchus with the abuses that provoked the war.

holding office alone but upright when he had colleagues. How could that be? This man, men of Athens, was appointed to the Council in the archonship of Nicophemus.[121] Now to attempt an account of all the crimes he committed in that year is not reasonable in a small portion of a day. But I shall give you a brief account of the ones most relevant to the charge that forms the basis of the present trial. [110] During the same archonship in which Timarchus was a member of the Council, Hegesander the brother of Crobylus was treasurer to the goddess,[122] and in collaboration like good friends they stole 1,000 drachmas from the city. A decent man, Pamphilus[123] of Acherdus, who had quarreled with the defendant and was angry with him, observed what had happened, and during an Assembly he stood up and said: "Men of Athens, a man and a woman are between them stealing 1,000 drachmas of your money." [111] When you were puzzled at what he meant by a man and a woman and what he was talking about, he paused for a moment and said: "Don't you understand what I'm saying? The man is Hegesander over there—now, though before he was himself Leodamas' woman; the woman is Timarchus here. How the money is being stolen I shall tell you." Then he gave a fully informed and lucid account of the affair. And after giving this information, he said: "So what do I advise you to do, men of Athens? If the Council convicts Timarchus of the offense, expels him, and hands him over to a lawcourt, give them their reward,[124] and if they don't punish him, withhold it and hold this against them until that day." [112] When the Council next entered the Council chamber, they expelled him in the straw vote but accepted him back in the formal ballot.[125] And because

---

[121] 361/0.

[122] That is, one of the board of treasurers of the sacred monies of Athena.

[123] Pamphilus is otherwise unknown.

[124] It was customary (though not inevitable) for the outgoing Council to be awarded a gold crown for its service; see P. J. Rhodes, *The Athenian Boule* (Oxford, 1972), pp. 14ff.

[125] The present passage is our most substantial piece of information on the disciplinary powers and procedures of the Council against its own members. There appears to have been an informal vote (I translate "straw vote," but the Greek verb *ekphyllophorein* suggests the use of leaves, *phylla,* though it is not known whether this is a literal indicator of practice in the fourth century) followed by a formal hearing.

they did not hand him over to a lawcourt or eject him from the Council chamber, though it pains me to mention it, still I must tell you that they did not receive their reward. So, men of Athens, do not show your anger against the Council and deprive 500 citizens of their crown for failing to punish this man, and then yourselves acquit him and preserve for the Assembly a public speaker who was useless to the Council.

[113] Yet one might argue that though in offices obtained by lot he behaves like this, in elective offices he is more upright. And who among you does not know that he was notoriously exposed as a thief? He was sent by you as auditor (*exetastēs*) of the mercenaries at Eretria;[126] and he was the only one of the investigators who admitted to receiving money. He did not address his defense to the question of fact but admitted his guilt and without hesitation directed his plea to the penalty. And you fined the ones who denied their guilt a talent each, while you fined Timarchus thirty minas. Yet the laws instruct that for thieves who admit their guilt, the punishment is death; the trial is for those who deny it.[127]

[114] As a result he developed such contempt for you that right away he took 2,000 drachmas in bribes during the deme ballots.[128] He claimed that Philotades of Cydathenaeum, a member of the citizen body, was a freedman of his and persuaded the deme members to reject him; he presided over the case for the prosecution in the court and, taking the sacrificial victims in his hand, swore that he had taken and would take no money, swearing by the gods who watch over oaths and calling down destruction on himself. [115] But it was proved that he had received twenty minas from Leuconides, Philotades' in-

---

[126] A city on the island of Euboea. Presumably this occurred at the time of the struggle for possession of Euboea between Athens and Thebes in 357 (see 3.85n). For the opportunities for peculation by falsifying the numbers for mercenaries, cf. 3.146. The *exetastes*, "auditor"/"assessor," was a financial official, associated by Aristotle (*Politics* 1322b) with the *logistai*, the financial officials responsible for auditing the accounts of public officials; for the role of the *exetastes* in military matters, cf. 2.177.

[127] See 1.91n.

[128] Under the Demophilus decree; see 1.77n.

law, by way of Philemon the actor,[129] money that he spent in a short time on the courtesan Philoxene;[130] so he abandoned the case and betrayed his oath. To prove I am telling the truth, please call Philemon, who gave Timarchus the money, and Leuconides, the in-law of Philotades, and read out the copy of the agreement under which he sold out the case.

[DEPOSITIONS, AGREEMENT]

[116] Now his behavior toward citizens and relatives, his shameful squandering of his inheritance, and his casual attitude to the abuse (*hybris*) of his own body are things you knew even before I spoke of them, and my account has given you adequate reminder. But there are two features of my accusation left, and I pray to all the gods and goddesses that I personally shall speak on these matters as I have resolved for the city's sake; and I would wish you for your part to pay attention to what I am about to say and follow it closely.

[117] My first theme is an advance account of the defense that I am told will be offered, in case, if I fail to mention it, the man who advertises that he can teach young men the art of speaking[131] tricks you with false logic and prevents a result to the city's advantage. My second theme is to exhort the citizens to right conduct (*aretē*). I see many of the younger generation present in court, and many of the older men, and no small number from the rest of Greece gathered to listen. [118] Do not imagine that they have come to see me; no, they would much rather know whether you not only know how to pass laws but also can judge between right and wrong, whether you know how to respect good men and whether you are willing to punish people who

---

[129] The individuals named here are otherwise unknown, with the exception of the comic actor Philemon, for whom we have inscriptional evidence for two victories as best actor at the Lenaea, one of the two state dramatic festivals.

[130] Evidently a well-known courtesan, but not mentioned in any other source.

[131] It is difficult to determine whether Demosthenes actually offered instruction, formal or informal, in rhetoric, or whether Aeschines is merely using Demosthenes' career as a professional speechwriter (1.94n) to present him as a teacher of rhetoric, exploiting the hostility to professional rhetoricians from the fifth century onward.

make their way of life a disgrace to the city. I shall speak to you first of all about the defense argument.[132]

[119] That consummate speaker Demosthenes claims that either you must expunge the laws or else you must pay no attention to my arguments. He says he is amazed if you don't all remember that every year the Council sells off the prostitution tax,[133] and that those who buy the right to exact the tax do not guess but have precise knowledge of the people who engage in this trade. While I have had the audacity to charge that Timarchus has no right to address the people when he has prostituted himself, Demosthenes claims that the practice itself calls not for an allegation from a prosecutor but for a deposition from a taxman who has collected the tax from Timarchus. [120] Men of Athens, see whether you find the reply I make to this simple and frank. I am ashamed for the city's sake if Timarchus, the people's adviser, the man who has the nerve to serve on embassies to the rest of Greece, will not attempt to cleanse his reputation of the whole business but instead will query the locations[134] where he offered himself and ask if the tax-collectors have ever collected the prostitution tax from him. [121] He should abandon this line of defense for your sake. I shall offer you another line of defense, an honorable and just one, which you should use, if you have nothing shameful on your conscience. Steel yourself to look the jurors in the face and say what a decent man should about his youth: "Men of Athens, I have been reared among you, from my childhood and adolescence, and my way of life is no secret. I am seen among you in the Assembly. [122] And I think that, if I were addressing any other body on the charge for which I am now on trial, your testimony would enable me to refute the accuser's statements easily. I think the rest of my life not worth living, not only if I have committed any of these acts but if it is your belief

---

[132] For anticipation of defense arguments, see 1.94n.

[133] The collection of taxes was put out to tender, the profit for the collector being the difference between the sum he paid the state and the sum he collected from those liable to the tax. The farming out of the prostitution tax reflects the recognition of prostitution as a legal (at least for noncitizens), though not respectable, activity.

[134] The text suggests that there was a list of brothels that served as the basis for tax collection.

that the life I have lived resembles the accusations made by my opponent, and I freely offer the punishment you inflict on me as a means for the city to defend itself in the eyes of Greece. I have not come to plead with you for mercy; no, destroy me, if you think me this sort of man."

This, Timarchus, is the defense that befits a noble and decent man, one who has confidence in his way of life and properly treats every attempt at slander with contempt. [123] In contrast, the argument that Demosthenes is trying to persuade you to use is not the speech of a free man but of a prostitute who is quibbling about locations. But since you take refuge in the names of the lodgings and demand that the case be proved on the basis of the establishment where you plied your trade, once you have heard what I am about to say you will not use this argument if you have any sense. It is not buildings or lodgings that give their names to the occupants, but occupants who give the titles of their individual practices to their locations. [124] Where a number of people have rented a single building divided among them, we call it an apartment building. Where one man lives, we call it a house. Surely if a doctor moves into one of the shops by the roadside, it is called a doctor's surgery. If he moves out and a blacksmith moves into the same shop, it is called a smithy. If it is a fuller, it is called a laundry, if it is a carpenter, it is called a carpenter's shop. If a pimp and prostitutes move in, it gets the name brothel from the trade itself. And so you have created a lot of brothels from your skill in the profession. So then, don't ask where you ever engaged in the acts, but defend yourself on the ground that you have not done so.

[125] Another argument, it seems, will be offered, contrived by the same sophist. He maintains that there is nothing more unjust than common report; and he offers examples picked up from the marketplace[135] and entirely consistent with his own life. First of all, he points out that the apartment building at Colonus[136] called "Demon's" is falsely named; it isn't Demon's. Then there's the Hermes called "An-

---

[135] As the administrative hub of the city and the main market, the Agora was a place for idlers to pass their time.

[136] Probably (given the nature of the building) the hill Colonus immediately to the west of the Agora rather than the small deme of Colonus Hippius a short distance from the city to the north. Nothing is known of Demon.

docides' Hermes," [137] which, he says, isn't Andocides' but a dedication
made by the Aegeis tribe. [126] And he offers himself as example by
way of a joke, like a good-humored man making jokes about his own
way of life. "Unless," he says, "I, too, must respond to the crowd when
they call me not Demosthenes but Batalus, because my nurse gave me
this nickname." [138] So if Timarchus was beautiful and is the butt of
jokes in slanderous distortion of the fact and not because of his own
conduct, surely, says Demosthenes, he doesn't deserve to be ruined
for this.

[127] Myself, Demosthenes, where dedicatory offerings and houses
and possessions, in short all voiceless objects, are concerned, I hear
many tales of all sorts and never consistent. For they have no capacity
for noble or base action; it is the man who happens to become associated with them, whoever he may be, who furnishes the common
account according to the scale of his own reputation. But where men's
lives and actions are concerned, of its own accord a true report spreads
through the city announcing an individual's conduct to the public at
large, and often predicting future events, too. [128] This statement is
so patently true and uncontrived that you will find that both our city
and our ancestors established an altar to Report [139] as a goddess of very

---

[137] The Hermes (often written "herm" in modern texts) was a nonrepresenta-
tional image of the god Hermes consisting of a tetragonal pillar surmounted by a
head and (in the archaic and classical periods) with an erect phallus projecting
from the front. These images stood at the front of private and public buildings.
The association of Andocides (rightly or wrongly) with a particular Hermes reflects both his complicity in the incident in 415 when almost all the Hermae in
Athens were mutilated overnight and the fact that Andocides subsequently prosecuted another for allegedly defacing Andocides' family Hermes (Lysias 6.11).

[138] The nickname is acknowledged by Demosthenes at 3.180. So it must have
admitted an innocent explanation. Yet here and at 2.99, Aeschines connects it
with passive homosexuality. Evidently we have two distinct derivations producing
identical or near-identical words. In its innocent sense, it may (this is uncertain)
have denoted a stammerer, in its indecent sense "anus."

[139] Greek *Phēmē*. The tendency to attribute divine status to what we would
term abstract qualities is from the first a marked feature of Greek thought and
appears both in creative literature and in actual cult. The existence of the altar is
confirmed by the later traveler Pausanias (1.17.1). The ancient commentators on

great power. You will find that Homer often says in the *Iliad* before some event that was about to happen: "Report came to the host," [140] and that Euripides declares that this goddess is able to reveal the character not only of the living, whatever it may be, but also of the dead, when he says:

Report declares the noble man, even when hidden in the ground. [141]

[129] And Hesiod actually describes her explicitly as a goddess. His words are quite clear for anyone who is willing to understand them. He says:

Report in no wise dies away completely, if many
people utter it. She, too, then, is a god. [142]

And you will find that people who have lived decent lives are admirers of these poems. For all men who have public ambitions believe that they will win their reputations from common report. But people whose lives are base do not respect this god. They see in her their undying accuser. [130] So recollect, gentlemen, the report you have encountered concerning Timarchus. Isn't it the case that as soon as

---

Aeschines state that it was founded after the victory of Cimon (see 2.172n) over the Persians at the Eurymedon in the 460s and reflected the fact that the Athenians knew of the battle before receiving Cimon's written report. It has been suggested plausibly that Pheme is not mere rumor but a mysterious force that promulgates information; hence the seriousness with which Aeschines can treat "report" here.

[140] The words, which have the appearance of an epic formula (that is, a ready-made semantic unit for insertion in the verse as necessary) make up "half" of a hexameter verse $— — — \smile \smile — \smile$. These words are not found in Homer. Either they come from a lost archaic epic (there was a tendency for the name of Homer to attach itself to epic poems other than the *Iliad* and *Odyssey*, though the specific reference here to the *Iliad* makes this unlikely) or, more probably, Aeschines has invented a plausible epic formula. *Phēmē* does not appear in the *Iliad*, though the similar figure of *Ossa*, "rumor," calls the Greeks to assembly at *Iliad* 2.93–94.

[141] Euripides fr. 865 Nauck.

[142] Hesiod *Works and Days* 763–764. This quotation, and the line of argument, came back to haunt Aeschines in 343, when Demosthenes used it to ground the "fact" of Aeschines' corruption in the (alleged) prevalence of the rumor to that effect, 19.243–244; cf. 2.144n, 1.152n.

the name is uttered you ask the question: "Which Timarchus? The whore?" So then, if I were offering witnesses, you would believe me. Yet if I offer the god as witness, will you not believe, when in all piety one cannot charge her with false testimony? [131] As to Demosthenes' nickname, he is rightly called Batalus, by common report and not by his nurse, having earned the name for unmanly and pathic ways. For if someone were to remove these smart robes of yours, and the soft tunics in which you write speeches against your friends, and carry them around and place them in the hands of the jurors, I think that, if someone were to do this unannounced, they would be at a loss whether they were holding the clothing of a man or a woman.

[132] And one of the generals will take the stand for the defense, I'm told, head held high and preening himself, with the air of a man who has frequented the wrestling schools and the philosophers' haunts. And he will attempt to discredit the whole basis of the dispute, maintaining that I have initiated not a prosecution but the start of an appalling coarseness. He will cite first of all your benefactors, Harmodius and Aristogiton,[143] and speak of their mutual loyalty and the good their relationship did for the city. [133] He will not shrink, they tell me, even from using the poems of Homer or the names of heroes, but will sing the praises of the friendship of Patroclus and Achilles, based on love, they say, and will now eulogize beauty, as though it had not long since been considered a blessing—if it is combined with self-control. If certain people, by slandering this physical beauty, bring ruin on those who possess it, he claims, your collective vote will be at odds with your individual prayers. [134] For he finds it strange, so he says, if in the case of sons as yet unborn all of you who are about to

---

[143] Harmodius and Aristogiton were lovers. According to Thucydides (6.54ff.), in the late sixth century the tyrant Hippias attempted to seduce Harmodius. On being rejected, he contrived to insult Harmodius' sister. The two lovers formed a conspiracy to kill Hippias. In the event, they panicked in the mistaken belief that the conspiracy had been discovered and killed the tyrant's brother, Hipparchus. Nonetheless, and despite the fact that the tyranny endured several years after the assassination (though the effect of the latter was to make Hippias' rule more repressive and therefore more unpopular), they passed into legend almost at death and were credited with the overthrow of the tyranny. As a special distinction, their descendants enjoyed almost total freedom from liturgies (see 1.11n).

sire children pray that they may be born noble in appearance and a credit to the city, but in the case of sons already born, who ought to be a source of pride for the city, if they stun people with their outstanding youthful beauty and become objects of lovers' rivalry, you will evidently disfranchise them under the influence of Aeschines. [135] And then he intends to make a direct attack on me, I'm told. He'll ask if I'm not ashamed to subject the practice to censure and risk, when I make a nuisance of myself in the gymnasia[144] and have been in love with many. And finally, so certain individuals inform me, in an attempt to encourage idle laughter among you, he says he will exhibit all the erotic poems I have written to individuals and claims he will provide testimony to quarrels and blows[145] that the practice has brought me.

[136] Personally, I neither criticize legitimate desire, nor do I allege that boys of outstanding beauty have prostituted themselves; nor do I deny that I myself have felt desire and still do. And I do not deny that the rivalries and fights that the thing provokes have befallen me. As to the poems they ascribe to me, some I admit to, but in the case of the rest I deny that their character is that presented by my opponents, who distort them. [137] According to my definition, desire for those who are noble and decent is characteristic of the generous and discerning spirit, but debauchery based on hiring someone for money I consider characteristic of a wanton and uncultivated man. And to be loved without corruption I count as noble, while to have been induced by money to prostitute oneself is shameful. The distance that separates them, the enormous difference, I shall try to explain to you in what follows. [138] Our fathers, when they were legislating about conduct

---

[144] Since Greeks usually exercised naked and the gymnasia played a major role in the physical training of (well-to-do) young men, they offered opportunities both for voyeurism and for seduction. The connection between the gymnasia and homoerotic pursuit is vividly depicted in Plato's *Charmides*. For predatory males cruising the gymnasia, see Aristophanes *Peace* 762–763.

[145] Fights over lovers (either young males or courtesans) were not unknown; see Demosthenes 54.14 and Lysias 3 and 4. However, our sources indicate that such behavior was not respectable; Aeschines indicates that he will be attacked not only as a hypocrite but as falling short of the conduct expected of his age and social station.

and activities dictated by nature, prohibited slaves from engaging in activities that they thought should belong to free men. "A slave," says the law, "may not exercise and rub himself down with oil in the wrestling schools." It did not add further: "But the free man is to rub himself down and exercise." For when the legislators in considering the benefits derived from the gymnasia prohibited slaves from participating, they believed that with the same law in which they prohibited these, they were also encouraging free men to go to the gymnasia. [139] And again the same legislator said: "A slave may not be the lover of a free boy or follow him, or he is to receive fifty blows of the public lash." But he did not forbid the free man from being a boy's lover or associating with and following him, and he envisaged not that this would prove harmful to the boy but that it would be testimony to his chastity. But since the boy is at this stage not responsible, and is unable to distinguish between real and false affection, it is the lover he disciplines, and he postpones talk of love to the age of reason, when the boy is older. And he considered that following and watching over a boy was the most effective way of securing and protecting his chastity. [140] In this way the city's benefactors, Harmodius and Aristogiton, those men of outstanding virtues, were brought up by that decent and lawful feeling—call it love or what you will[146]—to be men of such merit that when their deeds are praised, the panegyrics seem inadequate to their achievements.

[141] But since you speak of Achilles and Patroclus and of Homer and other poets, as though the jurors are men without education, and represent yourselves as impressive figures whose erudition allows you to look down on the people, to show you that we have already acquired a little knowledge and learning,[147] we, too, shall say something on the subject. For since they see fit to talk about wise men and take refuge in tales told in verse, look at the poets, men of Athens, who are acknowledged to be noble and edifying and see how great a distance

[146] The text translated here is an emendation (literally, "whether one must call it love or however one must [call it]"); the manuscript text would mean "whether one must call it love or inclination."

[147] Aeschines presents his opponents as talking down to the jurors; in contrast, in using the first-person plural, he associates himself with his audience.

they perceived between decent men, lovers of their equals, and those whose love is illicit, men who recognize no limits.

[142] I shall start with Homer, whom we count among the oldest and wisest of the poets. For Homer, though he often speaks of Patroclus and Achilles, is silent about love and gives no name to their friendship;[148] he thinks that the remarkable strength of their affection is obvious to the cultivated among his audience. [143] At one point, when Achilles is lamenting Patroclus' death, he mentions, as one of his most painful memories, that he has betrayed his promise to Patroclus' father Menoetius, that he had declared he would bring the son safe back to Opus, if the father would send him to Troy and entrust him to Achilles' care. And this makes it quite clear that it was for love that he had taken responsibility for his care. [144] The verses in question I shall now recite to you:

> Alas, pointless, then, the words I let fall on that day
> when I assured the hero Menoetius in his halls.
> I said I would restore his glorious son to Opus
> as sacker of Troy with his due share of spoil.
> But Zeus does not fulfill all of men's intents;
> for it is fated that both[149] stain the same earth red.[150]

[145] And it is not only here that he complains bitterly; so powerful was his grief for Patroclus that after his mother told him that if he did not go in pursuit of his enemies but left Patroclus' death unavenged he would return home and die in old age in his own homeland, while if he avenged it he would soon lose his own life, he preferred keeping faith with the dead man to survival. Such was the noble strength of purpose that drove him to punish his friend's killer that, though everyone urged him to bathe and take food, he vows he will do none of this until he brings Hector's head to Patroclus' tomb. [146] And while he is asleep at the pyre, as the poet tells us, Patroclus' ghost appears to

---

[148] The relationship of Achilles and Patroclus is not presented as homoerotic in Homer. They were presented as lovers in Aeschylus' *Myrmidons,* and this is taken for granted by speakers in Plato's *Symposium.*

[149] Achilles and Patroclus.

[150] *Iliad* 18.324–329.

him; and the memories he stirred, and the solemn instructions he gave Achilles, deserve both our tears and our admiration for their virtue and their friendship. He foretold that Achilles himself was not far from the end of his life and instructed him that, if at all possible, he should ensure that, in just the same way that they had grown up and lived together, in death, too, the bones of both should lie in the same vessel. [147] In his grief he speaks of the pursuits they shared in life, and says: "No more will we, as before, sit together apart from our other friends and deliberate on the most serious matters"; for he holds (I think) that the loss most keenly felt is loyalty and affection. To enable you to hear the poet's sentiments in verse, the clerk will read to you the epic lines in which Homer has described this. [148] To begin with, read the verses about taking vengeance on Hector.

> Yet, dear comrade, since I shall enter the earth after you,
> I shall not carry out your rites until I bring here Hector's
> armor [151] and head, those of your proud-hearted killer. [152]

[149] Now read out what Patroclus says as Achilles sleeps about their burial together and the pursuits they shared in life.

> For no more in life apart from our dear comrades
> shall we sit and take counsel. No, I am swallowed
> by hated doom, which fell to my lot at my birth.
> And for yourself, too, it is fated, godlike Achilles,
> to die beneath the walls of the noble Trojans,
> fighting with the enemy for fine-haired Helen.
> This, too, I shall tell you, and fix it in your heart.
> Place not my bones apart from your own, Achilles,
> but so the same earth may cover yourself, too,
> in the golden casket your lady mother gave you,
> just as we were raised together in your halls,
> when from Opus as a small child still Menoetius
> brought me to your house through grim man-slaying,
> on that day when I slew the son of Amphidamas,

---

[151] Patroclus had put on Achilles' armor to lead Achilles' troops into battle. Hector stripped the armor after killing Patroclus.

[152] *Iliad* 18.333–335.

in childish folly, not intending, in anger over dice.
There in his halls Peleus the knight welcomed me,
reared me unstinting and called me your companion.
Just so let the same vessel also cover our bones.[153]

[150] Now to show that he could have survived if he had not avenged
Patroclus' death, read out what Thetis says:

"Swift will be your fate, child, from what you say.
For straight after Hector your doom is waiting."
To her in turn spoke swift-footed godlike Achilles:
"Let me die now, since it seems I was not to save
my comrade from death, he who was far dearest to me."[154]

[151] And Euripides, as wise as any of the poets, took chaste love to
be one of the noblest emotions. He saw love as something worth pray-
ing for, and says somewhere:

Love that leads to decency and virtue
deserves men's envy. Might such love be mine![155]

[152] Again the same poet in his *Phoenix*, when defending him against
the false charge from his father and schooling people to judge not
from suspicion and slander but from a man's life, declares:

Oft have I been asked to judge disputes
and oft seen claims oppose each other,

---

[153] *Iliad* 23.77–91. Aeschines' text diverges from that of our manuscripts of
Homer. He adds, alters, and transposes lines. It has been suggested plausibly that
the changes represent Aeschines' own intervention rather than a distinct textual
tradition, and that their purpose is to enhance the intimacy of the relationship
between Achilles and Patroclus.

[154] *Iliad* 18.95–99. Aeschines again differs from the Homer manuscripts; he
has simplified the exchange (Achilles' reply in the Homer text is introduced by
"To her in anger spoke fleet-footed godlike Achilles," which taken out of context
might have suggested anger with Thetis) and changed the last line both to create
a self-contained quotation and to emphasize further the closeness of Achilles and
Patroclus. This episode, the paradigm of heroic choice, is used by Socrates in
Plato's *Apology* 28b–d to justify his refusal to abandon his way of life.

[155] The quote comes from Euripides' lost *Sthenoboea*, fr. 672 Nauck.

both witnessed, about the same event.
And thus do I, and any man who's wise,
reckon the truth, by looking to the nature
of a man and the way he spends his days.
And if any man enjoys bad company,
I've never questioned him—I know full well
he resembles those whose company he enjoys.[156]

[153] Observe the views expressed by the poet, men of Athens. He says that he has already decided many disputes, just as you now are judges, and he says that he bases his decision not on the testimony of witnesses but on a man's way of life and the company he keeps. He considers how the man on trial lives his daily life and the way he runs his household, on the ground that he will run the city's business in a similar way,[157] and whose company he enjoys. And finally he declared without hesitation that a man resembles those whose company gives him pleasure. So it is proper that you apply Euripides' reasoning to Timarchus. [154] How has he managed his property? He has squandered his inheritance, and, though selling his body and taking bribes in political life, he has wasted it all, and so he has nothing left but the resultant disgrace. Whose company does he enjoy? Hegesander's. And what are Hegesander's habits? The sort for which the laws forbid the practitioner to address the people. As for me, what charge do I make against Timarchus; what exactly figures in my written accusation? That Timarchus addresses the people when he has prostituted himself and squandered his paternal estate. And you, what have you sworn? That you will cast your vote on the charge brought by the prosecution.[158]

---

[156] From Euripides' lost *Phoenix*, fr. 812 Nauck. As with the quotation from Hesiod (see 1.129n), the words were later turned against Aeschines by Demosthenes (19.245).

[157] The tactic used here, of inserting "editorial" comment that has the effect of magnifying the support supposedly derived from the text cited, is identical to that in 1.19–20.

[158] At the beginning of the year, all 6,000 jurors empaneled for that year swore an oath whose clauses included promises to vote according to the laws and the decrees of Assembly and Council (or in default of a law according to "their most

[155] But I don't want to talk at excessive length about the poets. Instead I shall tell you the names of older men who are well known, and young men and boys. Some of these have had many lovers because of their beauty, while others are still in the bloom of youth now; but none of them has ever been exposed to the same accusations as those made against Timarchus. And in contrast I shall give you the names of men who have practiced shameful and blatant prostitution; remembering these will help you to put Timarchus in the proper category. [156] I shall start with the names of people who have lived in the honorable manner that befits free men. Men of Athens, you know that Crito[159] the son of Astyochus and Periclides of Perithoidae and Polemagenes and Pantaleon the son of Cleagoras and Timesitheus the runner were in their day the most beautiful not only of the Athenian citizens but in all Greece, and that they attracted the largest number of lovers, and the most decent. Yet nobody has ever found fault with them. [157] Again, among those who are young men or still children even now, there is Iphicrates' nephew, the son of Tisias of Rhamnus,[160] who bears the same name as the defendant Timarchus. Though he is good-looking, he is so foreign to shameful conduct that the other day, at the Rural Dionysia during the performance of the comic plays at Collytus,[161] when the comic actor Parmeno[162] spoke an anapaestic line to the chorus in which mention was made of certain "big Timarchian prostitutes," nobody suspected a reference to the young man; everyone saw a reference to you. So firm is your claim to the practice. And again there is Anticles the sprinter and Phidias the brother of

---

just opinion"), to give both sides a fair hearing, to cast their vote specifically on the subject under dispute, and to take no bribes. It is common for speakers to remind the jurors of the oath, either in general or with reference to specific clauses.

[159] Crito is known from inscriptions as a member of a propertied family. The rest are otherwise unknown.

[160] The father and son of this Timarchus (both called Tisias) are known from fourth-century inscriptions; Timarchus himself is known only from this passage. For Iphicrates, see 2.27n.

[161] Collytus was an urban deme, south of the Acropolis.

[162] We know little of Parmeno's life and career, beyond the fact that he was a renowned verbal mimic.

Melesias.¹⁶³ Though I could mention still more, I shall stop there, to avoid seeming to flatter any of them with my praise.

[158] Turning to those who share Timarchus' habits, I shall avoid making enemies and speak of those who least concern me. Who among you does not know of Diophantus, known as "the orphan," who arrested the foreigner and brought him before the archon for whom Aristophon¹⁶⁴ of Azenia was serving as assistant? He alleged that he had been cheated of four drachmas owed for this service and cited the laws that instruct the archon to take care of orphans,¹⁶⁵ when he himself had broken those which cover chastity. What citizen was not offended by Cephisodorus, known as the son of Molon,¹⁶⁶ who had defiled his most beautiful appearance with the most infamous acts? Or Mnesitheus, known as the cook's son, and many others whose names I purposely forget. [159] I don't want to pursue each of them by name spitefully. In fact, in my love of my city I would dearly wish to have a shortage of such cases to cite. But now that we have mentioned some examples of each type, dealing separately with the objects of chaste love and those who abused their own persons, I want you now to answer this question from me: to which category do you assign Timarchus, to the people who have lovers or to the prostitutes?¹⁶⁷ So then, Timarchus, do not try to desert the society you have chosen and defect to the way of life of free men.

---

¹⁶³ Not the Anticles of 1.53. Anticles is known as the winner of the Olympic *stadion* (single-lap race) in 340. Phidias and Melesias are otherwise unknown.

¹⁶⁴ Diophantus is otherwise unknown. For Aristophon, see 1.64n. The length of Aristophon's political career makes it impossible to date the incident precisely, though the fact that he was assistant (*paredros*) to the eponymous archon of the year in question would seem to place it early in the fourth century, before he achieved political prominence. The post of assistant to the archon both served as a rung on the political ladder for aspiring political leaders and offered a means for the archons (who were selected by lot but who appointed their assistants) to draw on administrative and political expertise.

¹⁶⁵ One of the duties of the eponymous archon was to take care of orphans (Aristotle *Constitution of Athens* 56.6–7; [Dem.] 43.75).

¹⁶⁶ Cephisodorus and Molon are otherwise unknown, as is Mnesitheus.

¹⁶⁷ Presumably Aeschines pauses here for the audience to shout out.

[160] If they try to argue that a man has not prostituted himself if he did not make a contract to hire himself out, and demand that I provide documentation and witnesses to this effect, firstly remember the laws concerning prostitution; nowhere does the legislator mention contracts. He did not ask whether anyone had disgraced himself under a written contract, but, however the activity takes place, he absolutely bars the man who has engaged in it from the public affairs of the city. And rightly so. If any man in his youth abandoned noble ambitions for the sake of shameful pleasure, he believed that this man should not in later years enjoy political rights. [161] Furthermore, one can easily detect the idiocy of this argument. We would all agree that we make contracts out of lack of trust for each other, so that the party who has not broken the written terms can obtain satisfaction in court from the one who has. Well, then, if the matter calls for litigation, the protection of the laws is still available for people who have prostituted themselves under a contract and are wronged, according to the defense arguments. And what case would each party make? Imagine that you're not hearing it from me but seeing the thing taking place. [162] Let's suppose that the one who hired is honest in the business and the person hired is dishonest and unreliable, or alternatively the opposite, that the person hired is reasonable and conforms to the agreement while the one who has hired him and had the pleasure of his youth has cheated him. Imagine that you yourselves are sitting in judgment. So then, the older man, when given his allocation of water to make his case, will present his accusation with gravity, looking straight at you, of course, and say: [163] "Men of Athens, I hired Timarchus to be my prostitute on the basis of the contract in the keeping of Demosthenes" (there's no reason why this shouldn't be what's said),[168] "and he is not doing what he agreed for me." And obviously he'll go on to tell the jurors of this agreement and explain what a person like this is required to do. And then won't he be stoned, this man who hires an Athenian in contravention of the laws?[169] Won't he

---

[168] Contracts were often lodged with third parties, commonly bankers. Here the effect is to drag Demosthenes into the fiction of debauchery, making him almost a pimp for Timarchus, just as in 1.131 Aeschines made him a fellow pervert.

[169] Based on Aeschines' interpretation of the law (1.15).

leave the court not only liable for compensation¹⁷⁰ but also convicted of serious outrage (*hybris*)?

[**164**] Or say that it is not this party but the one who was hired who brings the action. Now let clever Batalus¹⁷¹ come forward to speak for him, so we'll know what on earth he will say. "Jurors, somebody or other" (it makes no difference) "hired me to be his prostitute for money. And while I have done everything, and still do now, that a prostitute should according to the written contract, the defendant is in breach of the agreement." And then won't he be met with loud shouting from the jurors? Won't they all say: "Despite this do you invade the marketplace, wear the crown of office, do any of the things we do?" So then, the contract is no use.

[**165**] How, then, has it become an established practice to maintain that before now people have prostituted themselves by contract? This I shall now tell you. It is said that a certain citizen (I shall omit the name in a desire to avoid enmity),¹⁷² who failed to anticipate any of the problems I described to you just now, prostituted himself under a contract that was deposited with Anticles.¹⁷³ Since he was not a private citizen but entered public life and was subjected to insults, the result was that the city became accustomed to the expression, and this is why some people ask if the activity has taken place under a contract. But the legislator did not concern himself with the way the activity has taken place; no, the legislator condemned a man to disgrace if he hires himself out in any way whatsoever.

[**166**] Yet though these issues have been defined so clearly, Demosthenes will discover many diversionary arguments. The wickedness of his statements on the main issue might not arouse so much resent-

---

¹⁷⁰ Greek *epobelia,* a penalty of one-sixth of the sum in dispute paid to the winning party by the losers in certain private cases. We do not know the full range of cases to which it applied nor whether it applied only to failure to win or to conspicuous failure (i.e., failure to obtain a certain minimum proportion of the votes cast).

¹⁷¹ For Demosthenes' nickname, see above, 1.126; for the tactic of enmeshing Demosthenes in the alleged activities of Timarchus, cf. 1.163.

¹⁷² The lack of detail, while given a veneer of plausibility by the parenthesis, suggests that the story is an invention by Aeschines.

¹⁷³ Presumably the Anticles mentioned at 1.53.

ment. But the irrelevant arguments he will drag in to the detriment of
the city's system of justice deserve your anger. Philip will be there in
plenty; and the name of his son Alexander will be thrown in, too. For
in addition to his other faults, this man is a crude and insensitive
individual. [167] His offensive remarks against Philip in his speech are
uncivil and inappropriate, but less serious than the wrong I am about
to mention; for his abuse will be directed incontrovertibly against a
man, for all that he himself is not a man. But when with the use of
labored ambiguous language he drags in shameful insinuations against
the boy, he makes a laughing stock of the city. [168] In an attempt to
spoil the audit[174] I am about to undergo for my service on the embassy, he alleges that when he was giving the Council an account of
Alexander the other day—how he played the lyre to us while we were
drinking and recited speeches and debated with another boy—and
was telling the Council all he knew about the matter, I grew angry at
the jokes against the boy as if I were not one of the envoys but a
relative.[175] [169] In fact, I have not spoken with Alexander, naturally,
because of his youth.[176] But Philip I praise right now for his auspicious
statements. If his conduct toward us matches his present promises,[177]
he will make it a safe and easy task to praise him. I criticized Demosthenes in the Council chamber not out of a desire to curry favor with
the boy but because I felt that if you listened to such things, the city
would appear to share the speaker's lack of decency.

---

[174] For the *euthyna*, see 1.1n. The reference is to the second embassy to Macedonia of 346.

[175] The allegation appears to be that Aeschines is sexually attracted to Alexander, who would have been about ten at this time, an accusation that combines
suggestions of treason with hypocrisy (the man who distorts what the defense
represents as the normal homoerotic activity by the young Timarchus is himself
a voracious pursuer of young men) and possibly bad taste (since the ideal age for
the object of homoerotic pursuit was the mid-teens). The mockery of Alexander
may amount to laughing at the Macedonian "barbarians" for aping Greek culture,
or it could be mockery of alleged ineptitude by Alexander.

[176] As a young male, Alexander is a potential sexual target for older men; Aeschines shows discretion in avoiding contact that might compromise the boy.

[177] Philip made ambiguous promises during the negotiations for the peace. At
the date in question, these had yet to be tested.

[170] But in general, men of Athens, you should not admit lines of defense irrelevant to the main issue, first of all because of the oaths you have sworn,[178] and secondly to avoid being misled by a fellow who is a master of the art of speaking. I shall take my story back a little to give you the information. When Demosthenes had squandered his inheritance,[179] he went around the city hunting for rich young orphans[180] whose fathers were dead and whose mothers were in charge of the property. I shall omit many of them and mention one of the victims of appalling treatment. [171] He noticed a household that was rich but badly run. The head of the house was a proud but unintelligent woman, but the property was handled by a half-mad orphaned youth, Aristarchus the son of Moschus. He pretended to be in love with this young man, drew him into this intimate relationship, and filled him full of false hopes that he would very soon be a leading public speaker; and he showed him a list of names.[181] [172] And he encouraged and taught him to commit acts of a sort that the young man is now in exile from his fatherland, while this man, having got hold of the money that was to support Aristarchus in his exile, has robbed him of three talents; and Nicodemus of Aphidna has been violently murdered by Aristarchus, with both his eyes gouged out, poor wretch, and the tongue cut out with which he exercised free speech in confidence in the laws and in your authority.[182]

---

[178] For the jurors' oath, see 1.154n.

[179] Aeschines gives a distorted version of Demosthenes' early career (for which see 1.94n). In financial as in sexual activity, he presents Demosthenes as a kindred spirit of Timarchus.

[180] As the context makes clear, the Greek *orphanos* is not identical with our word "orphan," which denotes someone who has lost both parents; the Greek term refers to someone who has lost a father before reaching the age of majority.

[181] That is, the names of former pupils of Demosthenes, now successful politicians.

[182] The incident, about which we are badly informed, was evidently a notorious scandal (Aeschines alludes to it again at 2.148, as does Dinarchus [1.30, 47]). Nicodemus appears to have been a political associate of Demosthenes' enemy Midias; he indicted Demosthenes for failure to perform military service when the feud was at its height (see 3.52n, 3.148n). When he was murdered, and Demosthenes' young associate Aristarchus implicated, the incident naturally offered a useful weapon against Demosthenes. See further Demosthenes 21.103–104.

[173] So then, men of Athens, you put Socrates the sophist to death, because it was found that he had taught Critias, one of the Thirty who overthrew the democracy; [183] yet is Demosthenes to get his comrades [184] off in your court, this man who has exacted such terrible revenge from ordinary men loyal to the democracy for their free-speaking? At his invitation, some of his pupils have come to listen. For I'm told he declares to them, drumming up business at your expense, that without your noticing he will shift the ground of debate and your attention; [174] that he will bring confidence to the defendant the moment he appears in court and reduce the accuser to panic and fear for himself; that he will summon such loud and hostile heckling from the jurors by dragging in my political speeches and criticizing the peace that was brought about through me and Philocrates [185] that I will not even turn up in court to defend myself, when I submit to audit for my service as envoy; I'll be content if I receive a moderate punishment and am not condemned to death! [175] Under no circumstances must you allow this sophist to laugh and amuse himself at your expense. No, you must imagine you are seeing him back home from the court, preening himself in the company of his young men and telling them how successfully he stole the case from the jurors: [186] "You see, I led them away from the charges against Timarchus;

---

[183] Socrates was tried and executed in 399 for disbelieving in the city's gods and corrupting the youth. Aeschines distorts in narrowing the focus to Critias and in ignoring the religious dimension; he does, however, accurately pick up on one strand of the popular prejudice that led to Socrates' death.

[184] The Greek term is *hetairos,* which need be no more than "close associate/ friend," but since Demosthenes is presented in 1.172–173 as setting himself above the laws and curtailing the democratic rights of citizens, Aeschines probably also intends the sense of the word that became established late in the fifth century, referring to members of the oligarchic clubs that plotted the overthrow of the democracy.

[185] At this stage Aeschines was prepared to emphasize his active role in the peace negotiations and to associate himself publicly with Philocrates. As the Athenian attitude to the peace soured and Philocrates' unpopularity increased, culminating in his indictment by Hyperides in 343, Aeschines, though retaining his commitment to the peace, sought both to play down his own role in the negotiations and to dissociate himself from Philocrates.

[186] The taunt stung; Demosthenes uses this passage against Aeschines at 19.243.

I guided them toward the accuser, Philip, and the Phocians[187] and fixed their attention there, and I dangled fears before the eyes of my listeners; the result was that the defendant became prosecutor and the prosecutor found himself on trial, while the jurors forgot the case they were trying and listened instead to a case they were not trying." [176] Your duty is to resist these attempts firmly, to follow everything assiduously, and at no point to allow him to deviate or to press arguments irrelevant to the case. Just like in chariot races, you must keep to the actual track of the subject at issue. And if you do this, you will not be treated with contempt, and you will display the same attitude as legislators and jurors. Otherwise, you will give the impression of feeling anger in anticipation of crimes about to happen but losing interest in crimes actually committed.

[177] To put the matter briefly: if you punish wrongdoers, your laws will be noble and valid, whereas if you acquit them, the laws will still be noble but no longer valid. My reason for saying this I shall not hesitate to tell you frankly. And my account will serve as an example. Why do you think, men of Athens, that the laws are fine but the city's decrees are inferior and the judgments reached in court sometimes excite amazement? I shall explain the reasons for this. [178] It is because in making the laws you take account of all the principles of justice. You do not act for dishonest profit or favor or enmity, but consider only justice and the public good. And being naturally more intelligent, I think, than other men, as one would expect, you make the best laws. But in the Assembly and the courts you often lose sight of the arguments relating to the main issue; you are misled by deceit and posturing and admit the most unjust practice into your trials. You allow the defendants to bring counteraccusations against their accusers. [179] When you are distracted from the case for the defense

---

[187] That is, Demosthenes reverses the roles of prosecutor and defendant. Aeschines ignores the fate of Phocis in this speech, though it plays a more significant role in speeches 2 and 3. Unless Aeschines is merely guessing about the opposition arguments here, the defense exploited the issue in the Timarchus case. The settlement imposed on Phocis in the immediate aftermath of the conclusion of the peace was a blow to Athenian interests, expectations, and trust (always limited) in Philip. For Phocis and the Sacred War, see Introduction to Aeschines. The presentation of Demosthenes' boasts achieves plausibility by vividness but remains no more than unsubstantiated character assassination.

and your minds are on other matters, you become forgetful of the prosecution case, and you leave the courts without getting satisfaction from either side. Neither from the accuser (for his fate is not put to the vote) nor from the defendant (for by using his accusations against others to brush off the actual charges against him, he has evaded the court). And the laws are overturned, and the democracy is corrupted, and the practice becomes still more widespread. On occasion you are too ready to admit an argument that is not supported by an upright life.

[180] Not so the Spartans—and it is laudable to imitate the virtues of foreigners as well.[188] Once when someone was addressing the Spartan assembly, a man whose life had been disgraceful but who was a superlatively able speaker, and the Spartans, so they say, were about to vote as he advised, one of the Old Men came forward. These are the ones they revere and fear; they regard the office named after this age group as the most important, and they form it from men whose lives have been decent from childhood to old age.[189] One of these, it is said, came forward and vigorously berated the Spartans and even abused them along the following lines, that they would not long inhabit a Sparta unravaged by war if they listened to advisers like this in their assemblies. [181] At the same time he called upon another Spartan, not a gifted speaker but a man who had won glory in war and was outstanding in justice and self-discipline, and instructed him to utter as best he could the views expressed by the previous speaker; "So that," he said, "the Spartans may vote on the words of a good man, and close their ears entirely to the voices of men who are confirmed cowards and villains." This was the advice given to his fellow-citizens by an old man who had lived a decent life since childhood. He would have been keen to allow Timarchus or the pervert[190] Demosthenes to take part in public life!

---

[188] The justification for the digression anticipates possible resentment from the jurors at the comparison between Athens and Sparta in which Sparta emerges as superior. The incident narrated could be a piece of contemporary "folklore," but the resemblance to the alleged situation of Timarchus is so convenient that one suspects invention by Aeschines.

[189] A reference to the Gerusia, the council of elders at Sparta.

[190] The Greek term used, *kinaidos,* is more precise, in that it refers to the male recipient of homosexual penetration. See further 1.185n.

[182] But I don't want to give the impression of flattering the Spartans. So I shall speak also of our own ancestors. They were so severe in their attitude toward shameful behavior and took so extremely seriously the chastity of their children that one citizen who found that his daughter had been corrupted and had not preserved her maidenhood honorably until marriage sealed her up in an empty house with a horse, knowing that she would be killed by it if they were shut in together. To this day the foundations of this house are still standing in your city, and the spot is called "the place of the horse and girl."

[183] And Solon, the most illustrious of legislators, has drafted ancient and solemn laws on the orderly conduct of women. If a woman is caught with a seducer,[191] he does not allow her to wear finery or to enter the public temples, to prevent her from corrupting innocent women with her company. And if she enters them or wears finery, he allows anyone who encounters her to tear her clothing, remove her jewelry, and beat her, though he is not permitted to kill or maim her; Solon thus deprives such a woman of honor and makes her life intolerable. [184] And he allows for indictment (*graphē*) of procurers, male and female; and if they are convicted, he makes death the punishment. The reason is that when people who wish to sin hesitate through shame to come together, the procurers offer their own lack of shame for pay and advance the affair to the point of discussion and action.

[185] So then, this was the view of your fathers on the issues of shame and honor. Will *you* acquit Timarchus, a man guilty of the most shameful practices? A man, with a male body, who has committed the offenses of a woman?[192] Which of you, then, if he catches

---

[191] The Greek term is *moichos.* It and its cognate *moicheia,* "seduction," refer to a male who has unforced sex with a free woman without the consent of her *kyrios* ("guardian"—an Athenian female remained a legal minor all her life and was always under male control and protection). The penalties for the *moichos* could be severe (including the right for the aggrieved male to kill a *moichos* caught in the act). Those for the woman were scarcely less severe, since the ban on entry to public temples barred her from the one area in which Greek women played a significant public role. The embargo is confirmed by [Dem.] 59.87. The present passage is our sole source for the ban on wearing jewelry and fine clothes.

[192] The passage simultaneously appeals to Greek stereotypes of male and female character (it was widely accepted that women were less able than men to

his wife in misconduct, will punish her? Who will not seem stupid, if he shows anger at a woman who does wrong according to her nature but uses as his adviser[193] a man who had abused himself against nature. [186] What will be the state of mind of each of you when he goes home from court? The man on trial is not obscure; he is well known. And the law on the scrutiny of public speakers is not a poor one but quite excellent. It is to be expected that boys and young men will ask their relatives how the case has been judged.[194] [187] So what will you say, you who now have the power to vote, when your sons ask you if you convicted or acquitted? The moment you admit to acquitting him, won't you overturn the whole educational system? What's the use in keeping slave chaperones or appointing gymnastic trainers and teachers for our children, when the men who have been given responsibility for the laws are deflected from their duty when faced with disgraceful acts?

[188] I also find it surprising, men of Athens, if you, who hate brothel-keepers,[195] intend to let go people who have voluntarily prostituted themselves. Evidently this same man, who will not be allowed to obtain the priesthood of any of the gods, since under the laws his body is unclean, will draft in the text of decrees prayers to the Solemn Goddesses[196] for the good of the city. Then why be amazed at the failure of public policy, when speakers like this man attach their names

---

resist temptations) and hints at the different sexual roles, suggesting that Timarchus allows his body to be penetrated by other males. Although there is no evidence that this in itself laid a citizen male open to prosecution (unlike accepting money for sex), there was evidently a prejudice against it, and it may in the Athenian mind have been associated with male prostitution. The evidence of homoerotic scenes on vase paintings indicates that (face-to-face) intercrural rather than anal coitus was the "proper" position for homosexual acts between social equals, and Athenian comedy of the fifth century directs its mockery at males who succumb to penetration, not at males who play an active homosexual role.

[193] I.e., a speaker in the Assembly.

[194] For the attempt to shame the jurors with reference to their relatives, cf. 3.246; [Demosthenes] 59.110–111.

[195] Pimps in ancient texts are stereotyped as avaricious and unscrupulous.

[196] The *Semnai*, identified at Athens at least from the mid-fifth century with the *Erinyes* (Furies); they had a shrine below the Areopagus.

to decisions of the people? Shall we send abroad as envoy a man whose life at home has been disgraceful and entrust to him our most important interests? What would a man not sell when he has sold off the abuse (*hybris*) of his person? Who would this man pity when he has shown no pity for himself?

[189] Which of you is unfamiliar with the disgusting conduct of Timarchus? In the case of people who exercise, even if we don't attend the gymnasia, we can recognize them from a glance at their fit condition. In the same way we recognize men who have worked as prostitutes from their shameless and impudent manner and from their general behavior even if we're not present at their activities. For if a man has shown contempt for the laws and for morality on the most important issues, he has a certain attitude of mind that is visible from his disorderly manner.

[190] You will find that it is men such as this more than all others who have destroyed cities and have themselves encountered the worst disasters. Don't imagine, men of Athens, that wrongdoing has its origin in the gods and not in the willfulness of men, or that Furies pursue men guilty of impiety, as in the tragedies,[197] and punish them with burning brands. [191] No, unrestrained physical pleasures and a feeling that nothing is ever enough, these are what recruit to gangs of robbers, what fill the pirate ships, these are each man's Fury; these are what drive him to slaughter his fellow-citizens, serve tyrants, conspire to overthrow democracy. They take no account of the shame or the consequences for themselves; it is the pleasure success will bring that mesmerizes them. So eradicate natures such as this, men of Athens, and turn the ambitions of young men toward virtue.

[192] Of this you may be sure, and please be particularly mindful of what I'm about to say: if Timarchus is punished for his practices, you will be making a new start for discipline in the city; if he is acquitted, it would have been better if the trial had not taken place. For before Timarchus was put on trial, the law and the name of the courts inspired some fear. But if the leading and most notorious exponent of vice comes to court and gets away safely, he will inspire many more to

---

[197] Especially Aeschylus' *Eumenides,* where the chorus of Furies visibly pursues Orestes.

wrongdoing, and in the end what rouses you to anger will not be words but a crisis. [193] So don't wait to vent your wrath on a crowd, but do it on one man. And watch out for their cunning tricks and their supporting speakers. I won't mention any of them by name, so that they won't use this point to begin their speech by saying that they would not have come forward if they had not been mentioned by name. This is what I'll do. I'll remove the names and describe the practices and enable you to recognize their physical features. Each of them will have only himself to blame, if he mounts this stand and shows no shame. [194] Timarchus has three kinds of supporting speaker to help him, those who have squandered their inheritance with their daily expenditures, those who have misspent their youth and abused their bodies and are afraid not for Timarchus but for themselves and their way of life, in case they are brought to trial at some point, and others who are people without any restraint who have made unrestricted use of men like him and whose motive is that trust in the aid they offer[198] will make people more ready to do wrong. [195] Before you listen to their speeches in support of Timarchus, remember their way of life. Tell the ones who have done wrong to their own bodies not to pester you but to stop addressing the people; for the law does not examine the conduct of private citizens but of public men. Tell the ones who have squandered their inheritances to work and make their living in some other way. And tell the hunters of the young men who are easily caught to turn their attentions to foreigners and resident aliens; then they won't be deprived of their chosen passion and your interests will not be damaged.

[196] You have had from me all you could justly demand. I have informed you of the laws, I've examined the defendant's way of life. So now it is for you to judge my words; shortly I shall observe your acts. The final decision depends on your judgment. If it is your wish, if you vote justly and in your own best interests, we shall be more zealous in exposing lawbreakers.

---

[198] I.e., to anyone accused of such a crime.

2. ON THE EMBASSY

Context

With the exception of Demosthenes, those who negotiated the Peace of Philocrates had high hopes of its potential benefits. In the event, their expectations were disappointed. The peace released Athens from a war of which the population was tired, but it brought no tangible benefits. The vague promises hinted at by Philip and conveyed to Athens by at least some of its envoys failed to materialize. On the other hand, the settlement of the Third Sacred War caused profound resentment at Athens. Its effect was to eradicate Phocis as a political and military force, depriving Athens of an important ally against Thebes. In contrast, the advantages of the peace to Philip were all too obvious. He had been left with a free hand to deal with Phocis, and his settlement of the Sacred War had enhanced his prestige and influence in central Greece. He had emerged as the arbiter of interstate disputes in Greece and the protector of the temple at Delphi. The exclusion of the Thracian king Cersobleptes from the peace enabled him to reduce Cersobleptes to the status of vassal, depriving Athens of a potentially useful ally against Macedonia in the north. From the very beginning Athenian public opinion was suspicious of Philip. When invited in the immediate aftermath of the peace to join Philip in bringing Phocis to heel, the Athenians, under the influence of speakers like Demosthenes, had declined. In the years following the peace there were further sources of friction between Athens and Philip. In this context, the opponents of the peace began the task of painstakingly weakening or destroying its supporters. In 343 its most

visible supporter, Philocrates, was impeached by Hyperides. Philocrates fled the city, presumably aware that his chances of survival in
the prevailing climate were slim. In the summer of the same year,
Demosthenes' charge of ambassadorial misconduct, which he had
originally brought at Aeschines' final audit (*euthyna*) in 346, came to
trial. Ancient tradition reports that Aeschines was acquitted by a narrow margin, a mere thirty votes, from a judicial panel that had at least
500 (and more probably over 1,000) members. This was a technical victory only. Aeschines had arrayed some of the biggest names in
Athenian politics in his defense.[1] In coming close to defeating this con-
sortium, Demosthenes had begun his own inexorable rise to dominance in the Assembly and had demonstrated that popular dissatisfaction with the peace was approaching critical mass. Victory was not
necessary. Aeschines, in contrast, though technically the winner, was
substantially weakened as a political force.

The Case

This is one of the rare cases for which we have the speeches for
both sides. Demosthenes (19) charges Aeschines with betraying Athenian interests for money from Philip. Aeschines makes clear, and Demosthenes does not deny, that there was no accusation from Demosthenes after the first embassy. Demosthenes' charge is that Aeschines
was corrupted (or first gave signs of being corrupted) after this. He is
not specific about the date Aeschines allegedly came under Philip's
influence. The essence of his case is that during the debate on the
peace after the first embassy, Aeschines both forced the pace of deliberation, preventing a more general peace that would have included
other Greek states beyond Athens and its allies, and ensured that the
Phocians and Cersobleptes were excluded from the treaty. He then
delayed setting out on the second embassy to swear Philip and his
allies to the treaty, enabling Philip to finish dealing with Cersobleptes.
On his return from the second embassy he gave a false account of
Philip's intentions, with the result that the Athenians made no attempt to prevent Philip from gaining entry to central Greece (as they

---

[1] See 2.184.

had in 352) and declared a readiness to take to the field against Phocis if the temple at Delphi was not surrendered to Philip. The recognition that Athens would not support them led the Phocians to surrender to Philip, which resulted in the destruction of the Phocian cities. In presenting Aeschines as the collaborator of Philocrates, Demosthenes systematically suppresses his own very substantial contribution to the creation of the peace. More importantly, at no point does he offer anything remotely resembling evidence to support the charge of treason. There is no reason to suppose that Aeschines had been bought by Philip. He had, however (like many others), misread the intentions of Philip with Philip's active encouragement, and his response to some of the charges betrays an element of discomfort.

Whether Demosthenes believed the accusation is less clear. Some of his statements certainly reflect a desire to obtain a satisfactory result regardless of the truth, and it is tempting, particularly in view of Aeschines' portrayal of Demosthenes in the present speech, to conclude that the prosecution is entirely cynical. Aeschines is merely a means to attack the peace and its supporters. The truth may, however, be more complicated. The Athenians collectively tended to attribute failure to conspiracy rather than human error. In a world where politicians could amass large sums of money in gifts from interested parties, it was natural to see bribery everywhere. The adversarial nature of the Athenian political process, which meant that politicians tended to accuse their opponents of wrongdoing rather than stupidity, exacerbated this tendency. Certainly the Assembly and the panels of jurors were ready to suspect corruption behind political or military failure. Individual politicians may at different times have shared or manipulated this belief, and they may not always have been fully aware of the difference.

The Speech

As with the prosecution of Timarchus, Aeschines relies heavily on narrative. The effect of this, together with a tendency to treat allegations in chronological order, is once more to make neat classification of the different components of the speech difficult.

The introduction (1–10) consists of a bid for a favorable hearing and some preliminary character assassination against Demosthenes. It is followed after a brief transition (11) by a long narrative, which begins with an account of the courtship between Philip and Athens that led to the sending of the first embassy (12–19), emphasizing Demosthenes' active support for Philocrates and the peace. The narrative proceeds in chronological order to deal with the first embassy (20–39), where Aeschines displays his independence in the face of Philip and gives a forceful presentation of Athens' case while Demosthenes performs abysmally. The account of the return journey (40–56) adds duplicity and inconsistency to incompetence as defining features of Demosthenes and further emphasizes his full support for the peace as eventually passed.

In 57–69 Aeschines pauses to refute Demosthenes' allegation concerning Aeschines' conduct at the two successive Assembly meetings on the eighteenth and nineteenth of the month Elaphebolion. Demosthenes had alleged that Aeschines changed his mind overnight between the meetings, speaking against Philocrates on the first day and for him on the second. As well as rejecting this allegation, he charges Demosthenes with forcing the pace of debate, when the allies favored delay, and with favoring peace on exactly the terms proposed by Philocrates.

Aeschines never actually makes clear exactly what his own stance was on those crucial days. Instead he justifies his inclination to make peace by means of a narrative of Athenian difficulties in the preceding period (70–74), followed by a broad account of his arguments for pragmatic peace, consisting of an account of successes and failures in the fifth century (74–77), culminating in a digression on his source for fifth-century history, his father Atrometus (78), the aim of which is to appeal to the goodwill of the jurors. He defends his change from opposition to Philip in 348 to acceptance of peace in 346 (79) and closes this section with a complaint on the injustice of blaming envoys for peace terms resulting from failures by military commanders (80).

Aeschines now returns to Athenian deliberations on the peace and narrates Cersobleptes' attempt to be included in the peace treaty; he blames Demosthenes for his exclusion (81–88) and rejects Demosthenes' allegation that the delayed departure of the second embassy allowed Philip to defeat Cersobleptes (89–93).

Aeschines now interrupts his chronological account briefly to reject Demosthenes' allegation that he lied when he sought to avoid serving on the third embassy (94–96), then returns to the second embassy (97–118). Demosthenes again emerges as timid, deceitful, and incompetent, Aeschines as a man ready to confront Philip and to take risks for the city's sake. He presents himself as arguing for lenient treatment for Phocis and for an end to Philip's support for Thebes. He did everything he could (118). If events turned out badly, it was not his fault.

Aeschines again turns from narrative to argument. He begins with brief treatment of an uncomfortable issue, the report he gave on his return from the second embassy (119–120), which aroused high expectations about the peace. He refutes Demosthenes' claim that he was prevented from reporting the truth to the Athenians (121–123) and pours scorn on Demosthenes' allegation that Aeschines colluded with Philip in drafting the letter brought to Athens by the second embassy (124–129). Next he turns to the charge that he was responsible for the destruction of Phocis. He argues (130–135) that the cause was the exhaustion of Phocian finances and the misjudgments of the Phocian leader Phalaecus. Phalaecus was not the only one to miscalculate; there was a general uncertainty about Philip's intentions (136–137). But the main cause of the destruction of Phocis, he maintains, was the lost opportunity to influence the Sacred War because of the intervention of those, like Demosthenes, who prevented Athens from acceding to Philip's request that Athens send forces. Aeschines intervened to save the Phocian population when its enemies were arguing for savage punishment (138–143).

The rest of the speech moves from theme to theme in no apparent order. First Aeschines deals with the lack of evidence against him. With evident relish, Demosthenes has used the same argument as Aeschines had used against Timarchus, when he claimed that no proof is needed where everyone knows the facts and attributed a mysterious divine force to Report, which disseminates this information. In reply, Aeschines rather casuistically distinguishes between Report and slander (144–145). He uses his relatives to demonstrate his commitments in Athens as proof that he could not have betrayed his city and responds to Demosthenes' attacks on his family (146–152). He then refutes Demosthenes' allegation that he assaulted an Olynthian woman captured when the city fell (153–158). In 159–161 he reviews and rejects the case against him, appending a reply to Demosthenes' charge that he joined Philip in celebrating the destruction of Phocis (162–163).

He defends his policies against the charge of inconsistency (164–165), digressing once more (166) to savage Demosthenes' character. From Demosthenes he turns to his own impressive military career (167–171).

In 172–178, Aeschines sets the peace and its opponents in the context of a century and a half of Athenian history; peace appears as beneficial, war as both disastrous and dangerous to the democratic constitution. In 179 he appeals for pity for his relatives, who are here in court to plead with him. After an appeal for acquittal on the basis of his loyal service to the city (180–183), combined with a further attack on Demosthenes, the speech closes with a request that the supporting speakers take the platform (184).

The speech relies heavily on lucid narrative to carry conviction. It seeks to distance Aeschines from Philocrates (it would have been madness to try to defend Philocrates) and to associate Demosthenes closely with Philocrates. Through the medium of the narrative, Aeschines gives a plausible and consistent picture of himself as a loyal servant of the people, ready to confront Philip (an important detail, since he is accused of being in Philip's pay) and Thebes in the city's interests, and as a man whose policy and practice remain constant irrespective of his location. Demosthenes, in contrast, emerges as incompetent and cowardly in representing the city abroad but bold in attacking his colleagues back in Athens, inconstant in his policies, as well as duplicitous, scheming, and malicious. The reliance on chronological order gives the speech a fluency that carries the hearer along. The use of emotional appeal and character assassination as diversionary tactics when Aeschines deals with uncomfortable topics is effective.

An intriguing puzzle is posed by discrepancies between the speeches delivered by Aeschines and Demosthenes in the trial of 343. That they give conflicting accounts and interpretations of facts and motives is hardly surprising. However, on numerous occasions, each speaker attributes to the other statements and arguments that do not feature in the surviving speech. There is reason to believe that the speeches were revised for publication. Some discrepancies may be due to omissions or alterations made in the course of this revision. Some false attributions of argument or assertion may result from the erroneous anticipation of one speaker by his opponent when preparing the case for trial; that is, in some cases we may have genuine misstatements made at the trial and retained in the published version either deliberately or by oversight. On occasion we may be dealing with deliberate misrepresentation of the opponent's case. Probably no one cause will explain all such discrepancies.[2]

ON THE EMBASSY

[1] I ask you, men of Athens, to consent to give my speech a friendly hearing, bearing in mind the immensity of the danger and the vast number of accusations against which I must defend myself, the tricks and devices of my accuser and his cruelty. This man dared to ask men who have sworn[3] to give both litigants an equal hearing to refuse to listen to the party at risk. [2] And he did not say this in anger—nobody who lies is angry at the victims of his unfounded slander, nor do people who are telling the truth prevent the defendant from receiving a hearing; for the prosecution has no weight with the audience until the defendant has had an opportunity to defend himself and fails to refute the accusations that have been made. [3] But I do not think Demosthenes likes fair arguments. This is not his plan; his firm intention is to excite your anger. He has brought a charge of bribery, though from him the suspicion lacks plausibility; for anyone who tries to excite the jurors to anger on charges of bribery should personally avoid such conduct.

[4] For myself, men of Athens, as I listened to Demosthenes' prosecution speech, I have never felt fear as great as today, nor anger more intense than now, nor have I felt such extreme pleasure. I felt fear, and at this moment I am still worried, that some of you may get the wrong impression of me, captivated by his insidious and vicious antitheses. I was beside myself with indignation, when he accused me of drunken outrage against a free Olynthian woman.[4] But I was delighted when you shouted him down[5] as he was making this accusation; and I think

---

[2] For a recent discussion of this issue, see Harris 1995: 10–11.

[3] For the jurors' oath, see 1.154n. Demosthenes does not actually ask the jurors to refuse Aeschines a hearing, though he does warn them against Aeschines' vocal skills and urge them to listen with skepticism and even hostility (19.337–340).

[4] Demosthenes 19.196–198; see further below, 2.153–155.

[5] Literally, "you threw/drove him off," a metaphor from the theatre.

I have my reward for the decent life I have lived. [5] So for you I have praise and the warmest affection, because you put more trust in the way of life of people on trial than in the accusations from their enemies. But even so, I cannot omit a defense against this charge. For if anyone of the people standing in the viewing area[6] (and the vast majority of the citizen body must be here), or of you who are judging the case, has been convinced that I have treated not just a free person but anyone at all in the way described, I consider the rest of my life not worth living. And if in the course of my defense I do not prove both that the accusation is false and that the man who had the nerve to make it is an impious sykophant,[7] even if on every other charge I am patently innocent, I propose a penalty of death.[8]

[6] Another argument that struck me as strange and monstrously unjust was when he asked you if it was possible in the same city to condemn Philocrates[9] to death, because he convicted himself of the crime by refusing to stand trial, and to acquit me.[10] My own belief is that this very point would be the best reason for sparing me. If a man who convicts himself by failing to appear is guilty, then a man who acquits himself by handing himself over to the laws and his fellow-citizens is innocent.

[7] As to the rest of the prosecution case, men of Athens, my request to you is that if I omit any point and fail to mention it, you quiz me and declare whatever you want to hear, and that you form no adverse judgment in advance but listen with unbiased goodwill. I am

---

[6] Trials were open to members of the public, who were separated by a fence from the participants.

[7] See 1.1n.

[8] Aeschines uses the terminology of penalty assessment (*timasthai*), for which see 1.15n. This is not, of course, a formal proposal but a rhetorical demonstration of Aeschines' confidence in his innocence.

[9] Already active in the late 350s, Philocrates reached the peak of his influence in the 340s, culminating in the peace that bears his name. He was impeached for treason by Hyperides in 343 and fled. He was tried in absentia and convicted.

[10] There is no such question in Demosthenes 19. Either the question was removed by Demosthenes in the course of revising his speech for publication or Aeschines is replying broadly to Demosthenes' attempt to associate him with Philocrates and putting the charge in a form that allows him a crisp rejoinder.

not sure where I should begin because of the inconsistencies of the prosecution case. Consider whether you think I am being treated reasonably. [8] I am the one who is now on trial for his life; yet he has devoted most of his prosecution to Philocrates and Phrynon[11] and the rest of the envoys, and to Philip and the peace and the policies of Eubulus,[12] and I myself am merely included in all this. In his speech, it turns out, the only person with any concern for the city is Demosthenes, while all the rest are traitors. He has not paused in his insults against us or in directing unfounded slanders against not just me but the others, too. [9] So he treats me with contempt, but next thing with a random change of attitude, as if he were charging Alcibiades or Themistocles,[13] who surpassed all other Greeks in fame, he accuses me of having destroyed the cities in Phocis, lost you the territory in Thrace, and removed from power Cersobleptes, a friend and ally of

---

[11] Phrynon is treated scathingly by Demosthenes (19.189, 230). Apart from his role in the peace negotiations, which figures in passing in Aeschines and Demosthenes, and a mention in a fourth-century dedicatory inscription, he has left no mark on Athenian history.

[12] As with so many of the great figures of the fourth century, we know disappointingly little about Eubulus. He dominated Athenian politics during the 350s and early 340s. His foreign policy was based on avoidance of expensive and risky campaigns in distant parts or for unrealistic goals, combined with the maintenance of the military resources needed to defend essential Athenian interests.

[13] Alcibiades was one of the most controversial figures of late fifth-century Athens. He was one of the commanders of the ill-fated Sicilian Expedition of 415–413. Indicted for sacrilege, he fled to Sparta and helped stir up rebellion in the Athenian empire. Recalled, he enjoyed some success in the Peloponnesian War against Sparta but went into voluntary exile in Thrace after a debacle by his lieutenant. He is treated more generously in fourth-century sources than his achievements warrant. Themistocles was the creator of the Athenian navy early in the fifth century and the author of the Greek victory against the Persians at Salamis; he was also responsible for the effective fortification of Athens after the Persian Wars. He was eventually accused of plotting with the Persian king and fled to Persia, where he died. The point is that Demosthenes simultaneously tries to argue that Aeschines is a man of no significance and that he has done great damage. For Demosthenes' rejoinder (either in genuine anticipation or in revision of his speech for publication), see Demosthenes 19.29–30.

our city. [10] And he tried to compare me with Dionysius,[14] the Sicilian dictator (*tyrannos*); in great earnestness and with loud cries he urged you to watch out for me and described the dream of the priestess in Sicily. But despite this great exaggeration, he begrudged me credit even while slandering me and put the blame for events not on my speeches but on Philip's weapons.

[11] When a man displays audacity and trickery on this scale, it is difficult to remember what was said in detail and to reply while at risk to slanders one could not predict. But I shall begin with the issue that I think will make my arguments most lucid, intelligible to you, and fair, the discussions about the peace[15] and the selection of the envoys. This will be the best way for me to remember and be able to present my case, and for you to grasp it.

[12] I think that one thing you all remember for yourselves is that, when the envoys came from Euboea, after addressing the Assembly on the subject of peace with them,[16] they said that Philip, too, had asked them to report to you that he wanted to come to terms and be at peace with you. Not long after, Phrynon of Rhamnus was captured by privateers during the Olympic truce[17]—so he complained. And when he got back here after being ransomed, he urged you to choose an envoy

---

[14] Probably Dionysius I (dictator at Syracuse 405–367) rather than his inferior son Dionysius II (dictator 367–356, 346–344). The comparison does not figure in Demosthenes 19. The detail is so precise that it is unlikely to have been invented by Aeschines. Presumably it was omitted by Demosthenes in revision for publication (perhaps as overly melodramatic). According to the marginal notes (*scholia*) that survive in the medieval manuscripts of Aeschines, the dream (a variation on the story of Cassandra and the birth of Paris at Troy) predicted the tyrant's rise.

[15] I.e., the Peace of Philocrates.

[16] In the early summer of 348, following the failure of the Athenian expedition in support of Plutarch (cf. 3.86n). Athens had been at war with Philip since his capture of Amphipolis in 357. Since 349 Philip had been at war with Olynthus in the Chalcidice; in 348 he had begun to besiege the city, and Athens had provided some support for Olynthus. Philip was presumably hoping to undermine Athens' will to help Olynthus.

[17] Summer 348. The Olympic truce was intended to guarantee safe passage for those traveling to the festival and to protect the festival itself from disruption.

to Philip on his behalf, so that if possible he could recover the ransom. You were persuaded and chose Ctesiphon[18] as envoy on his behalf. [13] When Ctesiphon returned here from his mission, he reported to you on the matter on which he was sent and in addition stated that Philip said he had not wanted to go to war with you and wanted even at that point to be rid of the war. When Ctesiphon said this, and furthermore spoke of Philip's great kindness, the people readily accepted his claims and praised Ctesiphon; when nobody spoke in opposition, Philocrates of Hagnus proposed a decree, and the people voted unanimously for the proposal, which said that Philip should be allowed to send a herald and envoys here to speak of peace. For this was the very thing that was blocked before by some people who were determined to prevent it, as events themselves showed. [14] For they indicted the proposal as illegal,[19] entering Lycinus' name on the written indictment and proposing a penalty of 100 talents.[20] Subsequently the indictment went to court, and Philocrates, who was ill, invited Demosthenes as his supporting speaker,[21] not me. Demosthenes the anti-Philip came to the stand and spent the whole day on the defense, and in the end Philocrates was acquitted, while the man who brought the indictment failed to get a fifth of the votes.[22] And this is something

---

[18] Ctesiphon also served on the first and second embassies to Philip in 346; see further Introduction to Aeschines 3.

[19] For the *graphē paranomōn,* see 1.34n.

[20] For the assessment of the penalty in cases where it was not fixed by law, see 1.15n. Aeschines may conceivably exaggerate the penalty proposal, though we hear of other fines on this scale. The proposal was evidently meant both to eradicate Philocrates as a political force and to deter similar proposals in the future. Lycinus is otherwise unknown but was presumably a minor politician. We find such figures elsewhere acting as "front men" for political initiatives and prosecutions.

[21] Aeschines' aim is to associate Demosthenes with and dissociate himself from Philocrates. Since Demosthenes never answers these allegations (though he both could anticipate them and had the opportunity to dispose of them when revising for publication), we may accept Aeschines' account, which is also supported by Dinarchus (1.28).

[22] In order to deter casual recourse to the courts, the system imposed penalties for conspicuous failure. In most public actions, a prosecutor who failed to get 20% of the votes cast was fined 1,000 drachmas and probably (though this is controversial) lost the right to bring the same type of action again.

you all know. [15] At about the same time Olynthus was captured,[23] and many of our fellow-citizens were among the prisoners. These included Iatrocles the brother of Ergochares and Eueratus son of Strombichus.[24] Their relatives made a formal supplication[25] on their behalf and urged you to look after them. Philocrates and Demosthenes came forward to speak in their support, but not Aeschines. And they sent Aristodemus the actor[26] as envoy to Philip because of Philip's familiarity with and fondness for his skill. [16] On his return here from his mission, Aristodemus had pressing business and did not report to the Council. Before he could do so, Iatrocles came from Macedonia after being released by Philip without ransom.[27] At this point many people, hearing the same account about Philip from Iatrocles, expressed anger at Aristodemus' failure to report. [17] In the end, Democrates of Aphidna[28] came to the Council and persuaded it to summon Aristodemus. The Council members included my accuser Demosthenes. Aristodemus came forward and reported that Philip was very well disposed toward the city; he added that Philip also wanted to become its

---

[23] In the autumn of 348.

[24] Eueratus is otherwise unknown. Iatrocles later served on the first and second embassies to Philip in 346.

[25] Supplication, individual and collective, was a means of formalizing both a request and the commitment made by the individual of whom the request is made. It could involve ritualized gestures (touching the knee or cheek) or postures (such as taking refuge at an altar). Here the Greek (literally "placing supplication") suggests the placing of branches on an altar. Formal supplication of the Assembly (as here) was allowed at one of the regular Assembly meetings each prytany. From 1.104 it is clear that the rules for the Council of Five Hundred were similar.

[26] A distinguished tragic actor from Metapontum in Italy who was given Athenian citizenship. Aeschines at one stage in his acting career was part of his troop, according to Demosthenes 19.246.

[27] The Greek adds here *genomenos aichmalotos,* "who had been taken prisoner/the one who had been taken prisoner." The repetition (not in itself unusual in Aeschines) combined with the clumsy positioning suggests an intrusive explanatory note.

[28] A celebrated orator from the family of one of the "tyrannicides" (see 1.132n). His appearance in this context attests his pro-Macedonian leanings, for which we later find him attacked by politicians opposed to Macedonia (Hyp. 2.2–3).

ally, and he made this assertion not only in the Council but also in the Assembly. And at this point, Demosthenes voiced no opposition but actually moved that Aristodemus receive a crown.

[18] After these statements, Philocrates drafted a decree for the selection of ten envoys to Philip to discuss with him peace and the common interests of Athens and Philip. During the election of the ten envoys, I was proposed by Nausicles,[29] while Philocrates himself proposed Demosthenes,[30] the man who is now making accusations against Philocrates. [19] So eager was Demosthenes for the initiative that in the Council, to ensure that Aristodemus would suffer no loss by serving as envoy with us, he moved that envoys be chosen to go to the cities where Aristodemus was contracted to play and request his release from his penalties.[31] And to prove the truth of this, please take the decrees and read out the absentee deposition[32] from Aristodemus and call the people to whom he made it, so that the jurors will know who was Philocrates' collaborator[33] and who promised to persuade the people to give the rewards to Aristodemus.

---

[29] A politician and soldier. He led the Athenian force that in 352 supported Phocis and barred Thermopylae to Philip, for which he was awarded a crown by the Athenians. As well as proposing Aeschines, he himself served on the embassy. Aeschines could still call him a friend, and rely on his support, in 343 (2.184). Aeschines may associate him with Demosthenes' decrees after Chaeronea in 338 (3.159), and a later source ([Plutarch] *Lives of the Ten Orators* 844–845) associates him with Demosthenes and Hyperides in opposition to Macedonia; accordingly, it is often supposed that he had moved to a more firmly anti-Macedonian position. This may be so, though Athenian factions were never neat. In fact, Aeschines 3.159 may suggest that his name was not unacceptable to Macedonia and therefore that, if he had changed tack, his stance vis-à-vis Macedonia was not as strident as that of Demosthenes.

[30] Though this statement is never substantiated, it is not addressed by Demosthenes and is probably true.

[31] Evidently Aristodemus' contracts included penalty clauses for nonperformance.

[32] Greek *ekmartyria*. Athenian court rules barred hearsay evidence, with limited exceptions. One of these related to witnesses ill or abroad. The witness in such cases confirmed the written deposition to one or more individuals, who then attested in court that the witness had given this confirmation. Presumably Aristodemus was away touring.

[33] Greek *hetairos;* see 1.173n.

[DECREES, ABSENTEE DEPOSITION]

[20] So from the outset, the initiative for the whole business came not from me but from Demosthenes and Philocrates. During the embassy, Demosthenes took pains to eat in our company, not with my agreement but with that of my companions, Aglaocreon of Tenedos,[34] whom you chose to represent the allies, and Iatrocles. And on the journey he maintains that I urged him to join me in keeping watch on the brute, Philocrates;[35] this is a story he has concocted. How could I have invited Demosthenes to help me against Philocrates, when I knew he had both spoken in support of Philocrates, when the indictment for an illegal decree took place, and been proposed for the embassy by Philocrates? [21] Besides, this was not the kind of conversation in which we engaged; in fact, for the whole journey we had to put up with Demosthenes, an unbearably tedious man. When we were reflecting on what we should say and Cimon[36] said that he was afraid that Philip's presentation of his case would get the better of us, Demosthenes promised that he had unlimited founts of argument and would make such a case for our claims about Amphipolis[37] and the outbreak of the war that he would sew up Philip's mouth with a dry reed and persuade the Athenians to take back Leosthenes[38] and Philip to restore Amphipolis to Athens.

---

[34] Otherwise unknown. The allies in question are the remaining members of the Second Athenian Confederacy, which was founded in 377 but seriously diminished by the defection of a number of allies in 357 and the subsequent two-year Social War (see 1.108n).

[35] Cf. Demosthenes 19.13.

[36] Apart from his service on at least two (and possibly all) of the embassies to Philip in 346, Cimon is unknown. It has been suggested that he belonged to the family of the fifth-century general (2.172n).

[37] Amphipolis on the Strymon was founded by Athens in the fifth century and detached from Athens by Sparta in 424. Philip captured Amphipolis in 357. It was strategically important for its control of the gold mines of Mount Pangaeum, but in the fourth century it was also vitally important to Athens' self-image as a major Greek power.

[38] Leosthenes led the Athenian fleet that was defeated by Alexander, dictator (*tyrannos*) of Pherae in Thessaly, in 362/1, for which he was condemned to death in absentia for treason and his property confiscated. He took refuge in Macedonia. His son Leosthenes was also a general and was the hero of the ill-fated Lamian

[22] But, to avoid a lengthy account of this man's arrogance, as soon as we got to Macedonia, we arranged among ourselves that, when we came before Philip, the oldest should speak first and then the rest in order of age. It happened that Demosthenes was the youngest of us, so he claimed. When we were summoned—and please now pay close attention to this, for it will enable you to see the man's outstanding malice, his dreadful cowardice, his mean-spiritedness and machinations against messmates and fellow envoys of a sort that a man would not casually devise against his worst enemies. For he claims that his main concern is the city's salt[39] and the public table, when he does not belong to our land—it must be said!—or our blood. [23] And we, who have ancestral tombs in our homeland and share with you the pastimes and dealings that befit free men and have legally valid marriages[40] and in-laws and children, deserved your trust in Athens (or you would never have selected us), but on arriving in Macedonia we suddenly turned traitor. But the man without a single part of his body that he has not sold (not even the source of his voice),[41] as if he were Aristides, who fixed the tribute for the Greeks,[42] expresses indignation and contempt for bribe-taking.

[24] So listen to the speeches we made on your behalf and then those made by the great benefactor of the city, Demosthenes, so that I can reply in order and in detail to each of his charges. And I have the

---

War, when Athens revolted after Alexander's death. The alleged boast is intended both to be a measure of Demosthenes' arrogance and to attach to him some of the unpopularity of Leosthenes.

[39] As a symbol of hospitality; cf. 3.224. Demosthenes at 19.189–191, anticipating this attack, argues that Aeschines has betrayed the shared libations of the city.

[40] Before 451/0 a marriage was valid (i.e., it conferred legitimacy and citizenship on the offspring) if the father was Athenian, even if the mother was a foreigner. From 451/0 marriages between citizens and noncitizens were invalid, and by the mid-fourth century if not earlier they were subject to severe penalties. Allegations of non-Athenian or servile origin are not uncommon in political oratory. Demosthenes may have had non-Athenian blood on his mother's side, but this did not compromise his citizen status (see further 3.171n).

[41] The allegation (hinting both at speaking for pay and at *fellatio*) is repeated in similar words in 2.88; some editors delete the words in parentheses here as a later insertion, but I see no reason to deny Aeschines the repetition.

[42] For Aristides, see 1.25n.

very highest praise for you, the jurors, for keeping silent and giving us a fair hearing; so if I fail to refute any of the charges, I shall hold not you but myself to blame.

[25] Well, when the older men had spoken for our mission and our turn to speak came, I have already made a clear report to the Athenians as a whole on the details of what I said there and Philip's reply; at present I shall try to recall the main points for you.[43] [26] I began by speaking to him of our traditional goodwill and the assistance you gave to Amyntas, Philip's father;[44] I left out nothing but recalled everything in order. Then I turned to the good services he could attest personally. For shortly after the death of Amyntas and Alexander, the oldest of the brothers,[45] when Perdiccas and Philip were children, their mother Eurydice found herself betrayed by those she thought her friends. [27] Pausanias was returning to bid for power.[46] He was an exile at that point, but the situation was in his favor; he had many supporters and an army of Greek soldiers; he had captured Anthemous, Therma, Strepsa,[47] and some other places; the Macedonians were not united, and the majority favored Pausanias. At this point the Athenians elected Iphicrates[48] general to deal with Amphipolis (the

---

[43] The manner of Aeschines' reported speech to Philip is so similar to that in the published speeches (heavily reliant on narrative, with a preference for circumstantial detail and chronological sequence) that we can be confident that, though he has certainly adjusted details, Aeschines presents the essence of his speech in Macedonia. His account is evidently supported by his witnesses (2.44, 2.46).

[44] Specifically Athenian assistance in restoring Amyntas III to power after the two-year reign of his rival Argaeus (another member of the extensive Macedonian royal family) in the second half of the 380s.

[45] That is, the sons of Amyntas, Alexander, Perdiccas, and Philip. Alexander II succeeded Amyntas III in 369 and was assassinated in the following year by the pretender Ptolemy, who ruled as regent for Perdiccas.

[46] The invasion of Pausanias, who had been exiled by Amyntas III, belongs to the period of instability after the murder of Alexander II.

[47] Therma was on the northeast shore of the Thermaic Gulf, not far from modern Thessalonike, Anthemus slightly further east, and Strepsa at the top of the gulf.

[48] Iphicrates, a man of humble origins, was one of the great Athenian generals of the fourth century, associated with the revival of Athenian political and military influence in the early decades of the century. His distinguished military career began in the 390s and lasted to the Social War (see 1.108n). He died in the late

people of Amphipolis were themselves in control of their city and had the use of the territory at that point[49]). [28] Iphicrates arrived in the region with a few ships initially to assess the situation rather than to lay siege to the city. "It was then," I said, "that your mother sent for him, and according to the account of all present put your brother Perdiccas into Iphicrates' arms and placed you, still a small child, on his knees.[50] And she said to Iphicrates: 'Amyntas, who was the father of these boys, adopted you as his son[51] in life and was a friend of the city of Athens; the result is that as a private individual you are the brother of these boys and in your public role you are their friend.' [29] She then began to beg him passionately for herself, for you, for the throne, for your survival in general. Hearing this, Iphicrates drove Pausanias out of Macedonia and rescued the kingship for you." I went on to speak of Ptolemy,[52] who was appointed regent, and his ungrateful and unprincipled conduct. I told him that initially Ptolemy opposed our city on the issue of Amphipolis and that he made an alliance with the Thebans when the Athenians were in dispute with them, and then how Perdiccas,[53] when he came to power, went to war with our city over Amphipolis. [30] And I spoke of your goodwill in spite of the mistreatment you have received; I told him that when you had the advantage over Perdiccas in the war under the leadership of Callisthenes,[54] you concluded a truce with him in the continuing expectation

---

350s. It has been plausibly suggested that his presence in the north reflects an Athenian desire to capitalize on the instability in the region.

[49] That is, before Philip's capture of the city in 357.

[50] Despite its theatrical quality, this anecdote is unlikely to have been used in Macedonia (or if it was, it will have raised a smile from Philip). Hammond (in Hammond and Griffith 1979: 186 n. 3) observes that Philip and Perdiccas were teenagers at the date in question, and in all probability Philip was in Thebes as a hostage following the invasion by Pelopidas in 368.

[51] In return for Iphicrates' intervention against Argaeus.

[52] For Ptolemy, see 2.26n. The political realignment of which Aeschines complains here was a pragmatic response to an invasion by the Theban general Pelopidas in 368.

[53] In 365 Philip's older brother, Perdiccas III, murdered Ptolemy and took the throne.

[54] 363/2. We know no more of Callisthenes' career than we are told here. Aeschines' discomfort is palpable; in all probability, what brought about Callisthenes'

that you would receive some measure of fair treatment. And I tried to remove his suspicions on this matter, explaining that the people did not execute Callisthenes for the truce with Perdiccas but on other charges. And then I did not hesitate to accuse Philip personally and criticize him for continuing the war against our city. [31] And for all my statements, I provided as witness the letters of the individuals concerned, the decrees of the people, and Callisthenes' truce. As to the original founding of the site,[55] the so-called Nine Roads, and the sons of Theseus, one of whom, Acamas, is said to have received this territory as dowry for his wife, these were themes that it was appropriate to narrate at that point and that were dealt with in as much detail as possible; on this occasion, however, I suppose I must cut short my account. What I shall report is the evidence I provided not from ancient myths but from events in our own time. [32] When the Spartan alliance and the rest of the Greeks met,[56] one of those involved was Amyntas, Philip's father; Amyntas sent a delegate and, with complete freedom to cast his own vote as he chose, voted to join the rest of the Greeks in helping the Athenians to capture Amphipolis, Athens' property. And to witness my account I offered him the collective resolution of the Greeks and the names of the parties who voted, from the public records. [33] "When Amyntas in front of the whole of Greece renounced this territory not just in words but with his vote," I said, "it is not right for you, his son, to lay claim to them.[57] Now if you claim it on the ground that you captured it in war and can reasonably

---

trial and execution was his failure to win any gains for Athens in the north; his colleague Ergophilus was similarly tried for failing to deal effectively with the Thracian king Cotys, though according to Aristotle (*Rhetoric* 2.3.13) he was acquitted because popular anger had exhausted itself on Callisthenes the previous day.

[55] Aeschines traces the Athenian claim to Amphipolis back to myth. Greek heroic myth was generally accepted as reflecting real people and events. Nine Roads (*Ennea Hodoi*) was the name of the site colonized as Amphipolis by Athens in the fifth century.

[56] At the conference in Sparta that led to the Peace of 371.

[57] Demosthenes (19.253–254) claims that Aeschines never mentioned Amphipolis on the first embassy; the brevity of Demosthenes' treatment makes it suspect.

retain it, if you made war on us and took the city by force, then you have a right to it as an acquisition under the rules of war; but if you took from the people of Amphipolis a city that belongs to Athens, you are holding not their property but Athenian territory."[58]

[34] After these and other arguments, it was now Demosthenes' turn to play his part in the mission, and all paid close attention, expecting to hear perfect examples of verbal skill (for his extravagant claims had been reported to Philip himself and his associates [*hetairoi*[59]], as we heard later). With all listening so intently, this creature uttered an obscure prologue in a voice dead with fright, and after a brief narration of earlier events, suddenly fell silent and was at a loss for words, and finally abandoned his speech.[60] [35] Seeing the state he was in, Philip encouraged him to take heart and not to suppose that he had suffered a complete catastrophe, like an actor in the theatre; he should calmly and patiently recollect his arguments and make the speech he had planned. But Demosthenes, once he had become confused and had lost his place in his notes,[61] was now unable to recover; he tried once more to speak, and the same thing happened. In the ensuing silence the herald asked us to withdraw.

[36] When we were alone together, this fine fellow Demosthenes was very ill-tempered and claimed I had ruined the city and its allies. We were amazed, not just I but the other envoys as well, and we asked him why he said this. And he asked me if I had forgotten the situation in Athens and did not remember that the people were exhausted and eager for peace. [37] "Or are you full of confidence," he said, "because

---

[58] The argument might well impress an Athenian audience, but it rests on the untested assumption that Athens still "owned" a city that had revolted from it two generations earlier and had never been recaptured.

[59] A reference to Philip's inner circle of associates/advisers.

[60] Another theatrical metaphor. The account is implicitly rejected by Plutarch (*Demosthenes* 16), but Aeschines has witnesses to his account; Demosthenes' silence on the issue (even in the published version of his prosecution speech) also suggests that it is true. He was still a minor political figure at this stage and may well have been overwhelmed by the occasion.

[61] A tart reference to the fact that Demosthenes was at his best with written aids and was not a good improviser.

of the fifty ships that have been voted but will never be manned?[62] You have enraged Philip and made the kind of speech that would not turn war into peace but peace into all-out[63] war." As I was beginning to reply to this Philip's servants summoned us.

[38] When we went in and were seated, Philip tried to answer each of our arguments, starting at the beginning, though he devoted the most time to my statements, perhaps because, as I think, I had omitted none of the points that needed to be made. And he mentioned my name repeatedly in his speech. But to Demosthenes, who had performed so ridiculously, he made, I think, no reply on any point. This brought him so much pain he nearly choked. [39] Then Philip proceeded to speak of his goodwill, and the slur that Demosthenes had earlier directed against me among our fellow-envoys, that I would provoke war and hostility, fell apart on him. And at that point he was visibly beside himself with anger, so much so that even when we were invited to dinner his behavior was atrocious.

[40] When we were on our way home from the mission, suddenly to our surprise Demosthenes took to conversing affably with each of us on the road. Now before then I had no idea what the terms "monkey" (*kerkops*) and "sharper" (*paipalema*) and "turncoat" (*palimbolon*) and words like that meant.[64] Now with this man to initiate me I un-

---

[62] The fifty ships referred to here are those which the Athenians had voted to send under Proxenus as part of a force that would take delivery of the forts guarding Thermopylae from the Phocians. Early in 346 the Athenians learned that the Phocians were now unwilling to hand over the positions (see further 2.133n).

[63] Greek *polemos akeryktos*, literally "war without herald," i.e., a war that does not admit communications that might lead to truce or peace.

[64] The precise meaning of these terms, and the point of the passage, is not entirely clear. It is uncertain whether these are merely Aeschines' own terms for Demosthenes, terms used by Demosthenes on the road, or (perhaps most likely) slang terms used by Demosthenes and now applied to him by Aeschines. Obscenity has been detected (*kerkops* has been interpreted as "arse-licking shyster," *paipalema* as suggesting masturbation, e.g., "slanderous jerk," Brit. "wanker," "tosser"), but the sudden descent into obscenity would be ineffectual and unlike Aeschines' manner; probably the connotations are of trickery, duplicity, and unreliability.

derstand all the ways of wickedness. [41] He took each of us aside in turn and offered to raise a friendly loan for one man and help his private finances, and to obtain a generalship for another; in my case he followed me around congratulating me on my natural gifts and praising the speech I made; his praise was excessive and irritating. And when we were all dining together at Larisa, he joked at his own expense about the block he had experienced when speaking and described Philip as the cleverest man under the sun. [42] I expressed myself along much the same lines, observing how well he had responded from memory to each of the points we had made, and Ctesiphon, the oldest among us, talked of his own advanced age and years of experience and added that in the course of such a long life he had never yet seen such a pleasant and charming man. Then this Sisyphus[65] clapped his hands [43] and said: "Now this is something, Ctesiphon, you would not dare to say to the Assembly, nor would he" (meaning me) "dare to tell the Athenians that Philip is clever and has a good memory." We were slow and failed to see his plot (you will hear about this shortly); and he tricked us into a binding agreement that we would say all this to you. As to me, he also begged me earnestly not to omit to say that Demosthenes, too, had said something on the subject of Amphipolis.

[44] My account up to this point is supported by our colleagues on the embassy, whom Demosthenes has unceasingly insulted and slandered in his prosecution speech. But what he said on the platform in your presence you have heard yourselves; so I cannot possibly lie. I urge you to listen patiently to the rest of my account as well. I am fully aware that each one of you wants to hear about Cersobleptes and the charges relating to Phocis,[66] and I am eager to get to them. But if you do not hear what preceded those events, you won't be able to follow them so well either. If you allow me to make my case as I wish, since I am the one at risk, you will be able both to save me, if I am innocent,

---

[65] Sisyphus was a mythical king of Corinth. He managed to trick his way out of the underworld after death. His punishment when he eventually died again was to roll a huge boulder uphill; at the top the boulder would invariably roll back down. His name was a by-word for cunning.

[66] For Cersobleptes and Phocis, see Introduction to Aeschines.

since you will have adequate grounds for deciding, and to use the points agreed by both parties to assess the points under dispute.

[45] We arrived back here and gave a summary report on our mission to the Council and handed over the letter from Philip.[67] And Demosthenes was full of praise for us before the Council; he swore by Hestia[68] of the Council that he shared the city's pleasure at sending men of this quality on the embassy, men whose speaking skill and honesty were a credit to the city. [46] About me he said something to the effect that I had not disappointed the hopes of the people who selected me for the embassy. And finally he proposed formally that we should all be crowned with a garland of wild olive for our loyalty to the people and be invited to dine at the Prytaneum next day.[69] To show that there is no falsehood in anything I have said to you, let the clerk please take the Council decree and read out the depositions of our fellow envoys.

[DECREE, DEPOSITIONS]

[47] So then, when we were reporting to the Assembly on our mission, Ctesiphon was the first of us to come forward, because of his age. Among the points he made were the ones he had agreed with Demosthenes that he would say to you, about Philip's conversation, his appearance, and his dexterity at drinking. After him Philocrates said a few things, as did Dercylus,[70] and then I came forward. [48] After a general account of the embassy I came to the point I had agreed among the other envoys I would make and commented on Philip's retentive memory and skill at speaking. Nor did I forget Demosthe-

---

[67] The contents of the letter from Philip cannot be determined in detail; it certainly contained expressions of goodwill and references to benefits he would confer on Athens (Dem. 19.40, 7.33), which he claimed he would have specified had peace been guaranteed, the implication being that they were at the expense of other Greek states and could not therefore be revealed prematurely.

[68] Hestia was the goddess of the hearth. Just as each private house had a hearth that was sacred, so the Council chamber contained a sacred civic hearth.

[69] At 19.234 Demosthenes claims that at that stage he had no evidence of any wrongdoing on their part.

[70] A member of a propertied family, Dercylus served on all the embassies to Philip in 346. He later served as general in 319/8.

nes' request to me to say that it had been his task to make any point about Amphipolis that we might omit. [49] Last of us all Demosthenes stood up and, with the portentous manner he usually adopts, he scratched his head; seeing that the Assembly was about to give its approval and acceptance of my report, he said that he was amazed at both sides, both the audience and the returning envoys; they were letting slip the opportunity, the former for reaching a decision, the latter for offering advice, and wasting their time in entertaining themselves with foreign gossip on an occasion for their own business. For it was the easiest thing in the world to give a report on an embassy. [50] "I want to show you how the thing should be done." And he ordered the Assembly's decree[71] to be read out. After it was read, he said: "This is the motion on which we were sent, and we carried out the instructions written in it. Please take the letter we have brought back from Philip." Once it had been read, he said: "You have your answer and all that remains is for you to decide."

[51] There was uproar at his conduct, some yelling that he was a clever and succinct character, the majority that he was devious and malicious. "Observe now," he said, "my brevity in reporting on all the rest. Aeschines thinks Philip is a clever speaker but I do not; if someone removed the advantages luck has given him and bestowed them on someone else, he would not seem much inferior. [52] Ctesiphon thought his appearance impressive but I think Aristodemus the actor" (he was with us as our colleague) "is his equal. We're told he has a good memory; so do others. He was a good drinking companion; Philocrates who was with us was his superior. One of them says he left it to me to speak on Amphipolis; but the speaker in question would not leave room either for you or for me to speak.[72] [53] This is just rubbish," he said. "Myself, I shall draft a motion granting a truce[73] both for the herald from Philip and for the envoys who will come here from him, and requiring the Presidents (*prytaneis*),[74] when the envoys

---

[71] The decree authorizing the embassy to Philip.

[72] Cf. Demosthenes 19.253–254.

[73] The truce was required since Philip was still technically at war with Athens.

[74] The executive committee of 50 members of the Council of 500 (created by rotating the duty between the ten tribal contingents), whose duties included the preparation of business for the Assembly. Each contingent held office for one *prytaneia* (see 1.104n).

arrive, to hold a two-day meeting of the Assembly to deal not just with peace but also with an alliance, praising us who served on the embassy formally, if you think we deserve it, and inviting us to dine at the Prytaneum tomorrow."

[54] To prove that I am telling the truth, please take the decrees, to show you, the jurors, his inconsistency, his malice, his collusion with Philocrates in the affair, and his manipulative and dishonest character. And please call our fellow envoys also and read out their depositions.

[DECREES]

[55] This was not his only proposal; after this he proposed in the Council that the envoys from Philip, when they arrived, should be given seats at the Dionysia. Read this decree as well.

[DECREE]

Read out the deposition from our fellow envoys, to show you, the jurors, that Demosthenes cannot speak in the city's interest but readily practices his skills against those who have shared his meals and libations.

[DEPOSITION]

[56] So you can see that the active cooperation to bring about the peace was not between me and Philocrates but between Demosthenes and Philocrates; and I think I have given you ample proofs of my account. For the reports that we delivered you are my witnesses, and for what was said in Macedonia and events on our journey I have provided our colleagues as witnesses. You heard, and can still recall, the prosecution speech that Demosthenes made just now. His starting point was the speech I made on the peace.[75] [57] He distorted everything he said in that section of his case, and he was full of indignation at the circumstances of my speech. He claims that my speech was delivered in the presence of the envoys sent to you by the Greeks on the invitation of the Assembly with the purpose of joining the Athenians in war against Philip, if need be, or sharing in the peace, if it

---

[75] Demosthenes 19.13–16.

was decided that the advantage lay there.⁷⁶ Now observe his deception on a matter of great importance, and the extraordinary shamelessness of the man. [58] As to the envoys you sent to the rest of Greece when your war with Philip was still in progress, the dates of their selection and the names of the individuals who served are written down in the public records, and the men are physically present in Athens, not Macedonia. In the case of embassies from abroad, the Council schedules their appearance before the Assembly.⁷⁷ Now this man claims that the embassies from Greece were present. [59] So come to the stand, Demosthenes, in the time allotted for my speech, and give the name of any Greek city you like whose envoys you claim had arrived. Give the clerk the resolutions from the Council chamber relating to them to read out, and call the Athenian envoys sent out to the Greek cities as your witnesses. And if they attest that they were present and not abroad when the city was making the peace, or if you can provide evidence of their admission to the Council and the relevant decrees belonging to the time you allege, I am ready to quit the stand and propose a penalty of death.⁷⁸

[60] Now read out as well what the resolution of the allies⁷⁹ says; there it is explicitly written: "Since the Athenian Assembly is consid-

---

⁷⁶ In 348 Eubulus sent out embassies to encourage the Greeks to join Athens against Philip. Support for Athens was not forthcoming. In 346 embassies were sent to invite the Greeks to join in the negotiation of peace. It is to the latter initiative that Aeschines refers. His confidence, together with Demosthenes' evasiveness on the issue, suggests that Aeschines is correct to claim that they had not returned by the time of the Assembly meetings. Cf. 3.68.

⁷⁷ The agenda for the Assembly was set by the Council; no business could be presented to the Assembly without preliminary consideration by the Council (Aristotle *Constitution of Athens* 45.4).

⁷⁸ For the assessment of penalties, cf. 1.15n; for the rhetorical device, 2.5n.

⁷⁹ That is, the resolution of the congress of (the remaining) members of the Second Athenian Confederacy. The context makes clear the subordinate status of the allies. The real decision is to be taken by the Athenian Assembly; the allies can only seek to influence the outcome. Aeschines adds further details in 3.69–70; as well as proposing peace alone (without alliance), the allies wanted a common peace, with all Greek states free to sign up within a given period. A particular result would be to protect Phocis.

ering peace with Philip, and the envoys whom the Assembly sent to
the Greeks to summon the cities in defense of the freedom of Greece
are not yet here, it is the decision of the allies that when the envoys
have returned and reported on their missions to the Athenians and
their allies, the Presidents (*prytaneis*) should arrange for two meetings
of the Assembly as allowed by law, and that at these meetings the
Athenians should debate the peace. And whatever decision the Assembly reaches is to be the collective decision of the allies." Please read
out the resolution of the allied representatives.

[RESOLUTION OF THE ALLIED REPRESENTATIVES]

[61] Now please read out in comparison Demosthenes' decree,
where he instructs the Presidents (*prytaneis*) to arrange two Assembly
meetings after the City Dionysia and the meeting of the Assembly in
the precinct of Dionysus,[80] one on the eighteenth and one on the
nineteenth of the month;[81] in fixing the dates he slipped the meetings
through in advance, before the envoys from the Greek states were
present. And the allied decision, that I admit I, too, supported, instructs you to debate only peace, whereas Demosthenes instructs you
to debate alliance as well. Read out the decree.

[DECREE]

[62] You have heard both decrees, men of Athens. And they prove
that Demosthenes is representing envoys as present when they were
absent and that he has nullified the allied decision, though you were
willing to obey it. For the allies declared that the city should wait for
the envoys from the Greek cities, while Demosthenes, who changes
tack more rapidly and blatantly than any man alive, has prevented you
from waiting for them, not only by his arguments but by his acts and
his decree, by ordering you to decide at once.[82]

---

[80] The regular spring meeting in the theatre of Dionysus dealt with matters
relating to the festival; cf. Demosthenes 21.8. See further 3.204n.

[81] That is, Elaphebolion (roughly March).

[82] The reader who can shake off Aeschines' infectious indignation will note
that Demosthenes did no more than propose a motion; it was for the Assembly
to accept or reject his motion. The date of the meetings was approved by the
Athenians collectively.

[63] He has claimed that in the first Assembly after Philocrates had spoken, I took the platform and criticized the peace he was proposing, maintaining it was degrading and unworthy of the city, but on the second day on the contrary I spoke in support of Philocrates and succeeded in carrying the Assembly with me, by urging you to ignore mentions of the battles and trophies of our ancestors and not to give aid to Greece.[83] [64] His allegation is not merely false, it is impossible. Demosthenes himself will give one piece of testimony against himself; a second will come from the recollections of all Athenians, including yourselves; a third comes from the implausibility of the charge, and a fourth from a man of good character, an active politician, Amyntor.[84] For Demosthenes showed him his draft decree and asked whether he should hand it to the clerk; the contents he had drafted were not opposed to but the same as Philocrates' motion. [65] Please take Demosthenes' decree[85] and read it out. It can be seen that in this he laid down that in the first of the two Assembly meetings it should be open to anyone who wished to offer advice, while in the second the Chairmen (*proedroi*)[86] should put the proposals to the vote but offer no opportunity to speak. This is the one where he claims I spoke in support of Philocrates.

[DECREE]

[66] So we see that decrees remain as they were first drafted, while the arguments of malicious prosecutors (*sykophantai*) are directed to the situation of the moment.[87] My accuser presents a double speech

---

[83] Cf. Demosthenes 19.13–16, 313; Aeschines returns to the issue at 2.75, 138, 171.

[84] Amyntor is known only from this passage.

[85] Not the draft decree just mentioned but the decree setting the dates and terms for the Assembly meetings to discuss peace.

[86] For these officials, see 1.23n.

[87] Amid the conflicting claims of prosecution and defense it is difficult to reconstruct the two Assembly meetings with confidence. Though not crucial for the question of guilt, the issue is rhetorically important for both sides. For Demosthenes the interval of a night between Aeschines' (alleged) contradictory positions allows scope for the intervention of a corrupting influence, while it is equally important for Aeschines to rule out any opportunity for corruption. The issue is

from me, while the decree and the truth present a single speech. For
if the Chairmen (*proedroi*) did not offer an opportunity to speak at
the second Assembly, it was not possible to make a speech. What in
fact could have induced me, if I did share Philocrates' policy, to speak
against him before the same audience the day before, and after a single
night speak in support? To win prestige for myself, or to assist him?
But neither result was possible, only universal hatred and complete
failure.

---

complicated by the fact that Aeschines himself presents inconsistent accounts; in
330 (3.71) he offers a version that has speeches made on both days in order to
return Demosthenes' charges of 343 against him (see 3.71n). One would naturally
suppose that the earlier version is the more reliable, as nearer to the events, when
memories were fresher; but it is an inescapable fact that a mere three years after
the events, either Aeschines or Demosthenes is guilty of a gross but evidently
sustainable falsification of the content of the Assembly meetings. Aeschines' failure to cite witnesses (he uses only Demosthenes' procedural decree; the testimony
of Amyntor at 2.67 is actually in Aeschines' words, and we cannot exclude the
possibility that he expands and distorts in paraphrasing) raises a suspicion that in
the event, the distinction between the two Assembly meetings was not main-
tained, and that debate was allowed on the second day. On the other hand, the
amount of time devoted to demonstrating the content of the Assembly meetings
by Aeschines in contrast to Demosthenes, who offers no proof (nor does Aeschines at 3.71, when he talks of speeches on both days), argues some confidence on
the issue. Perhaps both are distorting the truth. It is possible (as suggested to me
by Athanasios Efstathiou) that the broad distinction between the two meetings
set out in Demosthenes' decree was retained, but that summary statements were
allowed before the vote at the second meeting. Aeschines may well have begun by
withholding support from Philocrates (at 3.71 he claims he spoke for the allied
resolution, for which see 2.74n) and publicly argued for the proposal either late
on 18 Elaphebolion (assuming one day of debate) or on 19 Elaphebolion (assuming debate at the second meeting). This change would be entirely explicable without recourse to Demosthenes' accusation of corruption. He may have been a late
convert to the inevitability of Philocrates' proposed peace and alliance as the only
terms Philip would accept. Or perhaps he knew throughout that peace on the
terms of Philocrates' decree was inescapable but chose to leave the unpleasant task
of arguing for it (and the consequent risk of attack if the peace proved a failure)
to others until compelled to intervene to ensure its success; the debate was clearly
heated (see 2.74n).

[67] Please call Amyntor of Erchia and read out his deposition. But I would like to give you an account of its contents in advance. "Amyntor testifies, in support of Aeschines, that when the Athenian people were debating the alliance with Philip under Demosthenes' decree at the second of the two Assemblies, when it was not permitted to address the people but the motions concerning peace and alliance were being put to the vote, [68] at this meeting Demosthenes, who was sitting next to him, showed him a decree drafted in Demosthenes' name and asked him whether he should pass it to the Chairmen (*proedroi*) for them to put it to the vote; it contained the terms on which Demosthenes proposed that the peace and alliance should be concluded, and these were identical with those that Philocrates had proposed." Please call Amyntor of Erchia and summon [88] him, if he refuses to appear.

[DEPOSITION]

[69] You have heard the testimony, men of Athens. Ask yourselves whether Demosthenes has incriminated me or, on the contrary, himself. But since he vilifies the speech I delivered and distorts the statements I made, I have no intention of distancing myself from them or denying any of what I said then, nor am I ashamed of them but in fact I am proud.

[70] I also want to remind you of the circumstances [89] in which you were deliberating. We began the war because of Amphipolis, and the situation was that our general in the war [90] had lost seventy-five allied

---

[88] For the process of *klēteusis,* available against reluctant witnesses, see 1.46n. Here the device looks like a sham to present Amyntor as an opponent of Aeschines and therefore a more reliable source of support for him, since 2.69 indicates that he testified.

[89] Aeschines interprets the notion of historical context very broadly, taking his audience back eleven years before 346 to Philip's seizure of Amphipolis and the outbreak of the Social War in 357.

[90] The general referred to is Chares, whose military career began in the early 360s and may have continued into the mid-320s. Chares was intermittently active in the north during the 350s and the 340s, and despite Aeschines' hostile evaluation here, he achieved some success in containing Philip's erosion of Athenian influence there; he later served with some distinction in the war that culminated in Chaeronea.

cities that Timotheus[91] the son of Conon had won over and brought into the confederation—I am committed to speaking openly and saving myself with a frank statement of the truth; if you take a different view, finish me off, for I have no intention of pulling back. [71] He had received 150 warships from the dockyards and had not brought them back (these facts are constantly presented to you by the accusers at Chares' trials) and had spent 100 talents not on pay for soldiers but on the pompous display of the commanders, Deiares, Deipyrus, and Polyphontes,[92] renegades assembled from all over Greece (apart from what went to his clique on the platform and in the Assembly); these men extorted contributions of sixty talents a year from the wretched islanders and seized cargo ships, and Greeks, on the open sea. [72] And in place of prestige and the leadership of Greece, our city acquired the stature of Myonnesus,[93] of pirates. Philip had expanded from Macedonia and now was not just disputing Amphipolis with us but Lemnos, Imbros, and Scyros,[94] our own possessions. Our citizens were deserting Chersonesus,[95] universally agreed to be Athenian territory, and you were forced to hold more special meetings[96] of the Assembly, amid anxiety and confusion, than meetings prescribed by law. [73] Our situation was so precarious and dangerous that

---

[91] Timotheus' father, the general Conon, was associated with the refortification of Athens and recreation of its fleet at the beginning of the fourth century. Timotheus was in turn a distinguished general; he played a major role in the resurgence of Athenian influence under the Second Athenian League. His career lasted from the 370s through to the Social War of 357–355. In 354/3 he was tried for treason and fined 100 talents; he withdrew to Chalcis in Euboea, where he died.

[92] Evidently mercenary commanders, but otherwise unknown.

[93] "Mouse Island," a small islet off the north coast of the Malian Gulf in west-central Greece, in the channel between the mainland and the north coast of Euboea.

[94] These islands, which are consistently mentioned together in fourth-century sources, were maritime stepping-stones between Athens and the Black Sea, which was vital for its grain supply.

[95] The modern Gallipoli, occupied by Athenian settlers.

[96] Greek *synklētos ekklēsia,* "summoned Assembly," that is, additional to the four regular meetings each prytany (though it has been argued that the term denotes not an additional meeting but a meeting summoned at short notice).

Cephisophon of Paeania,[97] one of Chares' friends and associates, was forced to draft a decree instructing Antiochus, the commander of the supply boats, to set sail as soon as possible to search out the general commanding our forces and, if he found him, tell him that the Athenian Assembly was amazed to discover that while Philip was making for Chersonesus, Athenian territory, the Athenians did not even know the location of the general and the force they had sent out. To prove the truth of my statements, listen to the decree and call to mind the war, and blame the peace on your commanders, not on your envoys.

[DECREE]

[74] This was the city's situation at the time we were discussing the peace. And the public speakers acting in unison stood up and made no attempt to offer measures for the city's rescue but urged you to look to the Propylaea[98] of the Acropolis and remember the naval battle against the Persians at Salamis and the tombs and trophies of our ancestors. [75] For my part, I said that, while you should remember all this, you should imitate our ancestors' wisdom but avoid their errors and their ill-timed ambition.[99] I called on you to emulate the

---

[97] A politician associated at different periods with the pragmatists who favored either accommodation or limited and targeted conflict with Macedonia and the hard-liners who favored a more vigorous policy against Philip.

[98] As the monumental entrance to the Acropolis, the Propylaea could serve as a symbol of Athenian power and traditions (cf. 2.105); it was the part of the Acropolis most visible from the Pnyx to the west. From the accounts of Demosthenes and Aeschines, it is clear that although there was a general desire for peace, the eventual approval of Philocrates' proposal was by no means inevitable. In addition to the vocal opposition to any peace with Macedonia described here, there was also at least one competing peace proposal, based on the resolution from the allied congress (see 2.60n). From Demosthenes 19.291 it appears that Eubulus was compelled to intervene and present the Athenians with a stark choice between the peace proposed by Philocrates and preparations for war. A fragment of the historian Theopompus (fr. 116 Jacoby) preserves part of the arguments against the peace from Aristophon of Azenia (see 1.64n); Aristophon stresses the resources available to Athens and argues that acceptance of the peace terms would be cowardice.

[99] The presentation of the ancestors here is bolder than it might appear at first sight. Like most societies, the Athenians mythologized the past; indeed, in Ath-

battle against the Persians at Plataea, the actions at Salamis, the battle at Marathon, the naval battle at Artemisium, and the campaign of Tolmides, who with 1,000 chosen Athenians passed securely through the central Peloponnese, which was hostile territory.[100] [76] But you should avoid the example of the expedition to Sicily,[101] which you sent to aid Leontini at a time when our enemies had invaded our territory and Decelea[102] had been fortified against us. The final act of folly was when they had been beaten in the war and the Spartans were inviting them to be at peace, retaining possession of Lemnos, Imbros, and Scyros as well as Attica and maintaining democracy and the rule of law.[103] They refused all of this but determined on a war they could not fight; and Cleophon the lyre-maker,[104] a man many remembered see-

---

ens the heroization of the ancestors was institutionalized through the public funeral oration, which dwelt on the successes and virtues of previous generations (cf. 3.152n).

[100] Tolmides was active at the apogee of Athenian expansionism in the middle of the fifth century and died in its cause at Coronea in Boeotia in 447. The campaign was a circumnavigation of the Peloponnese, in the course of which he burned the Spartan dockyards. Aeschines converts this to a land campaign comparable with the Theban invasions of Sparta in the fourth century. The other battles mentioned belong to the Persian Wars (490–479).

[101] The expedition against Syracuse (415–413), which ended with the near-annihilation of the Athenian forces.

[102] In 413, during the Peloponnesian War, the Spartans and their allies established a stronghold at Decelea in Attica. Aeschines' misdating in the text (the seizure of Decelea postdated the commencement of the Sicilian campaign) reflects either error or, more probably, a desire to emphasize the folly of invading Sicily.

[103] Again Aeschines distorts, presumably to enhance his argument. After the Athenian defeat at Aegospotami in 405, the Spartans at no time offered generous terms to Athens. The settlement of 404 involved the loss of the Athenian empire plus the fleet, and the destruction of the Long Walls (see 2.173) and the walls around the Piraeus; the Spartans also engineered the establishment of the oligarchy of the Thirty (see 1.39n). The Spartans had indeed offered more generous peace terms earlier, after the Athenian victories at Cyzicus in 410 and Arginusae in 406, when Athens' situation was precarious, but it had certainly not been "beaten."

[104] Cleophon was the leading figure in the Assembly in the last decade of the fifth century. He opposed peace after Cyzicus and Arginusae, and again opposed the proposed terms of the peace of 404. Like many of the leading politicians of

ing in chains, who had got himself falsely enrolled as a citizen to our shame and corrupted the people with distributions of money, was threatening to take a dagger and cut the throat of anyone who mentioned peace. [77] And finally they reduced the city to a condition where the people were grateful to conclude a peace under which they gave up everything, razed the walls, and accepted a garrison and a Spartan governor, and abandoned the democracy to the Thirty, who put to death 1,500 citizens without trial.[105] I admit that I urged you to avoid this folly and to imitate the achievements I mentioned just before. And I learned of these events not from outsiders but from my closest relative of all. [78] Our father Atrometus, the man you insult though you do not know him and never saw the man he was in his youth—despite the fact, Demosthenes, that you're descended from Scythian nomads on your mother's side[106]—went into exile under the Thirty and participated in the restoration of democracy. And our mother's brother, our uncle Cleobulus son of Glaucus of Acharnae, served with Demaenetus of the Buzygae when he defeated the Spartan admiral Chilon at sea.[107] So the city's misfortunes are well-known family stories I have heard often.

---

the period, he represented a significant and lasting change in Athenian politics, coming from a manufacturing or mercantile background rather than the landed gentry, which had traditionally provided political leadership. The comic playwrights of the late fifth century tended to exaggerate this social change, presenting the new politicians individually and collectively as men of noncitizen or even servile origins; Aeschines' depiction of Cleophon here is ultimately derived from such comic distortions. The distributions referred to are presumably the "two-obol payment" (*diobelia*), whose nature is obscure, but which is attested in late fifth-century inscriptions and attributed to Cleophon by Aristotle at *Constitution of Athens* 28.3. It is not to be confused with pay for attending the Assembly, which postdates the postwar oligarchy. It could be the Theoric Fund (for which see 3.24n) or possibly a hardship fund.

[105] For the Thirty, see 1.39n.

[106] For Demosthenes' family, see 2.23n and 3.171n.

[107] The Chilon incident is discussed by Harris (1995: 24). The foundation of the account seems to be an incident in 397/6 when the Athenian officer Demaenetus set off with a single ship and, despite Spartan pursuit, managed to join Conon, who had taken refuge in Cyprus after the defeat at Aegospotami (see

[79] But you criticize me for the speech I made as envoy to the Ten Thousand in Arcadia[108] and claim I changed position, when you yourself are virtually a slave and all but branded as a runaway. While the war lasted, I tried to the best of my ability to unite the Arcadians and the rest of Greece against Philip. But when no one in the world was supporting our city but some were idly watching what would befall us while others joined the fight against us, while the public speakers in Athens were looking to the war to underwrite[109] their daily living costs, I admit that I advised the Assembly to come to terms with Philip and conclude the peace. This is the peace you now consider shameful, though you have never yet held a weapon, but I declare that it is much more honorable than the war.

[80] Envoys, men of Athens, must be evaluated according to the context in which they served, generals according to the forces they commanded. The statues you set up and the honorary seats and the garlands and meals in the Prytaneum are not for those who have brought back peace but for those who have won battles. If the envoys are held responsible for wars while the generals are rewarded, your wars will be without truce or quarter. Nobody will agree to serve as envoy.

[81] It remains for me to speak about Cersobleptes and the Phocians and the other slanders I have been subjected to besides. Personally, men of Athens, on both the first and the second embassy I reported to you what I saw as I saw it, what I heard as I heard it. So what was it that I heard and saw about Cersobleptes? Both I and all my colleagues on the embassy saw Cersobleptes' son held hostage at

2.76n). From this minor incident Aeschines, either inventing freely or drawing on a family tradition that magnified his ancestor's role in history, creates a victorious sea battle.

[108] That is, during the initiative to unite Greece against Philip in 348 (see 2.57n and Dem. 19.11).

[109] Greek "making the war *chorēgos*" (see 1.11n). Aeschines is deliberately vague about the sources of alleged profit, but these will have included opportunities for bribery and blackmail from administrative activities relating to army and fleet (1.113n, 2.177n), profiteering from the military lists (3.146), and blackmailing generals with the threat of public actions. The full list is left to the hearer's imagination.

Philip's court.[110] And that remains the case to this day. [82] As it happened, on the first embassy, as I and my colleagues were setting off for here, Philip was leaving for Thrace, and he had agreed with us that he would not enter Chersonesus with his army while you were debating the peace. On the day you voted for the peace, no mention was made of Cersobleptes. When we had been elected to receive the oaths but had not yet set out on the second embassy, there was an Assembly where Demosthenes, my present accuser, was selected by lot to chair.[111] [83] At that meeting Critobulus of Lampsacus[112] came forward and said that he had been sent by Cersobleptes, and that he asked to offer his oaths to Philip's envoys and have Cersobleptes enrolled among your allies. After he had spoken, Aleximachus of Peleces[113] gave the Chairmen (*proedroi*) a motion to read out; its contents were that Cersobleptes' representative should give his oaths to Philip together with the rest of our allies. [84] When the motion was read out (and this is something I think you all remember), Demosthenes stood up from among the Chairmen and said he would not put the motion to the vote or destroy the peace with Philip and that he did not recognize as allies people who joined the ceremonies just as peace was being sealed, so to speak. For an earlier Assembly meeting had been available for this purpose. It was only when you all shouted and called the Chairmen to the platform that the motion was put to the vote.[114] [85] To

---

[110] The date Cersobleptes' son was taken hostage is uncertain; it may have been as early as 352, but 346 (i.e., between the first and second Athenian embassies) seems the most likely date, since, as Harris (1995: 191 n. 11) notes, the implication of this passage is that it was on the second embassy that Aeschines saw Cersobleptes' son at Pella.

[111] That is, Demosthenes, a member of the Council of Five Hundred for the year, was selected as one of the *proedroi,* for whom see 1.23n. The meeting took place on 25 Elaphebolion (2.90), mid- to late March in our calendar. Cf. 3.73n.

[112] Otherwise unknown.

[113] Otherwise unknown.

[114] Since Aeschines has witnesses, and since Demosthenes evades the issue even in the published version of his prosecution speech (and likewise in Dem. 18), we may accept this account with some confidence. However, when the motion was put to the vote, evidently the Assembly declined to admit Cersobleptes to the alliance (Harris 1995: 75).

prove that I am speaking the truth, please call Aleximachus, who drafted the motion, and Demosthenes' colleagues as Chairmen, and read the deposition.

[DEPOSITION]

So you can see that Demosthenes, the man who just now wept here when he mentioned Cersobleptes, tried to shut him out of the alliance. When the Assembly dispersed, Philip's envoys received the oaths of our allies in your generals' office. [86] My accuser has had the nerve to tell you I drove Cersobleptes' emissary Critobulus from the rites, in the presence of the allies and despite the Assembly decree, when the generals were sitting there. Where could I have gotten such power? How could the incident have been suppressed? And if I had dared to act this way, would you have let me, Demosthenes, without filling the Agora with shouting and yelling, if you saw me, as you claimed just now, driving the ambassador from the rites? Let the herald please call the generals and the allied representatives. Listen to their depositions.

[DEPOSITIONS]

[87] Is it not monstrous, men of Athens, that someone should dare to tell such enormous lies against his fellow-citizen (I correct myself—yours, not his), when his life is in danger? Surely our ancestors were right to prescribe, in homicide trials at the Palladium,[115] with cut sac-

---

[115] Homicide cases were allocated to different courts according to the status of the victim, the nature of the charge, or the nature of the defense. According to Aristotle (*Constitution of Athens* 57.3), the Palladium tried people charged with unintentional killing, the "planning" (*bouleusis*) of homicide (that is, causing a death through an intermediary, with or without intent; see further *Antiphon and Andocides,* trans. Michael Gagarin and Douglas M. MacDowell, The Oratory of Classical Greece 1 [Austin: University of Texas Press, 1998], p. 74), and the killing of a slave, metic, or other alien. The details are factually irrelevant, but Aeschines draws on Athenian respect for the homicide courts, their ancestors, and tradition to give emotional force to a simultaneous attack on Demosthenes' duplicity and appeal to the jurors to resist it on the grounds of the implications of wrongful conviction both for the defendant and for themselves.

rificial victims, that the party who obtained the verdict should swear[116] (and this custom remains your tradition to this day) that all the jurors who cast their vote for him had voted for truth and justice and that he had spoken no lie; that he should call down destruction on himself and his house if this were not so and pray for great good fortune for the jurors. Their action was entirely right and good for the city, men of Athens. [88] For if no one among you would willingly stain himself with a justified killing, he would certainly avoid committing an unjust one by taking away another's life or property or citizen rights, acts that have brought about the suicide of some and the execution of others by the state. Will you then forgive me, men of Athens, if I call him a pervert[117] whose body is unclean, even the part his voice comes from,[118] before giving manifest proof that the rest of the accusation concerning Cersobleptes is a lie?

[89] You have a practice that in my view is of the greatest merit, and of the greatest use for the victims of slander: you keep a record for all time among the public documents of the dates and the decrees and the individuals who put them to the vote. My accuser has told you that the reason for Cersobleptes' ruin was the fact that as leader of the embassy I took advantage of my influence with you and, when he insisted we should go to Thrace while Cersobleptes was under siege and formally demand that Philip stop, I refused and sat at Oreus with my fellow envoys arranging to get posts as foreign representatives.[119] [90] Now listen to the letter that Chares sent to the Assembly at that point saying that Cersobleptes had lost his kingdom and that Philip had taken Holy Mountain on the twenty-fourth day of Elaphebo-

---

[116] Oaths played an important role in homicide trials; in addition to the winner's oath mentioned here, both parties swore an oath at the outset, the prosecutor to the guilt and the defendant to the innocence of the latter, and all witnesses had to swear both to the defendant's guilt or innocence and to the truth of their testimony (see further 2.156n).

[117] Greek *kinaidos*. See 1.181n.

[118] See 2.23n.

[119] The Greek term *proxenia* has no precise equivalent in English. The *proxenos* is an individual chosen by a state to represent its interests within his own state; the office was often hereditary. The term is cognate with *xenos*, "host," "guest." For the accusation of delay at Oreus, see Demosthenes 19.155.

lion. Demosthenes was serving as Chairman in the Assembly on the twenty-fifth of that month, though he was one of the envoys.

[LETTER]

[91] Not only did we waste the remaining days of the month; it was Munichion [120] when we set out. I shall produce the Council itself as witness to this; for there is a decree of the Council instructing the envoys to go to receive the oaths. [121] Please read out the Council decree.

[DECREE]

Now read out its date.

[DATE]

[92] You hear that the decree was passed on the third of Munichion. And how many days earlier than my departure had Cersobleptes lost his kingdom? According to the general Chares and his letter, it was in the previous month, if Elaphebolion is earlier than Munichion. So could I have saved Cersobleptes, when he had been overthrown before I set out from home? [122] Then again, do you think that this man has spoken a word of truth about events either in Macedonia or in Thessaly, when he tells lies about the Council, the public records, the date, and the Assembly meetings? [123] [93] And is it true that after

---

[120] The Athenian month following Elaphebolion, corresponding roughly to April in our calendar.

[121] The author was Demosthenes (Dem. 19.150, 154), who presents the decree as part of his own attempt to hasten the departure of the embassy.

[122] There is no good reason to doubt the facts. But Aeschines does not indicate when he and his colleagues learned of the fate of Cersobleptes. Probably the envoys were in no hurry to head north, either before or after receiving the news, in the hope that Philip would settle matters in Thrace to his own satisfaction and present them with a fait accompli, thus avoiding any friction that might threaten the peace. The interruption of the chronological narrative (which resumes in 2.97) in 2.93–96 testifies to some discomfort on Aeschines' part.

[123] Some editors read "the date of the Assembly meetings" (referring to 2.90). But since one expects "the date" to refer to the Council decree (2.91), I have hesitantly retained the manuscript reading; "the Assembly meetings" would refer vaguely to Demosthenes' official presence at the Assembly on 25 Elaphebolion.

trying to exclude Cersobleptes from the treaty at Athens when serving as Chairman, you pitied him at Oreus? Are you bringing a prosecution now for taking bribes, when earlier you suffered the imposition of a fine from the Areopagus for failing to pursue the indictment for wounding that you brought against Demomeles of Paeania,[124] your cousin, after cutting your own head open? Do you make solemn speeches to these people as though they did not know that you are the bastard[125] son of Demosthenes the knife-maker?

[94] You tried to maintain that I first declined on oath to serve on the embassy to the Amphictyons[126] and then was guilty of misconduct. And you read out one decree but passed over another. In fact I was chosen to serve as envoy to the Amphictyons, but I was ill; I diligently gave my report on the embassy from which I had returned to you, and I did not decline to serve on the embassy but promised to serve if I were able.[127] And as my colleagues were setting out I sent my brother and nephew and my doctor to the Council, not to decline the post [95] (for the law does not allow one to take an oath in the Council declining election by the Assembly) but to give proof of my illness.

---

[124] Aeschines refers to this incident (for which he is our only primary source) again at 3.51. Demomeles' brother Demophon was one of Demosthenes' guardians, and the incident is presumably to be connected with Demosthenes' long-running dispute with the latter (see 1.94n). The quarrel was subsequently settled, since Demomeles was later the proposer of a crown for Demosthenes (Dem. 18.223).

[125] That is, the marriage of Demosthenes' parents is (presented as) invalidated by the (alleged) non-Athenian origin of his mother. See 2.23n.

[126] The Amphictyonic League existed to protect the holy places of Delphi. Although it included states from the Peloponnese, the membership (2.116) was predominantly from the immediately adjacent states. The embassy in question was to convey to Philip the Athenian resolution of 16 Scirophorion (early to mid-June in our calendar) to extend the peace to Philip's descendants and to take the field against the Phocians if they refused to hand the Delphic temple over to Philip. In the event, the envoys heard while still in Euboea that the Phocians had surrendered to Philip and returned to Athens with their mission uncompleted. Demosthenes deals with this issue at 19.120–127.

[127] Aeschines may be telling the truth; but an excuse for Aeschines or one of his associates to stay behind in case Demosthenes stirred up trouble in their absence would no doubt have been welcome.

When my colleagues turned back on learning of the fate of Phocis, the Assembly met, by which time I was present and physically fit. As the Assembly insisted that all of us who had originally been selected as envoys should nonetheless carry out our mission, I felt I should deal honestly with the people of Athens. [96] And when I was being audited for this embassy you lodged no accusation; your charge is concerned with the embassy to receive the oaths, and on this I shall give a clear and honest defense. It may suit you, and everyone else who tells lies, to distort dates, but my task is to tell the story in the order of events, beginning with the journey on the embassy for the oaths.

[97] To start with, of the ten envoys, together with an eleventh sent by the allies,[128] no one was willing to eat with him when we were setting off on the second embassy or to lodge in the same inn as him on the road, where possible. They could see that he had plotted against them all on the previous embassy. [98] There was no mention of a possible journey to Thrace. This was not in our instructions from the decree, which were simply to receive the oaths and carry out various other tasks; nor could we have achieved anything if we had gone there, since the fate of Cersobleptes had already been decided, as you have just heard. Nor is there any truth in his statements; he is lying, and, since he has no true accusation to bring, he is posturing.

[99] He had two attendants who each carried a bundle of bedding, and in one of them, he claimed, was a silver talent. This reminded our colleagues of his old nicknames. As a child he was known as Batalus for a certain readiness for humiliation and perversion.[129] When he left childhood behind he brought suits for ten talents against each of his guardians and got the name Argas.[130] As a man he acquired the further name common to all unscrupulous men, sykophant. [100] He was intending to use the journey to ransom prisoners-of-war, as he claimed and has now stated before you, though he knows that during the war Philip never exacted a ransom for any Athenian, and though he was told by all of Philip's friends that Philip would free the rest as

---

[128] Aglaocreon again (2.126).

[129] See 1.126n.

[130] For Demosthenes' suit against his guardians, see on 1.94. Aeschines presents the litigation as dishonest and intended to provide Demosthenes with an easy income as a *sykophantēs* (see 1.1n); hence the alleged nickname "Argas," "Idler."

well in the event of peace.[131] And though there were many unfortu-
nates, he was carrying a talent, just enough to ransom one man, and
not a very rich one at that.

[101] When we reached Macedonia, we held a meeting. We had
found Philip now back from Thrace. The decree defining our task as
envoys was read out, and we listed your instructions to us in addition
to the receipt of the oaths. Since nobody was mentioning the most
important subjects but they were spending their time on lesser matters, I made a speech that must be repeated to you. [102] And in
heaven's name, men of Athens, listen quietly to the defense, just as
you listened as my accuser offered the prosecution case in the way he
wanted, and show the same patience you have shown in listening to
my speech from the beginning. As I indicated just now, men of Athens, at the meeting of the envoys I said that they were strangely missing the most important order from the people. [103] "Receiving the
oaths and discussing various other matters and raising the issue of the
prisoners could all in my view have been carried out even if the city
had sent our slaves and entrusted the task to them. But to reach an
effective resolution of the whole situation, insofar as it is in our power
or Philip's, is a job for intelligent envoys. I am speaking," I said,
"about the expedition to Thermopylae[132] you can see is in preparation. And I shall give you convincing evidence that my assumptions
about it are not mistaken. [104] There are Thebans here; representatives have come from Sparta; and we have come with a decree of the
people stating that 'the envoys are to negotiate any other advantage
they can.' All the Greeks are watching to see what will happen. If the
Assembly had thought it appropriate for them to speak openly to
Philip, bidding him strip Thebes of its arrogance and rebuild the walls

---

[131] Demosthenes makes much of this at 19.166–172. No doubt Demosthenes
was indulging in a degree of posturing for the purposes of internal Athenian politics (it has also been suggested that he was seeking to undermine the peace by
putting Philip in a bad light at Athens in the event of refusal), but although Philip
could guarantee to free without ransom any Athenian prisoners under his control,
he could not offer such a guarantee for his allies.

[132] The narrow pass at Thermopylae was the entrance to central Greece from
the north.

in Boeotia,[133] they would have asked this in the decree. As it stands, they have used vagueness to provide themselves with an excuse, if they fail to persuade him, while they felt they should let us take the risk. [105] Men who are concerned for the public good should not take on the role of other representatives whom the Athenians could have sent instead of us, while they personally avoid the hostility of Thebes. Epaminondas was a Theban; he did not cower before the prestige of Athens but stated frankly in the Theban Assembly that they should transfer the Propylaea of the Athenian Acropolis to the front of the Cadmea." [134]

[106] While I was still saying this, Demosthenes yelled out loudly, as all our colleagues know; for on top of his other crimes he sides with Boeotia. And what he said was this: "This man is full of confusion and recklessness. I admit I am timid and the dangers I fear are remote; but I forbid us to cause friction between the states. For what I take to be advantageous is that we envoys should not interfere. [107] Philip is setting off to Thermopylae; I cover my eyes. Nobody is going to put me on trial for Philip's military exploits but for any statement I make that I should not or any action beyond my instructions." The outcome of the matter was that the envoys, when asked individually, voted that each of us should say what he thought advantageous. To prove I am speaking the truth, please call our fellow envoys and read out their deposition.[135]

[DEPOSITION]

[108] When the embassies came together at Pella and Philip was present, the Athenian envoys were called. First, we came forward on the basis not of age, as in the previous embassy (a practice that is

---

[133] I.e., the cities destroyed by Thebes in the years before and after the battle of Leuctra of 371; cf. 2.116.

[134] The citadel of Thebes, equivalent to the Acropolis at Athens.

[135] The presence of testimony from the other envoys appears to confirm Aeschines' account. Demosthenes' anxiety was well founded. Aeschines proposed to take, and subsequently took, a big risk, publicly alienating Thebes with no guarantee that Philip would turn against his Theban allies, to say nothing of the severity of the treatment of political failure at Athens.

respected and was held to be a credit to our city), but of Demosthenes' shamelessness. Though he claimed he was the youngest of all, he said he would not give up the position of speaking first or allow anyone (by which he hinted at me) to get control of Philip's ears and to leave no chance for anyone else to speak.

[109] He began his speech with a veiled slander against his fellow envoys, to the effect that we had not all come with the same purpose or the same opinions. Then he recounted the services he had performed for Philip, first his support for Philocrates' decree, when Philocrates was charged with illegal legislation for proposing that Philip be allowed to send envoys to Athens to discuss peace, and second he read out the decree that he himself had drafted granting a truce for the herald and the embassy from Philip, third the one requiring the Assembly to decide the question of peace on specified days. [110] And he added an observation to the effect that he had been the first to bridle the individuals who were trying to close the door on peace,[136] not with arguments but with the timing. And then he cited another decree, that the Assembly should also consider an alliance, and after that as well the decree granting seats of honor at the Dionysia to Philip's envoys. [111] He went on to mention his own attentiveness, his provision of cushions and his nights on watch because of people who envied him and desired to mock his ambition,[137] and gave an absolutely ridiculous account that made his colleagues cover their faces, of how he entertained Philip's envoys, how he hired mule teams for them when they were leaving and accompanied them on horseback,[138] not shrinking into the shadow like some people but making a

---

[136] Aeschines elsewhere sneers more explicitly at Demosthenes' flamboyant metaphors (3.72, 166–167).

[137] Presumably Demosthenes was trying to prevent any incident involving the Macedonian representatives that might both embarrass him and cause hostility between Athens and Macedonia.

[138] Here and at 3.76 Aeschines presents Demosthenes' behavior to the Macedonian representatives as servile flattery (likewise Dinarchus 1.28); Demosthenes (19.235) presents his treatment of Philip's envoys as meant to display Athenian generosity in terms intelligible to Macedonians, though the brevity of his treatment of the issue suggests an awareness that it did not display him in a good light in Athenian terms. At 18.28 he observes rather lamely that failure to provide the-

public display of his favor for their cause. [112] And then he also corrected those statements of his:[139] "I did not say you were handsome, for a woman is the most beautiful thing there is. Nor that you were a good drinker, which I regard as praise fit for a sponge. Nor that you had a retentive memory, an encomium in my view for a hack sophist." To avoid a long story, this was what he said in the presence of representatives from virtually the whole of Greece. The laughter it provoked was of a quite uncommon sort.

[113] When he eventually finished and there was silence, I was forced to speak after such bad taste and such an embarrassing excess of flattery. Of necessity I made a brief introductory response to the slander he had uttered against his fellow ambassadors, saying that the Athenians had sent us as envoys not to defend ourselves in Macedonia but because on the basis of our way of life we had been judged at home worthy of the city. [114] I spoke briefly about the oaths we had come to receive, and I mentioned the other matters you instructed us to raise. For the elaborate and eloquent speaker Demosthenes had mentioned none of the essential topics. Above all I spoke of the expedition to Thermopylae and the cult sites and Delphi and the Amphictyons;[140] I urged Philip if at all possible to settle the situation there not with arms but with a trial and a vote. If that was impossible (this was obvious, since the army was there, already assembled), I said that anyone who was going to determine the fate of the cult sites of Greece should give careful thought to the question of piety and listen attentively to attempts to give advice about ancestral traditions. [115] I gave an account beginning with the founding of the temple and the first confer-

---

atre seats would not have excluded Philip's envoys, since they could have paid to see the performance.

[139] The statements made to the Assembly after the return of the first embassy (2.51–52).

[140] Aeschines' speech as described here is consistent with the surviving speeches in its reliance on narrative and its careful preparatory creation of atmosphere, here the solemn history of the Amphictyons leading to the denunciation of Thebes for its treatment of the other Amphictyonic cities of Boeotia. The denunciation was evidently meant to take the Thebans by surprise, since the narrative would most naturally be understood as directed toward the impiety of the Phocians in seizing and plundering the temple at Delphi.

ence of the Amphictyons, and I read out their oaths. In these the men of early times bound themselves not to destroy any Amphictyonic city or to bar access to flowing water in war or in peace, and to take to the field against anyone who broke this oath and destroy their cities; and if anyone were to rob the god's property or connive in or advise any action against the temple's contents,[141] they would punish him with hand and foot and voice and all their power. A solemn curse was appended to the oath. [116] After reading this out I asserted that in my opinion it was unjust to let the Boeotian cities lie in ruins. To demonstrate that they were Amphictyonic and parties to the oath, I listed the twelve peoples who shared responsibility for the temple: Thessalians, Boeotians (not just the Thebans), Dorians, Ionians, Perraebians, Magnesians, Dolopians, Locrians, Oetaeans, Phthiots, Malians, and Phocians.[142] And I showed him that each of these peoples, the greatest and the smallest, had an equal vote and that the delegate from Dorium and Cytinium[143] had equal power with the Spartans (for each people cast two votes), likewise among the Ionians the delegate of Eretria and Priene[144] had equal power with the Athenians, and all the rest in the same way.

[117] I declared that the principle of this campaign was holy and just, but I urged that, when the Amphictyons assembled in the temple and could safely vote, the individuals responsible for the original seizure of the temple should be punished, not their countries but those who had planned and executed it, and that the cities should suffer no punishment if they offered up the guilty parties for trial. "But if you use your military might to ratify the Theban crimes,[145] you will get no

---

[141] The temple and precinct at Delphi contained a fabulous collection of votive offerings; the remains of the treasuries built by various Greek states to house their offerings can still be seen lining the sacred way winding up to the temple.

[142] With the exception of the Dorians (a group that included the Spartans in the Peloponnese) and the Ionians, all are peoples of central Greece, i.e., close to Delphi.

[143] Cytinium was a city in the small central Greek state of Doris, northwest of Delphi, Dorium a small town in the western Peloponnese.

[144] Eretria was a city in Euboea, Priene a Greek city in Asia Minor (modern Turkey).

[145] That is, by leaving Thebes in control of Boeotia.

gratitude from the side you aid—for you could not yourself do them a service as great as that of the Athenians in the past,[146] and they do not remember that—while you will be wronging the side you abandon,[147] and they will be more committed enemies, not your friends."

[118] I do not want to waste time by giving you a detailed account of what was said there; so I shall summarize it and leave the topic. Fortune and Philip were responsible for what was done, but I was responsible for my loyalty to you and for my speech.[148] For my part I said what was just and in your best interests, but the result was not what we prayed for but what Philip brought about. Well, then, who deserves praise, the man who had no intention of doing any good, or the man who left nothing undone that was in his power? But for now I leave much unsaid for lack of time.

[119] He said that I deceitfully claimed that within a few days Thebes would be humbled and that I panicked the Euboaeans while encouraging you in empty hopes.[149] I want you to realize what he is up to, men of Athens. At Philip's court I affirmed, and I reported to you on my return, that I thought it right that Thebes should be part of Boeotia, not Boeotia part of Thebes. He represents me not as reporting but as promising it. [120] And I told you that Cleochares of

---

[146] Aeschines may have no specific incident in mind. Thebes could be regarded (with the rest of Greece) as a beneficiary of Athenian action during the Persian invasions of 490 and 480–479; Athens had joined forces with Thebes against Sparta in 394 and had sheltered the Theban exiles after the Spartan garrison seized the Cadmea in 382.

[147] Phocis.

[148] This argument ("I did all I could but events were beyond my control") is used with great effect by Demosthenes thirteen years later in the speech *On the Crown* (Dem. 18.192–195, 208) in reply to Aeschines 3. Cf. 2.165n.

[149] Although it was clear to all that Philip intended to march south to end the Sacred War, his precise plans for the settlement remained unclear. Philip did not commit himself to any specific course of action, while listening with apparent sympathy to all representations (cf. 2.136). Aeschines seems to have left Macedonia with high hopes of Philip (cf. 1.169; Dem. 5.10, 19.22, 74) and to have conveyed these hopes to the Assembly. The mention of Euboea relates to part of an anticipated deal with Macedonia in which Athens would regain Euboea in compensation for Amphipolis. Aeschines' response at 2.120 is disingenuous.

Chalcis[150] said he was amazed at the sudden consensus between you and Philip, especially when our instructions were to negotiate any other advantage we could; men like himself from small cities, he said, were alarmed by the secrets of more powerful states. Demosthenes represents this not as an anecdote I told but as a promise to hand over Euboea. My view was that a city that was about to debate the whole situation should not refuse to listen to what any Greek had to say.

[121] One slanderous claim on which he laid great emphasis was that he wanted to report the truth but was prevented by me and Philocrates.[151] For myself, I would like to ask you if any Athenian when sent out as envoy has ever been prevented from reporting to the people on his mission and, despite being treated with such disrespect by his colleagues, has proposed that the perpetrators be praised and invited to dinner. Now Demosthenes on his return from the second embassy, the one where, he claims, the Greek cause was ruined, did not praise us only in his resolution. [122] When I had reported on my statements about the Amphictyons and Boeotians to the Assembly, not briefly and hastily as now but with word-for-word accuracy, as far as I could, and the people were giving me an enthusiastic reception, I called on him together with the rest of our colleagues. When asked if my report to the Athenians was true and identical with what I said to Philip, amid general affirmation and praise from our fellow envoys he stood up last of all and said that what I was now saying was not the same as in Macedonia—my speech there was twice as good. And you who will give a verdict are my witnesses for this. [123] Yet what better opportunity than that could he have had to expose outright any lie I was telling the city? You say that on the earlier embassy you did not realize I was part of a plot against the city, that you became aware on the second embassy, the one where you clearly supported me. You make accusations about the first embassy while simultaneously claiming you have no complaint, and you base your charge on the embassy for the oaths. Yet though you criticize the peace, it was you who proposed

---

[150] Otherwise unknown.

[151] Demosthenes claims he attempted to write independently to the Assembly and to depart alone but was overruled by his colleagues (19.174, 323).

alliance as well. And if Philip deceived the city, his purpose in lying was to gain the peace that was to his advantage. Well, then, the earlier embassy was critical for this, but when the second embassy took place, everything had been settled.

[124] See from his own statements the lies he has told. These are the mark of the charlatan.[152] He says I went down the river Loedias by night in a small boat to meet Philip and that I composed the letter that came here for Philip.[153] You see, Leosthenes,[154] who was in exile from Athens because of his persecutors (*sykophantai*), was incapable of composing a clever letter, the man some people are prepared to declare the most able speaker after Callistratus[155] of Aphidna. [125] Nor could Philip himself, to whom Demosthenes proved unable to make a response on your behalf.[156] Nor Pytho of Byzantium,[157] a man proud of his skill in writing. No, it seems, the job needed me, too. And you say that I often spoke alone with Philip in broad daylight, but you accuse me of sailing down the river by night—so vital was a night letter! [126] That there is no truth in what you say those who ate with me are here to attest: Aglaocreon of Tenedos and Iatrocles[158] the son of Pasiphon, with whom I spent the night throughout the whole period. They know that I was never away from them for a

---

[152] Greek *goēs,* the language of magic; see 3.137n.

[153] The letter brought back by the second embassy. For the accusation, see Demosthenes 19.36–40. Demosthenes does not present this level of detail. Either Demosthenes cut this material from his published version or Aeschines embroiders the allegation to make it more preposterous (see Harris 1995: 10, with 178 n. 6).

[154] See 2.21n.

[155] The general and politician Callistratus played a major role in the creation of the Second Athenian League in the early 370s. His military career lasted until 361, when he was tried and condemned. He went into exile but subsequently returned to Athens and was executed (Lycurgus 1.93).

[156] See 2.34–35.

[157] Pytho was a distinguished orator. He had served as envoy for Philip to Athens in late 344 or early 343, when he conveyed Philip's willingness to amend the peace of 346 in order to meet any Athenian dissatisfaction with its terms.

[158] See 2.15 and 2.20 for these two envoys.

whole night or part of a night. And we have brought our slaves and offer them for torture.[159] I am willing to break off my speech, if my accuser agrees. The public executioner will come and torture them in front of you all, if you order it. What remains of the day is enough to do this, since this is a measured day and my trial is set at eleven amphoras.[160] [127] If the slaves agree that I spent the night away from my messmates at any time, show me no mercy, men of Athens, but stop the proceedings and put me to death. But if you are proved a liar, Demosthenes, the penalty you must pay is this: admit before these people that you're effeminate and not of free birth. Call my slaves here to the stand and read out the deposition of our fellow envoys.

---

[159] The evidence of slaves was only admissible in court if extracted under torture. The agreement of both parties to a legal action was required if such evidence was to be obtained, and the procedure was for one party to issue a challenge (as Aeschines does here) demanding that his opponent either surrender his slaves for torture or accept the offer of the challenger's slaves for torture. In cases that went to arbitration (the bulk of private cases), such a challenge could not be offered seriously in court, since the evidence containers were sealed at the end of the arbitration process. Public cases did not go to arbitration, and so in theory evidence could continue to be collected (e.g., depositions drafted) up to and during the trial. The offer to set the torture time against Aeschines' time-allowance here is a variation on a common motif designed to express confidence, the challenge to the opponent to offer a refutation within the speaker's time (cf. 2.59). The challenge is not taken up here and is evidently made in the confident expectation that Demosthenes will refuse (the penalty for Demosthenes outlined in 2.127 is intended to guarantee this).

[160] Unlike the practice in private cases, several of which could be tried in a day by a single panel of jurors, a panel would try only one public case in a day. Aristotle gives further information on the "measured day" at *Constitution of Athens* 67.3–5. The quantities are for water poured into the *klepsydra,* or water-clock, a container with a hole at the base to allow the water to run out (and a stopper to stop the flow during the reading of documents—this applied only to private cases). For the allocation of the time to different parts of the process within public hearings, see 3.197. Although a water-clock from the late fifth century (evidently used by the tribe Antiochis) has been found, the relation of this to those in use in the courts is unclear; accordingly, we do not know how long an amphora of water would take to run out. The Antiochis water-clock (which holds two *choes,* one-sixth of an amphora) would give just over six-and-a-half hours for eleven amphoras.

[DEPOSITION, CHALLENGE]

[128] Since he refuses the challenge and says he will not rely on the torture of slaves, take this letter that Philip sent. Clearly it must be a very clever deception imposed on the city, if writing it kept us awake.

[LETTER]

[129] You hear, men of Athens, that Philip says: "I have given my oaths to your envoys"; he has written the names of his allies who were present and of their cities, and he says he will send you those allies who were late. Don't you think Philip could have written this in daylight without my help?[161]

[130] But heavens above, in my opinion my opponent has only one concern, to enhance his reputation during the course of his speech. If a moment after stopping he will be thought the most unscrupulous man in Greece, he does not care a bit. How could anyone trust the sort of man who has tried to argue that Philip got past Thermopylae[162] not through his own stratagems but through my public speeches? And he counted the days for you during which I reported here on the embassy, while the couriers of Phalaecus,[163] the Phocian dictator (*tyrannos*), took the news there, and the Phocians through their trust in me allowed Philip to pass through Thermopylae and surrendered their

---

[161] The citation from Philip's letter is selected for the *reductio ad absurdum* of Demosthenes' position. Demosthenes (19.36) states that the letter exonerated the Athenian envoys (i.e., those on the second embassy of 346) for their delay in returning to Athens (they traveled south from Pella with Philip, who delayed taking the oaths to them until he was within easy reach of the pass at Thermopylae). This does not inculpate Aeschines, but it does indicate that the letter was open to malign interpretation. At 19.38 Demosthenes cites selectively from the letter for *his* purposes. The exchange is an interesting illustration of the susceptibility of documentary evidence to manipulation.

[162] That is, when he marched south after receiving the second Athenian embassy.

[163] Phalaecus, one of a rapid succession of Phocian leaders during the Third Sacred War, was in power from 351 until he was deposed in 347. He returned to power in 346 (cf. 2.133n). When Philip marched south to settle the Sacred War, Phalaecus reached an agreement with Philip under which he and his mercenaries were allowed to depart unmolested and Phocis was surrendered to Philip. For the calculation of dates, see Demosthenes 19.57–60.

cities to him. [131] This is the account contrived by my accuser. But the Phocian cause was ruined first because of Fortune,[164] which controls everything, second because of the long duration of the ten-year war. It was the same factor that established the power of the Phocian dictators and destroyed it. They came to power through their audacious seizure of the temple money, and they changed their constitutions with the support of foreign troops; they lost power through lack of money, once they had used up all they had on mercenaries. [132] The third factor that brought them down was the internal fighting that usually arises when armies are short of money, and the fourth was Phalaecus' ignorance of future events. For the campaign by the Thessalians and Philip became clear not long before peace was concluded with you. Envoys came from Phocis requesting military aid and promising to hand over Halponus, Thronium, and Nicaea, the positions that control the entrance to Thermopylae. [133] Though you passed a resolution that the Phocians should hand over these positions to the general Proxenus,[165] that fifty ships be manned and there should be an expeditionary force of men under forty, instead of handing over the positions to Proxenus, the dictators (*tyrannoi*) imprisoned the envoys who had offered to hand the forts over to you,[166] and the Phocians were the only Greeks who did not conclude a truce with the truce officers when they were announcing the truce for the Mysteries.[167] And later, when Archidamus the Spar-

---

[164] For the role of Fortune, cf. 2.118.

[165] A descendant of the tyrannicide Harmodius, Proxenus was general in 349/8 and in 347/6. He had been tried and convicted on a political offense by 343 (Dem. 19.280), presumably in the settling of scores that followed the Athenian disillusionment with the Peace of Philocrates.

[166] The offer was made by Phalaecus' successors after he was deposed in 347 (cf. 2.130n) and repudiated by Phalaecus on his return to power. Presumably Phalaecus had heard of the feelers being put out by Philip and Athens, and no longer regarded Athens as reliable. The envoys are the Phocian delegates returning from Athens.

[167] Early in 346. The truce for the Eleusinian Mysteries, like that for the Olympic games (see 2.12n), was intended both to allow celebrants to travel unmolested and to prevent disruption to the festival. The Mysteries, a cult of panhellenic importance celebrated at Eleusis in Attica in honor of the goddesses Demeter and Core/Persephone in the autumn month of Boedromion (roughly September),

tan [168] offered to take over and defend the positions, they declined and replied that he should worry about Sparta's dangers, not theirs. [134] At that point you had not yet reached a settlement with Philip; it was on the same day you were deliberating about the peace [169] that you heard from Proxenus' letter that the Phocians had not handed over the positions to him and the officials who were announcing the Mysteries had revealed that the Phocians were the only people in Greece who had not accepted the truce and that they had actually imprisoned the envoys who came here. To prove the truth of my statements, please call the truce officers and Proxenus' envoys to Phocis, Callicrates and Metagenes; [170] you must also hear the letter from Proxenus.

[DEPOSITIONS, LETTER]

[135] You hear, men of Athens, the dates being read out from the public records for comparison, and the witnesses as well testifying to you that before I was elected envoy, Phalaecus the Phocian dictator was refusing to trust the Spartans and us and was putting his faith in Philip.

[136] But was he the only man who could not predict the future? What was your own collective position? Didn't you all expect Philip to humble Thebes, because he could see their audacity and because he was reluctant to enhance the power of people he could not trust? Didn't the Spartans along with us use their embassy to pursue a pol-

---

lasted several days and culminated in the revelation to the initiates of secret objects. In the classical period, the process of initiation became more complex with the introduction of the Lesser Mysteries in the winter month of Gamelion (roughly January). The reference here is to the latter.

[168] By the time Archidamus, the son of Agesilaus, came to the throne in 360, Sparta's power had effectively been broken by Thebes. Like his father, Archidamus served as a mercenary in order to raise the funds Sparta would need if it was to regain control of Messenia. He died fighting in Italy in 338.

[169] That is, the Assembly meeting early in 346 when the decision was taken to send the first embassy (2.18).

[170] Callicrates is a common Athenian name; whether the individual named here is to be identified with any of the other bearers known from the period is uncertain. Metagenes may be the same as the witness against Timarchus at 1.100.

icy opposed to that of Thebes and end by clashing with them openly in Macedonia and threatening the Theban envoys? Weren't the Theban envoys themselves worried and frightened? Didn't the Thessalians laugh at the rest and declare that the campaign was for their own sake? [137] Didn't some of Philip's associates (*hetairoi*)[171] tell some of us explicitly that Philip would restore the Boeotian cities? Didn't the Thebans have all their forces in the field because they were anxious about the situation? When Philip saw this, didn't he send us a letter inviting you to take to the field in full force to aid the cause of justice? And wasn't it the people who are now set on war and who call peace cowardice who prevented you from taking the field after peace and alliance had been concluded, claiming they were afraid that Philip would seize our troops as hostages?[172] [138] Was I the one who prevented the people from imitating their ancestors or you and your fellow conspirators against the public interest? Was it safer and more honorable for the Athenians to march out when the Phocians were at the height of their madness, when they were at war with Philip and were holding Halponus and Nicaea (before Phalaecus handed them to the Macedonians), and the people we were to support were rejecting the truce for the Mysteries, and we were leaving the Thebans in our rear; or when Philip invited us, when we were bound by oaths of alliance, and when the Thessalians and the rest of the Amphictyons were participating? [139] Wasn't this a better occasion than the other, when because of your cowardice and spite the Athenians brought their belongings in from the country?[173] This was when I was serving on

---

[171] For Philip's *hetairoi*, cf. 2.34. Whether the *hetairoi* in question were simply thinking aloud or were actively pursuing Philip's policy of keeping everyone guessing is unclear.

[172] The reference is to Philip's invitation to the Athenians as his allies (under the new peace treaty) to participate in the settlement of the Sacred War in the summer of 346. The Athenian failure to participate not only risked alienating Philip, but prevented Athens from playing a significant role in the Amphictyonic decision on the fate of Phocis.

[173] For the Athenian panic on learning that Philip had gained access to central Greece, cf. 3.80; Demosthenes 19.125, 18.36.

the third embassy,[174] the one to the Amphictyons. You dare to claim that I went on it without having been elected,[175] yet though you are my personal enemy you have not seen fit even to this day to impeach me for misconduct as envoy. Though you certainly do not begrudge me capital punishment.

[140] Well then, the Thebans were pressing Philip with their entreaties, and our city was in a state of panic thanks to you, and the Athenian hoplites were not there; the Thessalians had joined the Theban side through your lack of judgment and the Thessalian hostility to Phocis that went back to early times, when the Phocians took some Thessalian hostages and whipped them; and Phalaecus had left under truce before the arrival of myself, Stephanus, Dercylus,[176] and the Amphictyonic representatives; [141] the people of Orchomenus were deeply afraid and had asked for a truce guaranteeing their physical safety on condition that they left Boeotia. With the Theban envoys present and Philip facing the prospect of open hostility from Thebes and Thessaly, the situation was lost not through my fault but through your betrayal and your position as Theban representative (*proxenia*).[177] And I think I can offer convincing factual proof of this. [142] If there were any truth in your claims, I would now be accused by the Boeotian exiles for having caused their exile and by the Phocian exiles for having prevented their return home. In fact, because they do not take account of the outcome but recognize my loyalty to their cause, the Boeotian exiles have gotten together and chosen supporting speakers for me, and representatives have come from the Phocian cities that I

---

[174] Aeschines treats as a single mission the third embassy (see 2.94n) and the fourth, which was made up of the same envoys (including Aeschines, who had claimed illness when appointed to the third embassy); this embassy was sent to Delphi, where the Amphictyons were to meet.

[175] Demosthenes 19.126.

[176] Stephanus is known to us as a minor politician connected with the pragmatists who opposed the stridently anti-Macedonian stance of politicians like Demosthenes; he is best remembered for his association with the courtesan Neaera, who is the target of [Demosthenes] 59. For Dercylus, see 2.47n.

[177] For the role of the *proxenos,* see 2.89n.

saved on my third embassy, the one to the Amphictyons, when the
Oetaeans were making a case for throwing the adult males from the
cliffs and I brought them before the Amphictyons so that they had an
opportunity to speak in their defense. Phalaecus had been allowed to
leave under truce, and the innocent were in danger of being killed, but
thanks to my support they were spared.[178] [143] To prove the truth of
my account, call Mnason of Phocis and his fellow envoys and the
chosen representatives of the Boeotian exiles. Take the stand, Liparus
and Pythion, and show your gratitude by saving my life as I saved
yours.

[SUPPORTING STATEMENT OF THE BOEOTIANS
AND PHOCIANS]

Wouldn't it be terrible if I were convicted when my accuser is Demosthenes, the Theban representative (*proxenos*) and the most unscrupulous man in Greece, and my supporting speakers are Phocians
and Boeotians?

[144] He had the nerve to say that I am the victim of my own
words.[179] He says that when I was prosecuting Timarchus I said that
everyone had heard the rumor of his life as a prostitute, that Hesiod,
a good poet, says:

> Report in no wise dies away completely, if many
> people utter it. She, too, then, is a god.

And he says that this same god has now come to accuse me, since
everyone agrees that I am in receipt of Philip's money. [145] You may
be sure, men of Athens, that there is an enormous difference between
common report and malicious accusation (*sykophantia*). Common
report has no connection with slander, but malicious accusation is

---

[178] The fate of Phocis was formally decided by the Amphictyonic Council.
There was evidently strong pressure for severe action against Phocis. In the event,
partly because of Aeschines' intervention and partly perhaps because of Philip's
influence behind the scenes, the Phocian cities were destroyed, and the Phocians,
now settled in small hamlets, were condemned to repay the money stolen from
the temple. Demosthenes (especially 19.65–66) presents the fate of Phocis as disastrous, but the outcome could have been far worse.

[179] Demosthenes 19.243–244, responding to Aeschines 1.128–129; cf. 1.129n.

slander's sister. I shall clarify the difference between them. Common report is when the mass of citizens of their own accord with no ulterior motive talk of an event as real; malicious accusation is when one individual presents an accusation to the general public and slanders someone at every Assembly and in the Council. We sacrifice to Report publicly as a goddess, while we bring charges[180] against sykophants publicly as criminals. Don't mix the most noble of things with the most disgraceful.

[146] There were many of his allegations that angered me, but especially when he accused me of being a traitor. For these charges inevitably presented me as brutal and cold-hearted and guilty of many other previous crimes. As to my life and my daily activities, I think that you are able to judge. But there are things that are invisible to the general public but are of the greatest importance to decent men— things that are very numerous and to my credit. For these I shall bring members of my family up here for you to see, so you will know the pledges I left at home when I went to Macedonia.[181] [147] You, Demosthenes, made up all these things you said against me; but I shall tell my tale honestly, as I was taught.

This is my father Atrometus, almost the oldest of the citizens. He has already lived for ninety-four years. When he was young, before he lost all his property through the war,[182] he was an athlete;[183] exiled by

---

[180] Greek *probolē,* an action involving accusation before the Assembly. According to Aristotle's *Constitution of Athens* (43.5), up to six individuals (both citizen and resident alien) could be accused by this process once per year in the sixth prytany.

[181] The rhetorical force of this and what follows is underpinned by the fact that there seems to have been a legal requirement (at least according to Dinarchus 1.71) that a public speaker, as was the case with a number of other officials, should have legitimate children and land in Attica; though there is reason to doubt that the law was applied strictly, it testifies to a desire that officials and politicians have a visible stake in the country's well-being.

[182] The Peloponnesian War (cf. Introduction to Aeschines, p. 3).

[183] Aeschines presents his father as coming from a propertied background, which allowed the leisure for athletics, and (by implication) his trade as schoolmaster as arising from financial disaster. The fact that Aeschines takes refuge in the tenuous connection of his family to the Eteobutadae (the clan, *genos,* that presumably formed the inner core of the phratry to which Atrometus belonged)

the Thirty, he fought in Asia[184] and proved his excellence in times of danger. By birth he belonged to a phratry[185] that shares altars with the Eteobutadae, which is where the priestess of Athena Polias comes from, and he took part in the restoration of democracy, as I mentioned a little earlier.[186] [**148**] On my mother's side, too, all my relatives are in fact of free citizen birth. And I see her before me now,[187] fearful for my safety and distraught. And yet, Demosthenes, my mother went into exile in Corinth with her husband and shared the city's sufferings; while you, who maintain you are a man (I would not dare to assert that you are in fact a man), were charged with desertion and saved yourself by buying off the man who indicted you, Nicodemus of Aphidna.[188] This man you and Aristarchus later killed, and you dare to enter the Agora, though you are unclean.[189] [**149**] And Philochares[190] here, our oldest brother, is a man whose way of life (despite your slanders) is not ignoble, a man who spends his time in the gymnasia, who served with Iphicrates and has been general now for three years in succession; he has come to beg you to save my life. Aphobetus here, our youngest brother, has served as your envoy to the Persian king and was a credit to the city; he was an honest administrator of your revenues, when you elected him as custodian of the public funds; he has sired children according to the laws, without putting his

---

casts doubt on the claim. The fact that he sees fit to make it tells us not a little about Athenian social prejudices.

[184] Presumably as a mercenary.

[185] See 3.18n.

[186] 2.78.

[187] Greek, literally "she appears before my eyes"; the language does not make absolutely clear whether she is alive and in court or present only in Aeschines' imagination and infirm or possibly dead, though as Michael Gagarin points out to me, the different terms used to refer to the mother and father (2.148, "This is my father") together with the absence of any mention of the mother in 2.179 strongly suggests the latter.

[188] For this scandal, see 1.172n.

[189] For the sacred character of the Agora, see 1.21n.

[190] We owe our knowledge of the careers of Aeschines' brothers to Demosthenes' sneering references at 19.237–238 and Aeschines' response here.

wife in bed with Cnosion,[191] as you did. He is here to show his contempt for your abuse;[192] a lying insult goes no deeper than the ears.
[150] And you dared criticize my in-laws; you are so shameless and
lost in ingratitude that you feel neither affection nor reverence for
Philodemus[193] the father of Philo and Epicrates, the man who secured
your enrollment in the deme, as the oldest members of Paeania know.
I am astonished that you have the nerve to insult Philo, and furthermore among the most upright citizens of Athens, who have come here
to give judgment in the best interests of the city and are more concerned with our way of life than with our speeches. [151] Do you think
they would wish to have 10,000 infantrymen like Philo with bodies as
fit as his and minds as decent, or 30,000 perverts (*kinaidoi*)[194] of your
sort? You try to turn the obliging nature of Epicrates, Philo's brother,
into a subject for abuse.[195] And who has ever seen him misbehaving
either in daylight, as you allege, in the procession for the Dionysia, or
at night? For you cannot claim that nobody noticed; he was too well
known. [152] I have three children, men of Athens, by Philodemus'

---

[191] Identified by Hyperides (1.13) as a friend of Demosthenes. The ancient
commentators on the present passage say that Demosthenes was his lover when
Cnosion was a youth, though the authority for the statement is uncertain.

[192] See Demosthenes 19.199–200, 237–238, 249, 281. Demosthenes becomes
far more abusive (and entertaining) at 18.129–130, 258–260.

[193] Philodemus, Aeschines' father-in-law, was a man of property (in 330 Demosthenes alleged that Aeschines inherited five talents from Philodemus' son,
Philo, 18.312). Aeschines is our sole source for Philodemus' role as Demosthenes'
sponsor for enrollment in the deme of Paeania at the age of 18, but there is no
reason to doubt the statement. Demosthenes does not in the extant version of the
prosecution speech insult Philodemus or Philo, though he does insult Epicrates
in passing (19.287). Possibly Demosthenes' abuse was toned down for publication,
but equally Aeschines may have interpreted the insult to Epicrates as a slur on the
whole family, especially as it enables him to convict Demosthenes of ingratitude.

[194] See 1.181n.

[195] Demosthenes (19.287) alleges that Epicrates has participated in comic
processions (presumably involving indecency and ritual abuse) without a mask.
"Obliging nature" is in the Greek *euagōgia,* literally "ability to be led easily"; the
word suggests that Epicrates was a weak character, and the allegation may contain
some truth.

daughter, the sister of Philo and Epicrates, a daughter and two sons. I have brought them here with the rest for the sake of a single question as evidence that I shall now offer the jurors. I ask you, men of Athens: do you think I would have betrayed to Philip not just my country, the friends with whom I associate, and my right to share the temples and graves of our ancestors, but these, the ones I love most of all the people in the world, that I would have set more store by his friendship than their safety? What passion could have overcome me? When have I ever behaved wrongly for money? It is not Macedonia that makes men good or bad but their nature. We are not different men now that we are back from the embassy but the ones you sent.

[153] In my political life I have become enmeshed to an extreme degree with a charlatan [196] and a criminal, a man who could not speak the truth even by accident. When he is telling a lie, he first swears an oath by his shameless eyes, and he not only presents imaginary events as fact but even gives the day when he claims they happened. And he falsely adds someone's name, claiming he happened to be there, in imitation of people telling the truth. But those of us who are innocent are lucky in one respect, that he does not have the intelligence to match his posturing ways and his skill with words. Just look at the stupidity and clumsiness of the man who made up a lie against me like the one about the Olynthian woman, where you stopped him in mid-speech. He was slandering the man furthest removed from conduct of the sort in front of an audience that knew the facts. [154] Observe how long he was in fabricating this accusation. There is a man named Aristophanes of Olynthus [197] living in the city. Demosthenes was introduced to him by some people, and, on discovering that he is a skilled speaker, he won him over with gross flattery; and he tried to persuade him to give false evidence against me before you. If Aristophanes would come forward and agree to malign me and allege that I am guilty of drunken violence against a female related to him who was captured in war, Demosthenes promised to give him 500 drachmas at once and another 500 once he had testified against

---

[196] Greek *goēs;* see 2.124n, 3.137n.

[197] Otherwise unknown. His appearance for Aeschines indicates that Olynthian exiles at Athens were still pursuing factional disputes predating the fall of the city to Philip. For the alleged assault, cf. 2.4 and Demosthenes 19.196–198.

me. [155] Aristophanes replied, and I have it on his own account, that Demosthenes had not misjudged the poverty resulting from his ex-ile—indeed, he had gauged it with absolute accuracy—but had com-pletely misjudged his character; Aristophanes would not do anything of the kind. To prove I am telling the truth, I shall provide Aristoph-anes himself as my witness. Call Aristophanes of Olynthus and read out his deposition, and call the people who heard him and brought word to me, Dercylus son of Autocles of Hagnus and Aristides son of Euphiletus of Cephisia.[198]

[DEPOSITIONS]

[156] You hear the witnesses giving evidence and swearing to its truth.[199] But as to those unholy rhetorical tricks of his, which he ad-vertises to the young men and has now used against me, do you re-member how he wept in grief for Greece and also praised Satyrus[200] the comic actor because when he saw some guest-friends (*xenoi*) of his, now prisoners, digging in Philip's vineyard and bound in chains, over drink he begged Philip to free them?[201] [157] From this start he went

---

[198] Aristides was a member of a family already attested as wealthy in the fifth century. His brother (also called Euphiletus) may be the friend of the general Phocion in 318 mentioned by Nepos (*Phocion* 4.3), which tallies with the appear-ance of Aristides for Aeschines here (along with Phocion, 2.170, 2.184). For Der-cylus, see 2.47n. The alert reader will note that what the Athenian witnesses con-firm is the fact that Aristophanes claims to have been offered a bribe, not the attempted bribery itself.

[199] Except in homicide trials (see 2.87n), there was no requirement for wit-nesses to take an oath; it was, however, possible for a witness to take a voluntary oath, and a litigant could challenge his opponent's witnesses to take an oath.

[200] Athenaeus makes Satyrus a native of Olynthus (13.591e), but the anecdote about his conversation with Philip, which takes place while Philip is still celebrat-ing the capture of Olynthus, would seem to rule this out.

[201] Demosthenes' version (19.193–195) has Satyrus secure the release of the daughters of a dead friend (Diodorus [16.55.3], in narrating the incident, takes his cue from Demosthenes). Demosthenes may have altered for publication or Aes-chines may misrepresent the allegation, either because he falsely anticipated the allegation and thought the detail not worth changing either in court or in revi-sion, or in order to exaggerate Demosthenes' appeal for pity (Harris 1995: 178 n. 6).

on to say, raising that shrill, vile voice of his, that it was monstrous that the man who played the part of Cario or Xanthias[202] should show such nobility and spirit, when I, the adviser to the greatest of cities, the man who counsels the Ten Thousand in Arcadia, could not curb my arrogance but got drunk when Xenodocus, one of Philip's associates (*hetairoi*),[203] was entertaining us and dragged a female prisoner by the hair, grabbed a whip, and beat her. [**158**] Now if you had believed him or if Aristophanes had supported his lie, I would have been ruined unjustly on shameful charges. So are you going to let a man who brings down the curse of heaven on his own head (not on the city, I hope) live among you? You purify the Assembly;[204] will you include prayers in your decrees on this man's proposals when you send out an army or a fleet? Note that Hesiod says:

> Many a time a whole city has paid for an evil man
> who sins and devises criminal acts.[205]

[**159**] There is one more thing I want to say beyond what I have said already. If there is any kind of wickedness among mankind and I cannot show that Demosthenes is an expert in it, I set my penalty at death.[206] But in my view, a man on trial has many disadvantages. The danger he faces distracts his mind from the anger he feels and makes him concentrate on arguments that will save his life, in case he misses anything. So I want to remind both you and myself of the charges against me. [**160**] Consider them one by one, men of Athens. What decree am I accused of proposing? What law have I repealed or prevented from being passed? What agreement have I made on behalf of the city? Which of the clauses you approved in the peace treaty have I erased, or what clause of my own have I added that you did not vote for? [**161**] There were some public speakers who did not like the peace. Well then, shouldn't they have spoken out against it then, instead of

---

[202] Slave names from comedy.

[203] By implication a Macedonian (though not all Philip's *hetairoi* were Macedonian); Demosthenes (19.196) calls the host Xenophron and makes him an Athenian and the son of one of the Thirty (for whom, see 1.39n).

[204] See 1.23n.

[205] Hesiod *Works and Days* 240–241.

[206] See 2.5n.

putting me on trial now? There were some people who were getting
rich by the war from your levies and the public revenues. Now that
has stopped, since peace does not support idleness. So should men
who are not victims but criminals wronging the city take revenge
on the man who supported peace, while those of you who benefit
from peace desert the men who have served the public interest well?
[162] Yes, because I joined in singing Philip's paeans when the Phocian
cities were razed, my accuser says.[207] And what clear proof can be offered for this? I was invited to dinner with the rest of the envoys, and
the invited guests at the dinner amounted to no fewer than 200, including the Greek delegations. And among all these I could be clearly
seen joining in the singing instead of keeping silent; so Demosthenes
claims, when he was not there and has not presented anyone who was
there as witness. [163] And who could have seen me, unless I was
leading the singing in the manner of choral performances?[208] Now if
I was silent, your charge against me is false. But if, while our country
was safe and no public misfortune had befallen our citizens, I joined
in the paean with the rest of the ambassadors, when the god was being
honored and there was no disgrace for Athens, I was behaving piously,
not committing a crime, and I should in justice be spared. And this
makes me a man without pity, while you are a man of piety, when
you bring charges against men who have shared your libations and
your food.

[164] You have also accused me of incoherence of policy because I
served as envoy to Philip when previously I had sought to unite the
Greeks against him.[209] Yet if you wish, you may also bring this charge
against the rest of the Athenian population. You[210] made war on

---

[207] Demosthenes 19.128; Demosthenes found the allegation worth reviving
thirteen years later, this time with reference to Chaeronea (18.287). The Athenian
envoys were evidently placed in an awkward situation. Even if they joined the
singing (and Aeschines' discomfort on the issue suggests that some did, including
him), it is to be remembered that the Athenian Assembly had declared a readiness
to make war on Phocis (cf. 2.94n); the Phocians had been awkward and embarrassing allies, and only in retrospect did they become martyrs for Greek freedom.

[208] I.e., as chorus leader.

[209] Demosthenes 19.9–16. See 2.57n.

[210] Addressed to the audience.

Sparta, and after their disaster at Leuctra you sent aid to the same people.²¹¹ You restored the Theban exiles to their country, and then later you fought them at Mantinea.²¹² You made war on Eretria and Themison, and then later you rescued them.²¹³ And there are countless other Greek peoples you have dealt with like this in the past. Both states and individuals must adjust to the prevailing situation to secure their best advantage. [165] What should a loyal adviser do?²¹⁴ Won't he give the city the best advice in the prevailing circumstances? And what should a dishonest accuser do? Won't he suppress the circumstances and criticize the action? And how should we recognize the born traitor? Surely he will behave the way you have treated people who cross your path and who have trusted you, writing lawcourt speeches for money and passing these on to the opponents? You wrote a speech for the banker Phormion for pay and you handed it to Apollodorus, who was prosecuting Phormion on a capital charge.²¹⁵

---

²¹¹ Having made peace in 374, Sparta and Athens returned to a state of war almost immediately. Peace was negotiated in 371, but the refusal of Sparta to acknowledge Thebes' claim to dominance over the whole of Boeotia led to a Spartan invasion of Boeotia and Spartan defeat by Thebes at Leuctra. When the Thebans proceeded to invade the Peloponnese, Athens sent aid to Sparta.

²¹² For the Theban exiles, see 2.117n. The battle of Mantinea was fought during the fourth Theban invasion of the Peloponnese in 362. Thebes won, but the general Epaminondas died in the fighting.

²¹³ The campaign against Themison, dictator (*tyrannos*) of Eretria, dates to 366, when he seized Oropus from Athens (he subsequently handed it over to Thebes). The "rescue" relates to the Athenian expulsion of a Theban force from Euboea in 357.

²¹⁴ This again is a theme taken up by Demosthenes in 330 (18.190, 194, 209, 301). Cf. 2.118n.

²¹⁵ Three speeches in the Demosthenic corpus belong to different phases in the long-running property dispute between the banker Phormion (a former slave) and Apollodorus, the son of his former owner Pasion: Demosthenes 36 (for Phormion), Demosthenes 45 and 46 (for Apollodorus against one of Phormion's witnesses). Demosthenes 36 is generally accepted as genuine. Demosthenes 45 may be Demosthenic, while Demosthenes 46 is almost certainly not by Demosthenes and may (though this is disputed) have been written by Apollodorus himself. If Aeschines refers to this phase in the dispute, he is paradoxically both unjust (since

[166] The household of Aristarchus the son of Moschus was prosperous when you entered it; you destroyed it.[216] You received three talents from Aristarchus when he was going into exile; this was to support him in exile, and you cheated him of it, without any consideration for your public claim to be an admirer of his beauty. But you were not really; honest love has no place for deviousness. All this, and acts like this, mark the traitor.

[167] He also spoke about military service and called me "that noble soldier."[217] And I think I may speak on this subject as well without giving offense; my concern is for the danger that now faces me rather than for his insults. For where or when or to whom shall I speak on this subject, if I do not mention them today? When I ceased to be a child I served as a border guard for this country for two years; to prove this I shall provide my fellow ephebes[218] and our commanders as witnesses. [168] The first expedition I served on was what's termed "service by divisions."[219] Along with others of my age group and Al-

---

Phormion won, it is unlikely that Demosthenes exposed his strategy to his opponent in advance) and overgenerous (since, if Dem. 45 is genuine, Demosthenes actually wrote for both sides at different points in the dispute). Aeschines' reference to a capital charge fits ill with this reconstruction, however. Unless there were further trials unknown to us, either Aeschines is confusing the suit in question with an earlier attempt by Apollodorus to sue Phormion (Dem. 45.4) that did not come to court, or he is deliberately exaggerating.

[216] Cf. 1.171.

[217] Demosthenes 19.113. In the surviving version Demosthenes says not "noble" but "remarkable," "wondrous" (*thaumasios*); the description is, of course, sarcastic. Possibly Aeschines adjusts the phrase in order to introduce a term that can be turned to his credit.

[218] The *ephēbeia* was a period of military service, consisting of guard duty, undertaken by Athenian males (though possibly restricted to the hoplite class and above) on reaching the age of majority. It was probably an old institution. It was substantially reorganized in the wake of the defeat at Chaeronea in 338.

[219] By the 320s (Aristotle *Constitution of Athens* 53.7), limited army drafts for campaigns were based on age groups (that is, year groups of citizens registered under the year they achieved majority). "Service by divisions" may have consisted of a levy based on part of an age group, or it may refer to the older system, under which all those registered for military service were drafted in turn, irrespective of age.

cibiades' mercenaries,[220] I was part of the escort force to Phlius. When we came under attack near the place called the Nemean Ravine, my role in the fighting was such as to receive the praise of my commanders. And I served in all the successive campaigns where the force was conscripted by age groups. [169] I fought in the battle at Mantinea,[221] where my conduct was no disgrace nor unworthy of our city. I served in the expeditions to Euboea and was among the picked force in the battle of Tamynae,[222] where my conduct under danger won me a crown there and again from the people on my return here, when I brought the news of the city's victory and my fellow envoy to Athens from the army, Menites the division commander (*taxiarchos*)[223] for Pandionis, reported on my conduct in the danger we faced.

[170] To prove I am speaking the truth, take this decree and call Menites, the men who served with me on the campaigns for the city, and Phocion[224] the general—not at this point as my supporting speaker (*synegoros*), unless the jurors approve, but as a witness open to malicious prosecution by my opponent, if he tells a lie.[225]

---

[220] In 366. The Athenians were escorting a supply train to the city of Phlius, under siege from opposing cities in the Peloponnese. The general Chares took the opportunity to inflict a defeat on the forces of Sicyon (Xenophon *Hellenica* 7.2.17–23).

[221] See 2.164n.

[222] See 3.86n.

[223] The *taxiarchos* (often anglicized as "taxiarch") was the commander of the heavy infantry (hoplite) contingent for the tribe, in this case Pandionis. Menites is not otherwise known.

[224] A distinguished general and statesman, born in 402/1. Though ready to fight Macedonia as necessary, he favored a policy of cautious pragmatism. He served as envoy to Philip after Chaeronea in 338 and to Antipater in 322 after the unsuccessful Athenian bid for freedom following the death of Alexander, and opposed sending aid to Thebes when it revolted from Macedonia in 335. He was tried and executed for treason in 318 as a result of the interaction of disputes between Alexander's successors and internal Athenian politics.

[225] It was open to any litigant to sue any of his opponent's witnesses for false testimony by *dike pseudomartyrion*. Penalty consisted of compensation paid to the aggrieved party, and three convictions brought loss of citizen rights. No such penalty attached to statements made by supporting speakers; Phocion later appears as supporting speaker for Aeschines (2.184).

[DECREE, DEPOSITIONS]

[171] So I was the first to bring news of the city's victory and your sons' success. And the first return I ask is that you spare my life. I am no enemy of democracy, as my accuser maintains, but an enemy of wickedness. Nor do I prevent you from[226] imitating Demosthenes' ancestors (he hasn't any) but call on you to emulate those policies that are honorable and protect the city. And now I shall go back in time to describe them in slightly greater detail.[227]

[172] In earlier times our city enjoyed prestige after the battle against the Persians at Salamis.[228] Though the walls had been razed by the barbarians, we were at peace with Sparta, and our democratic constitution remained secure. But when trouble was stirred up by certain individuals, we went to war with Sparta, and both inflicted and suffered a great deal of harm. Then Cimon[229] the son of Miltiades entered negotiations with Sparta as their representative (*proxenos*),[230] and we made a truce for fifty years[231] that we kept for thirteen.

---

[226] The reading adopted by Dilts ("And I do not allow you to imitate Demosthenes' ancestors, etc.") has greater manuscript authority but in my view gives an inferior sense. The text adopted here both avoids the tacit association of the jurors with Demosthenes' (allegedly) bad ancestry and offers an ironic response to the allegation at Demosthenes 19.16 that Aeschines on 19 Elaphebolion urged the Athenians to ignore the examples of their collective ancestry (cf. 2.63n).

[227] The highly tendentious and chronologically confused narrative that follows is heavily dependent on the account of Andocides' speech *On the Peace* (And. 3) of 392/1, in which Andocides, arguing for the acceptance of peace terms on offer from Sparta, seeks to associate peace with the preservation of, and war with danger to, the democratic constitution. Demosthenes anticipates and rejects Aeschines' praise of peace at 19.88–91.

[228] In 480.

[229] A distinguished general and politician, active in the struggle against Persia after the invasion of 480–479 and the creation of the Delian League and its metamorphosis into the Athenian empire. He favored the maintenance of friendly relations with Sparta. Ostracized in 461, he was recalled in 452. He fell ill when campaigning in Cyprus in 449 and died.

[230] For the *proxenos,* see 2.89n. The statement comes from Andocides (3.3).

[231] Aeschines takes over a misstatement of Andocides (3.4), who presents the five-year peace of 451 as a fifty-year peace.

[173] During this period we fortified the Piraeus and built the north wall,[232] we built 100 ships in addition to those we already had, we equipped a force of 300 cavalry and bought 300 Scythians, and we kept our democracy stable.

Then our political system was invaded by individuals who had neither free birth nor moral restraint, and we embarked on war again because of the Aeginetans.[233] [174] This war caused us no small damage, and we became eager for peace. We sent Andocides[234] and his fellow envoys to Sparta and so enjoyed thirteen years of peace, which raised the democracy high.[235] We deposited 1,000 talents in coin on the Acropolis, we built another 100 triremes and constructed the shipyards, we established a force of 1,200 cavalry and an equal number of archers, the Long Wall to the south was built,[236] and nobody attempted to overthrow the democracy.

[175] When we were persuaded to go to war again because of the Megarians,[237] we abandoned our territory to be ravaged and lost much

---

[232] The reference is to one of the three "Long Walls" connecting Athens to Piraeus, its port city, in the fifth century; the wall was actually built before the peace of 451, as was the fortification of the Piraeus, which was undertaken by Themistocles. The statement (and likewise the figures in this chapter) comes from Andocides 3.5. The Scythians referred to here are the slave archers, whose duties included keeping order at public meetings.

[233] Andocides 3.6. The reference is to the final conquest of Aegina (458), which was in itself painless for Athens, though it coincided in time with a period of (ultimately unsuccessful) Athenian expansion. The confusion may be due to the importance of Aegina in Spartan propaganda leading up to the Peloponnesian War, which began in 431. Aeschines follows Andocides in reversing the chronological relationship between the war against Aegina and the peace of 451.

[234] The grandfather of the orator, a fact mentioned by Andocides with evident pride (3.6). The reference is to the Thirty Years' Peace of 446/5.

[235] The metaphor comes from Andocides 3.7, as do the following figures. The reserve fund of 1,000 talents postdated the recrudescence of war in 431, whereas the construction of the shipyards predated the Thirty Years' Peace.

[236] Linking Athens with Phalerum, the smaller, older harbor. The statement comes from Andocides 3.7; in fact, the south wall was built at the same time as the north wall (see 2.173n).

[237] The reference is to the outbreak of the Peloponnesian War in 431. In the negotiations leading up to the outbreak of war, the Spartans made much of the decree excluding Megarians from the Agora at Athens and the harbors of the

of our prosperity; and we began to desire peace, which we achieved through the efforts of Nicias son of Niceratus.[238] And again during that period we deposited 7,000 talents on the Acropolis, thanks to this peace, and we acquired no less than 300[239] seaworthy and fully equipped triremes, our annual income in tribute was over 1,200 talents, we held the Chersonese and Naxos and Euboea, and we sent out our largest number of colonies during those years.[240] [176] But though we were enjoying so much prosperity, we were persuaded by the Argives[241] to go to war with Sparta, and finally, thanks to the bellicosity of the public speakers, we ended up with a garrison in the city, with the Four Hundred[242] and the godless Thirty,[243] when we did not ne-

---

empire. Although Thucydides' account in the first book of his history suggests that the Megarian decree was a minor issue, the Spartan insistence that war could be avoided if the decree was rescinded caused some Athenians at the time to put the blame for the war on the Megarian decree; in time, this belief came to prevail. The devastation mentioned relates to the Spartan annual invasions of Attica in the early years of the war.

[238] In 421. Nicias was a successful politician and general; he was one of the commanders of the Athenian expedition against Syracuse in Sicily in 415–413 and was captured and executed after the destruction of the expeditionary force. In what follows, the figures come from Andocides 3.8–9.

[239] The manuscripts of Andocides give a figure of 400 (*tetrakosias*), those of Aeschines 300 (*triakosias*); the text of Andocides is usually altered on the basis of the present passage and Thucydides 2.13.8; against, see Gagarin and MacDowell 1998: 151 (cited in 2.87n).

[240] This slightly distorts Andocides 3.9. Having mentioned the Chersonese, Naxos, and Euboea, Andocides observes only that it would take a long time to describe all the Athenian colonies; it is not clear whether Andocides is referring to existing or new colonies; Aeschines took him to mean the latter.

[241] In 414; the fact is taken from Andocides 3.9 and 3.31.

[242] In 411 a short-lived oligarchic regime was set up. The new regime was never accepted by the Athenian fleet and was ultimately overthrown by dissent among the oligarchs. If the translation "a garrison in the city" is correct, Aeschines by accident or design advances the date of the imposition of a Spartan garrison, which actually postdated the Athenian surrender of 404, confusing the two oligarchic coups. The Greek could conceivably mean "garrisoning of the city," referring to the reduction of Athens to a fortress within its own territory by the Spartan occupation of Decelea (for which, see 2.76n); cf. Thucydides 7.28.2.

[243] For the Thirty, see 1.39n.

gotiate a peace but were forced to accept one imposed on us. Once political order had returned and the democracy had been restored from Phyle,[244] Archinus and Thrasybulus[245] became the popular leaders and bound us by oath "to bear no grudge against each other,"[246] and as a result the world thought our city exceptionally wise. [**177**] At this point, when the democracy had sprung up afresh and recovered its original strength, persons who had had themselves fraudulently enrolled as citizens constantly attracted to themselves the corrupt element in the city and pursued a policy of war and more war. In peace they spoke of danger they foresaw and tried to stir up ambitious and over-hasty minds, while in war they never lifted a weapon but got themselves made army auditors (*exetastai*) and naval inspectors (*apostoleis*).[247] These are men who father children[248] on their mistresses, men disfranchised for malicious prosecution (*sykophantia*). And they are placing the city in extreme danger. They support the name of democracy not with their conduct but with flattering words; they are trying to destroy the peace that keeps democracy safe, while they champion the wars that destroy democracy.

---

[244] In 403 a small band of exiles seized Phyle on the border between Athens and Boeotia. From there they established themselves in the Piraeus, from which they overthrew the Thirty.

[245] Archinus was among the moderate oligarchs when the Thirty came to power; he was subsequently exiled and returned with the democrats in 403. There were two politicians of the name Thrasybulus, one belonging to the deme Collytus and the other to the deme Steiria. Aeschines refers to the latter. A military leader in the latter part of the Peloponnesian War, he led the democratic exiles at Phyle and played a role in the resurgence of Athenian influence in the latter part of the 390s; he died fighting in Asia Minor in 389.

[246] For the amnesty of 403, see 1.39n.

[247] For the *exetastai,* cf. 1.113. The *apostoleis,* "dispatchers," were concerned with the efficient dispatch of the Athenian fleet. Their powers included the detention of errant trierarchs in certain circumstances and a judicial role in disputes between successive trierarchs serving on the same ship. Aeschines implies that the authority of both officials offered scope for abuse; presumably he has in mind opportunities for bribes, blackmail, or revenge on personal enemies.

[248] The Greek verb used (*paidopoieisthai*) implies not only physical procreation but also formal acknowledgment, i.e., the conferring of rights exclusive to legitimacy and citizenship upon illegitimate and non-Athenian offspring.

[178] These people have now formed ranks and come against me, claiming that Philip bought the peace and got the better of us in every aspect of the treaty, and that he has breached the peace that he devised to his own advantage. They put me on trial not as envoy but as guarantor for Philip and the peace; and they are holding me accountable for anticipating events, though I had only words at my disposal. I can point to the same man as my eulogist in his decrees whom I have had as my accuser in court. I was one of ten envoys, but I am the only one being held to account.

[179] There are people here to join me in imploring you: my father—do not deprive him of his hopes for his old age; my brothers, who would not want to live if I were taken from them; my in-laws; and these little children who do not yet recognize the danger but who will be pitiful if anything befalls me. I beg and implore you to give careful thought to them and not hand them over to their enemies or to this unmanly and effeminate person.

[180] First of all, I urge and implore the gods to save my life, secondly you who have the vote in your hands, to whom I have offered a defense against each of the charges to the best of my recollection; and I beg you to save me and not hand me over to this speechwriter, this Scythian.[249] All of you who are fathers with sons or who care for your younger brothers, remember that I have issued a call for chastity that will never be forgotten through my prosecution of Timarchus. [181] And as to all the rest whom I have never vexed with my conduct, an ordinary man in fortune and as decent as any of you, and in political struggles the only one of all of them who has not colluded against you, I urge you to save me. I have served the city with complete loyalty as envoy and have single-handedly stood up to the clamor of the sykophants, which before now many men who have shown courageous spirits in war have failed to resist. It is not death that is terrible, it is humiliation in death that is to be feared. [182] Isn't it pitiful to face the mocking gaze of an enemy and have one's ears filled with his insults? But still I have endured it; I have exposed my life to danger. I was brought up among you; my way of life has been your way of life.

---

[249] For Demosthenes' birth, see 2.23n, 3.171n. For Demosthenes the Scythian, cf. Dinarchus 1.15.

There is nobody among you whose private life is worse because of my pleasures, who has been deprived of citizenship on my accusation at the time of the ballots,[250] or who was put at risk by me when subject to account for official conduct.

[183] I have a little more to say before I step down. Men of Athens, it was for me personally to decide to do you no wrong, but it was for Fortune[251] to decide if I should face no accusation; she threw in my lot with a slanderer, a barbarian, a man who has shown no respect for shared rites, libations, or table, who is trying to frighten off anyone who will argue against him in the future, and therefore has come with a false charge that he has fabricated against me. If you choose to protect the champions of peace and your security, the city's interests will acquire many supporters who will be ready to face danger for your sake.

[184] As supporting speakers I call[252] on Eubulus to represent the politicians and men of character, Phocion to represent the generals, a man who has also surpassed everyone in justice, and to represent my friends and contemporaries Nausicles and all the others I have mixed with and whose pursuits I have shared.[253]

My own speech is finished; my life I and the law now place in your hands.

---

[250] See 1.77n.

[251] Cf. 2.118, 131.

[252] See 3.202n.

[253] For Eubulus, see 2.8n; for Phocion, 2.170n; for Nausicles, 2.18n.

3. AGAINST CTESIPHON

INTRODUCTION

Context

By the time Aeschines and Demosthenes faced each other in court again, their positions had to a large extent been reversed. Demosthenes' influence had increased, partly because those who had argued most vigorously for peace in 346 had been unable to demonstrate any tangible benefit, whereas those who had predicted the inexorable expansion of Philip's power had been proved right, and partly because Demosthenes had proved himself effective after the outbreak of the hostilities that culminated in Chaeronea. It might be expected that the Athenians would hold him responsible for the disaster, and it seems that political attacks were made on him at that time (Dem. 18.249). But the prevailing view seems to have placed more weight on his efforts on the city's behalf than on their failure. He was chosen to give the oration in honor of the dead of Chaeronea. He was also entrusted with a number of important public duties. He was among those made responsible for ensuring the city's supplies in the wake of the disaster. In 337 he was selected as his tribal representative among the board of *teichopoioi* ("wallbuilders") entrusted with the task of improving the city's fortifications. He supplemented the state funds provided for the work on the fortifications with money of his own.

In 336, Ctesiphon, a political ally of Demosthenes,[1] proposed a

---

[1] Probably not to be identified with the Ctesiphon who served as Athenian envoy to Philip in 346 (2.12n). That there was hostility in 343 between the envoy Ctesiphon and Demosthenes (who speaks disparagingly of him: 19.12, 315) is no obstacle to identifying the two, since political affiliations in the Athenian system

crown for Demosthenes as a reward for these efforts, and more generally for his continuing service to the city. Aeschines challenged Demosthenes to defend his public record by prosecuting Ctesiphon for bringing an illegal measure. The case did not come into court until 330. The reasons for the delay are unclear, but presumably Aeschines was waiting for the right opportunity. Chaeronea had failed to dent Demosthenes' popularity. But the failure of the revolts of 335 (Thebes) and 331 (Sparta), in which even Demosthenes refused to become actively involved, together perhaps with Alexander's irresistible momentum in Asia (which ruled out the prospect of Persian assistance for Greek opponents of Macedonia), may have suggested to Aeschines that the patent bankruptcy of anti-Macedonian politics offered a promising background for an attack on Demosthenes.

The charge against Ctesiphon was based specifically on alleged procedural irregularities in the terms of the proposal, and more broadly on alleged falsehood in Ctesiphon's supporting statement in justification of the award. The alleged irregularity was twofold, consisting of the proposal to crown an official who had yet to submit to the final audit for his term of office and the announcement of the award in the theatre, both breaches of the laws, according to Aeschines. Opinions differ on the validity of Aeschines' technical objections. In reply to the second charge, Demosthenes argues (18.120–121) that the law allowed for exceptions to the rule against the proclamation of individual honors in the theatre, and Aeschines himself admits (3.47) that there was scope for exceptions; although he blusters to the effect that this applies only to crowns given by foreign states, his argument remains highly tendentious. The first charge is more difficult to evaluate. Although the majority of modern scholars have accepted Aeschines' argument,

---

(see Introduction to Aeschines, n. 8) were more fluid than in modern party-based democracies and relations with Macedonia were an issue on which allegiances changed with time. Nor is the fact that that Ctesiphon was in 346 the oldest of the Athenian envoys (2.42), since age was no bar to political activity. But Aeschines' failure to associate Ctesiphon with Demosthenes' alleged subservience to Macedonia is surprising if the defendant in this trial is the envoy of 346, while the brevity of Aeschines' attack on Ctesiphon at 3.213–214 is strange if the target had played a prominent role in interstate politics, as is Ctesiphon's alleged defense at 3.214 ("He says he expects to be seen as an ordinary man," i.e., as distinct from a politician).

Harris has argued[2] that Aeschines misrepresents the laws: what was forbidden was not the crowning of an official before his audit, but the crowning of an official *for the term of office* for which he was still subject to audit; he further argues that Ctesiphon is proposing to crown Demosthenes for his lifetime achievements, not for his activities as *teichopoios*. The proposed reconstruction of the law is supported by the tenor of Demosthenes' defense at 18.111–113, where he accepts that he was still subject to audit but maintains that the decree praised him not for his conduct in office but for his donation to the fortifications. It is possible that the law was genuinely ambiguous.[3] But even on this narrow interpretation of the law, Ctesiphon may be vulnerable. Although the proposed decree cannot be reconstructed in detail, evidently it praised Demosthenes' donation to the funds for the fortifications for which he was responsible as *teichopoios;* it is difficult to separate the donation from the office as neatly as Demosthenes does at 18.110–119.[4] However, if Ctesiphon's decree was flawed in this respect, the breach of the law was evidently a common one, since at 18.114 Demosthenes is able to provide precedents for awards to officials still in office for donations made in the course of their duties.

The real target, of course, is the broader issue: Ctesiphon's justification of the award on the ground that Demosthenes has shown consistent loyalty and concern for the Athenian people. It is illegal to make false statements in public documents. Here the issue turns on the evaluation of Demosthenes' career, and Aeschines seeks to persuade the jurors of his own damning view of Demosthenes' influence, while Demosthenes counters with a defense of his record.

In comparison with the earlier courtroom clashes, this one was

---

[2] Harris 1994: 140–148.

[3] If 3.31 ("Another law forbids the crowning of officials subject to audit") reflects the exact wording of the law, the crucial issue of the acts for which crowning was forbidden was left unexpressed.

[4] The connection of the decree to Demosthenes' term of office is closer still if the work on the ditches for which Demosthenes is praised in Aeschines' quotation from the decree at 3.236 took place in the context of the larger project of the work on the fortifications of 337 (Demosthenes appears to connect ditch and wall at 18.299) rather than as part of the emergency measures in the immediate aftermath of Chaeronea (3.236n). The clause in question may have been part of the praise of Demosthenes' voluntary financial contribution.

(at least in its effects) insignificant. Aeschines' prosecution of Timarchus was intended to block Demosthenes' attack on Aeschines, and through him his associates and their policies. Demosthenes' prosecution of Aeschines in the matter of the embassy was an important part of the bid to topple the supporters of peace, and for Aeschines personally a matter of life and death. But no great issues of policy were affected by this final encounter. It owes its interest to the individuals involved, as the culmination of a relationship based on a hostility so powerful that it may have been personal as well as political, to the broader policy issues raised as they plead their case before the bar of history as well as before the Athenian jurors, and to the fact that Aeschines' attack provoked in Demosthenes' defense speech, *On the Crown* (18), what for many is the finest example of classical Greek oratory. One interesting aspect of the duel is the complex dialogue between the speeches of 330 and those of 343.[5] Aeschines takes an obvious delight in turning against Demosthenes charges the latter had used against him in the earlier trial, while Demosthenes picks up some aspects of Aeschines' defense of 343 and develops them, almost as though he were showing Aeschines how it should be done.

In the event, the prosecution failed miserably. Aeschines failed to get one-fifth of the votes, was fined, and left Athens.[6]

The Speech

Once more Aeschines relies heavily on narrative. After an opening reference to the conniving tactics of the defense (1), he contrasts the orderly practice of the past in the Assembly with the undisciplined present, specifically the readiness of politicians to make illegal proposals (2–4), and concludes that the jurors have a duty to protect the constitution (5–8).

In 9–31 Aeschines presents the first technical objection, that Demosthenes could not be proposed for an award, since he had not submitted to audit. In 9–12 he explains that the bar on awards for men yet to submit to audit exists to prevent guilty men from influencing the outcome of political trials. He then counters the first anticipated

---

[5] The details of this dialogue are picked up in the individual notes.
[6] See Introduction to Aeschines.

defense argument, that Demosthenes' task was not technically an office (13–16). He next anticipates and refutes the claim that since Demosthenes contributed his own money, he could not be financially accountable to the state (17–23), by demonstrating that all officials are subject to final audit; and he argues further that Demosthenes was especially liable because he was simultaneously *teichopoios* and overseer of the Theoric Fund (24–27).[7] In 28–31 he refutes the claim that Demosthenes was exempt from audit because he was appointed by his tribe, not by the Assembly.

In 32–48 Aeschines presents the second technical objection, that the law does not allow crowning in the theatre, only in the Assembly. In anticipation of a defense plea that the law allows exceptions, Aeschines insists that the law code cannot contain such contradictions. The law cited by the defense deals with the announcement of honors from foreign states, not domestic awards.

After this preliminary skirmishing, Aeschines turns to the real business of the speech. The law does not allow false statements in public documents, and Ctesiphon's praise of Demosthenes is a false statement (49–50). The refutation of Ctesiphon's praise occupies the rest of the speech. First the private life of Demosthenes is subjected to criticism (51–53). Aeschines then turns to Demosthenes' political career (54–167). He divides Demosthenes' career into four periods (54–57) and then subjects each period to a narrative in chronological sequence. The first period (58–76) lasted from the beginning of hostilities over Amphipolis (357) to the Peace of Philocrates (346). Demosthenes supported Philocrates in pushing through a hasty peace on disadvantageous terms. Aeschines appends a brief attack on Demosthenes for hypocrisy (77–78). The second period (79–105) lasted from the peace of 346 to the outbreak of hostilities over Amphissa (339). During this period Demosthenes reversed his policies in order to protect himself from the hostility caused by the results of his peace. He tried to create suspicion of Macedonia and organized an alliance, on terms disadvantageous to Athens, with Euboean politicians who had shown themselves disloyal to Athens. The third period (106–158) was from the beginning of the Amphissaean War to the battle of Chaeronea in 338. After Aeschines had rescued the situation at Delphi, when

---

[7] For the Theoric Fund, see 3.24n.

Athens was falsely accused by a member of the Amphissaean delegation, Demosthenes contrived to lose the advantage Athens had gained,
setting Athens against the Amphictyons for the sake of the bribes he
received from Amphissa; he once more made a disadvantageous alliance, making unreasonable concessions to Thebes. The fourth period
(159–167) brings the narrative from the defeat at Chaeronea to the
present (330). After taking to his heels in battle, Demosthenes has
shown a consistent pattern of timidity, making empty gestures against
Macedonia but ignoring any opportunities for inflicting real damage.

Aeschines now turns from narrative to argument. In 168–170 he
describes the ideal statesman, with which he contrasts the background
and character of his opponent (171–176). He contrasts the ease with
which the city now gives crowns (177–188) with the more restrained
past, then disposes of the anticipated reply that his opponent must be
compared with contemporary, not past, figures by arguing that politicians who receive an award are measured against absolute, not relative, standards of merit (189). In 190–200 he contrasts the strictness
of earlier generations in dealing with illegal legislation with the laxity
of contemporary practice. The jurors should display comparable firm-
ness now, either refusing Ctesiphon permission to have Demosthenes
as supporting speaker or keeping Demosthenes to the point (201–
202), on the model of Aeschines' own honest presentation of the
prosecution (203–206); Aeschines also gives the jurors specific advice
on their response to Demosthenes (207–212). After a brief attack on
the character of Ctesiphon (213–214), Aeschines returns to anticipation of the defense case, warning the jurors of the attacks on himself
they may expect and replying to them (215–229), digressing to make
further allegations against Demosthenes (221–225).

In 230–235, Aeschines presents a number of arguments against
acquittal. He then returns to Demosthenes' career, rejecting the
depiction of him as public benefactor (236–240). In 241–242 he
seeks to place Ctesiphon's use of a supporting speaker in a bad light,
then returns to the offenses of Demosthenes and the iniquity of honoring him (243–245), which will set a bad example for the young and
undermine the moral authority of the jurors as individuals (246–247).

The next section urges the jurors to look carefully at the credentials
of men proposed for public honor in order to retain control of democratic power (248–251) and argues for severe punishment (252–253).

A brief reminder of how Greece will view the acquittal of Demosthenes (254) precedes the closing reflections. In 255–256 Aeschines reminds the jurors that they are deciding the fate of their own city, invites them to question the motives of any of their number seen voting for Demosthenes, and dismisses his boasts of his achievements with contempt. The tone becomes more elevated in 257–259, as Aeschines asks the jurors to imagine the great men of Athens' past supporting his case, culminating in an appeal to the heroic dead of the Persian Wars, before placing the duty to arrive at a fair judgment in the hands of his hearers (260).

Modern readers often find this speech disappointing. Certainly it is disorganized in places, particularly toward the close, and though intermittently powerful, it is uneven. One unifying feature is the presentation of Demosthenes. The decree under attack described him as a consistent public benefactor. Aeschines, in contrast, presents us with a figure whose policy is inconsistent but is ultimately governed by the single constant of venality. His actions throughout tend to be dictated by bribes already received or the hope of future bribes, from Philip, Amphissa, Euboea, Persia. Likewise, within Athens itself, lawsuits and legislation are exploited as a means of obtaining money. But the vehemence of the attack on Demosthenes underlines a notable silence in the speech. Although Philip's name occurs repeatedly, criticism of his actions is infrequent and muted. In 343 Demosthenes' hostility to the peace left him free to present Philip as a predator and Aeschines as his venal underling. Aeschines, doubly constrained by his commitment to the peace and his need to maximize Demosthenes' responsibility for Athens' troubles, is unwilling or unable to exploit audience hostility to Philip, and this inevitably deprives the speech of the vigor of Demosthenes' prosecution of 343, despite Aeschines' adoption of lines of attack derived from Demosthenes. The silence about Philip's activities in the late 340s produces a political analysis that will have had little appeal for his audience, many of whom may have participated in the Athenian decisions.[8]

But despite its weaknesses and its failure to achieve its goal, there

---

[8] This is particularly the case with Aeschines' silence about Philip's seizure of the grain ships and the Athenian declaration of war on Philip in 340; see 3.54n.

is evidence that the speech was admired by contemporary politicians. The later prosecution speeches against Demosthenes by Hyperides and Dinarchus (which were successful) utilize arguments derived from Aeschines and even reproduce individual turns of phrase.

As with the speech *On the Embassy,* there are signs that *Against Ctesiphon* was revised for publication. Given the spectacular failure of the prosecution, it may seem surprising that Aeschines chose to publish. However, quite apart from the evidence that the speech was admired by contemporaries, publication of the speeches of 343 and 330, for both Aeschines and Demosthenes, gave the forensic texts a second life as pamphlets in a battle for Athenian public opinion, and ultimately for the verdict of posterity.

AGAINST CTESIPHON

[1] You can see the extent of the intrigues and the forces ranged against me, men of Athens, and the pleas that certain people have been making in the Agora to prevent the normal course of justice in the city. I, however, have come here with my confidence first in the gods, and second in the laws and in you. I believe that no intrigue carries more weight in your courts than the laws and justice.

[2] I wish, men of Athens, that meetings of the Council of Five Hundred and the Assembly were properly controlled by the people who preside over them and that the laws passed by Solon for the good conduct of public speakers were enforced. Then it would be possible for the oldest citizen to come first to the platform in a dignified manner, just as the laws prescribe, and offer the city the best guidance on the basis of his experience without interruption or clamor, and only then in second place for any other citizens who wished to state their opinion on each issue one by one in turn according to age. In this way, in my opinion, the city would be administered most effectively and there would be fewest trials.

[3] But all the practices that in the past were agreed to be beneficial have nowadays been eliminated, and there are people who are all too ready to draft illegal proposals that are then put to the vote by others, who have not been selected Chairman[9] by lot in the fairest way but

---

[9] For the *proedros,* see 1.23n.

have maneuvered to secure their seat. And if any other member of the Council gains the position of Chairman properly by lot and announces your vote honestly, the group that views politics as no longer a public activity but their own private preserve threatens to impeach him in their attempt to enslave ordinary men and maintain their own despotic power.[10] [4] They've put an end to regular trials under the laws and prefer to bring cases under decrees[11] amid anger. As a result, the most respected and prudent announcement is no longer heard in the city: "Who wishes to speak of those who are above the age of fifty? And then the rest of the Athenians in turn." The disorderly conduct of public speakers is no longer subject to the control of the laws, the Presidents (*prytaneis*), the Chairmen (*proedroi*), or the presiding tribe,[12] which makes up a tenth of the city.

[5] In this situation and in the city's current circumstances, whose nature you appreciate, there is one part of the constitution left, if my understanding is correct; that is the indictments for illegality.[13] If you remove these or give way to those who are attempting to remove them, I warn you that without realizing it, you will have surrendered your political power to a few men.

[6] You are well aware, men of Athens, that there are three kinds of constitution in the whole world, dictatorship (*tyrannis*), oligarchy, and democracy, and dictatorships and oligarchies are governed by the temperament of those in power, whereas democratic cities are governed

---

[10] It is interesting to compare the rhetoric here and later in the speech (3.251) with Demosthenes 3.30–32. In both cases the speaker presents himself as an outsider and his opponents as having a stranglehold on politics. Though the similarity suggests the presence of a rhetorical commonplace (found as early as Aristophanes *Wasps* 697ff.), it also reveals the extent to which the positions of Aeschines and Demosthenes had been reversed between the two courtroom duels. The allegation derives its rhetorical force from the democratic ideology (even in the age of the expert politician) of equal access to political influence.

[11] That is, by the procedure of *eisangelia,* in which the prosecutor brought the charge before the Assembly or the Council instead of initiating a *graphē* (see 1.2n) before the relevant magistrate. Until about 330 the *eisangelia* was not subject to the penalties for frivolous prosecution that attached to the *graphē* (see 2.14n).

[12] For the *prytaneis,* see 2.53n; for the presiding tribe, see Aeschines' account at 1.33–34 with 1.33n, 1.34n.

[13] For the *graphē paranomōn,* see 1.34n.

by the established laws.[14] None of you should fail to note, in fact everyone should be clear in his mind, that when he enters the courtroom to judge an indictment for illegality, he is about to give a verdict that day on his own right to free speech. This is why the legislator made this the first clause in the jurors' oath: "I shall vote according to the laws."[15] He was well aware that when the laws are protected for the city, the democracy, too, is preserved. [7] With this firmly in mind, you should hate people who draft illegal decrees and regard no offense of this sort as insignificant but attach great importance to every one of them. And you should not allow any man to deprive you of this right, neither the supporting speeches from generals who have been colluding with certain public speakers to harm the constitution, nor the entreaties of foreigners, whom some people bring to the stand and so get off free from the courts, even though their political conduct contravenes the laws. No, just as each of you would be ashamed to desert the post assigned to him in war, so now you should feel ashamed to desert the post of guardians of the democracy that the laws have assigned to you today.

[8] Another thing you should bear in mind is that just now the whole citizen body has placed the city in your care and entrusted the constitution to you; and some of them are here listening to this trial, while others are off dealing with their personal concerns. Show your respect for them and remember the oaths you have sworn and the laws, and if I prove that Ctesiphon has drafted a measure that both contravenes the laws and is dishonest and against the city's interests, overturn the illegal proposals, men of Athens, confirm the democratic constitution for the city, and punish the men whose political activity is opposed to the laws and to your best interests. And if this is your frame of mind as you listen to the speeches about to be made, I am confident that your verdict will be just and true to your oath and beneficial to you yourselves and to the whole city.

[9] Now on the general issue of the prosecution, I believe what I have said is reasonable. But I want to speak briefly about the laws that

---

[14] Substantially repeated from Aeschines 1.4.

[15] For the jurors' oath, see 1.154n.

are in force to deal with individuals subject to audit,[16] which Ctesiphon has certainly breached with the decree he has drafted.

In earlier times there were certain individuals who held the most
important offices and managed the revenues and took bribes in every
area.[17] They won the support of public speakers on the Council and
in the Assembly and prejudiced the outcome of their audits far in
advance with votes of praise and crowns and public proclamations.
The result was that at the audits of officials, accusers found themselves
in great difficulty, and the jurors much more so. [10] For many of the
individuals subject to audit were escaping scot-free from the courts,
though it was made clear to all that they had stolen public money. Not
surprisingly. For the jurors, I think, were embarrassed by the thought
that the same man in the same city, who was one day proclaimed at
the public contests as the recipient of a golden crown from the people
for his virtue and his integrity, might be seen a short while later leaving
the court convicted of theft at his audit. So the jurors were forced to
cast their vote not on the offense facing them but to save the people
from disgrace.

[11] A legislator noticed this and passed a law, and a very good one,
explicitly forbidding the crowning of men who are subject to audit.
And though the legislator has taken this sensible precaution, arguments have been invented to subvert the law; and if you are not told
of them, you will not notice you have been tricked. Some of these
men who attempt illegally to crown men subject to audit are decent
men (if anyone who drafts illegal proposals can be described as decent); at any rate, they make some attempt to cover their shame. They
add a clause that the man subject to audit should be crowned "when
he has presented his account and submitted to audit for his office."
[12] The offense against the city is the same, since the audits are being
pre-empted by votes of praise and crowns, but the drafter of the decree
is demonstrating to his hearers that, though he has drafted an illegal
proposal, he is ashamed of his offense. But Ctesiphon, men of Athens,

---

[16] For the audit (*euthyna*), see 1.1n.

[17] The account that follows, though it probably reflects the recognized purpose
of the law in question, should not be taken as an authoritative account of its
origin; for the narrative structure, cf. 1.13; the structure recurs at 3.41.

has bypassed the law in force to deal with individuals subject to audit and rejected the pretext I mentioned to you just now; he has proposed that Demosthenes be crowned before he presents his account, before he submits to audit, while he's still in office.

[13] They will also advance another argument[18] opposite to the one just mentioned, men of Athens, to the effect that duties a man carries out when he has been elected on a decree are not an "office" (archē) but an "assignment" (epimeleia) and a "public service" (diakonia). They will maintain that offices are the posts that the Thesmothetae[19] assign by lot in the Theseum[20] and those the people fill by show of hands at the election meetings of the Assembly (the generals, the cavalry commanders, and other offices of this sort), while everything else consists of "duties assigned by decree."

[14] In reply to their claims, I shall provide your law, which you passed with the intention of ruling out such excuses. There it is stated explicitly, "The offices (archai) filled by election"—the legislator says, including them all in a single term and describing as "offices" all posts filled by the people by show of hands—"and (he adds) the overseers of public works"—and as Commissioner for Walls[21] Demosthenes is overseer of the most important of the works—"and all who manage an aspect of public administration for more than thirty days and those who assume the presidency of a lawcourt"—the overseers of public works all have the presidency of a court.[22] And what does he instruct them to do? [15] Not "serve" but "hold office after scrutiny in the lawcourt," since the offices filled by lot, too, are not free from this requirement but are filled only after scrutiny has been passed, and "submit a written account to the auditors," as with the other offices. To prove I am telling the truth, he will read out[23] the actual laws to you.

---

[18] The argument does not in fact appear in Demosthenes 18.

[19] The title (literally "legislator") given to six of the nine archons.

[20] Probably to the east of the Agora; in modern times traditionally confused with the temple to Hephaestus on the high ground to the west of the Agora.

[21] Greek teichopoios, literally "wall-maker." See Introduction to Aeschines 3.

[22] To deal with individual dereliction of duty and to provide a tribunal for settling disputes arising out of individual responsibilities in the relevant area.

[23] Referring to the clerk of the court; cf. 1.2, 1.11, 1.147.

[LAWS]

[16] So when these people use the terms "duties" and "assignments" for what the legislator calls "offices," it is your job to remember the law and confront their insolent claims with it; and you must reply to them that you refuse to tolerate an unprincipled sophist who thinks he can nullify the laws with his words; indeed, the better the speech of a man who drafts illegal measures, the greater the anger he will encounter. Men of Athens, the public speaker and the law must say the same thing. When the law says one thing and the public speaker another, your verdict should go to the just claim of the law, not the insolence of the speaker.

[17] Now as to what Demosthenes calls his irrefutable argument, I want to give you a brief warning in advance.[24] He will say: "I am a Commissioner for Walls—I admit it. But I donated 100 minas to the city and the task has been carried out on a larger scale than required. So what am I to be audited for? Unless there's such a thing as an audit for patriotism." Now hear my response to this excuse; it is both fair and in your best interests.

In this city, ancient and great as it is, of all who come into public life in any way at all, there is no one who is not subject to audit. [18] I shall demonstrate this to you first of all with the cases where one would not expect it. For instance, the law requires that priests and priestesses be subjected to audit, both all collectively and each one of them individually, people who merely receive the relevant privileges and offer prayers to the gods on your behalf; and they are not just audited individually but also by whole clans, the Eumolpidae, the Ceryces,[25] and all the rest. [19] Then again the law requires that trierarchs[26] be subject to audit. These are not people who've handled

---

[24] Cf. Demosthenes 18.111–118.

[25] A clan, *genos,* was a group believed to be based on kinship. The units were very old, and it was common for a *genos* to form the inner core of a phratry or "brotherhood" (*phratria*), a larger kinship group. Although most Athenians belonged to a phratry, the *genos* was considerably more exclusive (cf. 2.147n). The Eumolpidae *genos* supplied one of the two major priests of the Eleusinian Mysteries; the Ceryces (literally "heralds") supplied the other.

[26] The trierarch, "trireme commander," was originally a rich citizen charged (under the *leitourgia,* "liturgy," system of capital taxation) with the maintenance

public funds, or filched a lot of your money while spending a little of their own and claim they are making a voluntary donation when they are only giving you back what is yours, but people who have indisputably spent their inherited property on their ambition for public service.

Now not only the trierarchs but also the most important tribunals in the city must face the jurors' vote. [20] First of all the law requires that the Council of the Areopagus[27] should present their accounts to the auditors (*logistai*) and submit to audit and makes even its stern members, who have the most solemn responsibilities, face your vote. Won't they then receive a crown? No, it is not their tradition. Have they no ambition for honor? They certainly do. They are not satisfied if their members simply avoid wrongdoing but punish them for any mistakes; in contrast, your public speakers have an easy time. Second, the legislator has made the Council of Five Hundred subject to audit, [21] and so strong is his distrust of men facing audit that right at the beginning of the laws he says: "An official subject to audit is not to leave the city." "Hercules!" a man might reply. "Just because I have held office am I not to leave the city?" Yes, to prevent you from exploiting public money and policy for your own advantage and then running away. Then again, he does not permit a man subject to audit to consecrate his property or to make a dedication or to be adopted[28]

---

and captaincy of a warship for a year. By the end of the fifth century, joint trierarchies, when two men shared the cost, had come into being; from 357 there were further changes that spread the financial burden over boards of wealthier citizens. See further 3.222. Here the reference is to individuals actually charged with the captaincy as well as part of the financial burden, or to hired captains, for which we have evidence before and after 357.

[27] For the Areopagus, see 1.81n.

[28] Adoption in Athens was very different from adoption in most modern societies. The adoptee was almost always an adult, and the purpose was to provide an heir to an adopter who had no male issue in order to prevent the family from dying out and its property and cults from passing outside the bloodline. A man who was adopted terminated his formal membership in his natural family. Theoretically an official facing a fine could use adoption to remove himself from the succession within his natal family, allowing his father's estate to pass in due course directly to his sons. This would prevent the state from recovering the fines from

or to dispose of his property by will or to do a range of other things. In sum, the legislator holds the properties of men facing audit as security, until they account for themselves to the city. [22] Yes, but there are people who have neither received nor spent any public money but have been involved in some area of public activity. Even a man such as this is ordered to present his account to the auditors. And how is a man who has neither received nor spent money to present an account to the city? The law itself gives the answer and provides instruction on what should be written. It tells him to enter precisely this: "I have neither received nor spent any of the city's money." There is not a position in the city that is not subject to audit, investigation, and examination. To prove I am telling the truth, listen to the laws themselves.

[LAWS]

[23] So when Demosthenes at his most brazen asserts that because of his voluntary donation he is not subject to audit, give him this answer: "Was it not your duty, Demosthenes, to let the auditors' herald make this, the announcement sanctioned by ancestral custom and law: 'Who wishes to bring an accusation?' [29] You must allow any citizen who wants to maintain that you made no donation but spent only a small portion of the large sums at your disposal on the building of the walls, when you had received ten talents from the city for this purpose. Don't take honor by force, and don't snatch the votes from the jurors' hands; don't put yourself above the laws in your political career but under them. For this is what keeps the democracy safe."

[24] So much for my response to the empty excuses these people will offer. Now what I shall try to show you from the public records is that Demosthenes was truly subject to audit when the defendant proposed his decree, since he was holding both the office of Controller of

---

what would have been his inheritance, and if the debt exceeded his assets, it would protect his sons from losing their citizen rights (a debtor to the state was automatically disfranchised until the debt was discharged, and his loss of rights was inherited by his sons). Hence presumably the inclusion of this with other restrictions whose effect is to create a limited freeze on assets.

[29] See 1.1n.

the Theoric Fund[30] and the office of Commissioner for Walls and has not yet presented his account or submitted to final audit for either of these posts. Read out the archon year, the month, the day, and the Assembly meeting when Demosthenes was elected to the post of Controller of the Theoric Fund.

[ENUMERATION OF THE DAYS]

Well then, if I were to prove nothing beyond this, it would be right to convict Ctesiphon. His guilt is proved not by my speech for the prosecution but by the public records.

[25] In the past, men of Athens, there was an accountant (*antigrapheus*) elected by the city who reported to the Assembly on the revenue every month. But because of your confidence in Eubulus,[31] those elected Controllers of the Theoric Fund performed the accountant's duties (before Hegemon's law[32] was passed) and the duties of the Receivers (*apodektai*),[33] and controlled the dockyards and were constructing an equipment store; they were also Commissioners for Roads and had charge of virtually the whole of the city's government. [26] My aim in saying this is not to accuse or criticize them but to prove to you that, though the legislator does not permit a man who is subject to audit for a single office, however insignificant, to be

---

[30] The Theoric Fund was set up to enable the poor to attend theatrical performances (though it was not means-tested). It may have been created at the beginning of the fourth century, but if so, it was reorganized in the middle of the century. The scope of the activities covered by the fund was widened after its creation to cover attendance at other festivals and also public works (cf. 3.25–26, though Aeschines exaggerates there to suit his immediate rhetorical purpose).

[31] For Eubulus, see 2.8n.

[32] We are badly informed on Hegemon's law, which evidently limited the power of the Theoric treasurers. The context (esp. 3.26) dates it after Demosthenes' tenure. Little is known about Hegemon; if the later lexicographer Harpocration is right to present him as favoring friendship with Macedonia (which agrees with Demosthenes' inclusion of him with Aeschines and Demades at 18.285), the law may have been intended to blunt the influence of Demosthenes and his associates.

[33] A board of ten officials (one from each tribe) that took receipt of money due to the state and was responsible for the relevant records.

crowned until he presents his account and submits to audit, Ctesiphon had no hesitation in proposing to crown Demosthenes when he was holding every office in Athens rolled into one.

[27] To show that he was also holding the office of Commissioner for Walls when the defendant drafted his decree and was handling public money and imposing fines [34] like every other official, and was presiding over court hearings, I shall provide Demosthenes himself as my witness. In the archonship of Chaerondas, [35] on the twenty-ninth of Thargelion, at a meeting of the Assembly, Demosthenes proposed to hold tribal assemblies [36] on the second and third of Scirophorion, [37] and he gave orders in that decree for the election of representatives for each tribe who would be responsible for the work on the walls and treasurers (quite rightly), so that the city would have people with personal responsibility from whom it could receive an account of the sums expended. Please read out the decree.

[DECREE]

[28] Yes, but straight away he tries to wriggle out of this by saying that he was not made Commissioner for Walls by lot or elected by the people. And Demosthenes and Ctesiphon will have much to say on this. However, the law is succinct and lucid and briskly disposes of their tricks. But I want to give you a little advance information about them. [29] There are, men of Athens, three kinds of public office. One of these, and the most obvious to everyone, is the officials elected by lot or show of hands; the second kind consists of all the people who handle public business for more than thirty days and the Overseers of Public Works; thirdly, it is written in the law that if any people on their appointment hold the presidency of a court, "these, too, are

---

[34] Greek *epibolai;* the term refers to the summary fines on a small scale that magistrates could impose on their own authority in their areas of responsibility. Both the fines and the court hearings mentioned here relate to the complex and expensive activity of upgrading the fortifications (cf. 3.27).

[35] 338/7.

[36] Greek *agora,* the regular word for meetings of public bodies other than the popular Assembly (*ekklēsia*).

[37] Thargelion and Scirophorion (the last two months of the year) correspond roughly to May and June in our calendar.

to hold office after scrutiny." [38] [30] When one excludes the officials elected by the people and the ones selected by lot, we are left with the individuals chosen by the tribes, districts,[39] and demes to handle public money. This happens when (as now) some task is imposed on the tribes, such as digging trenches or building triremes. You will see from the actual laws that I am speaking the truth.

[LAWS]

[31] Now remember what has been said: the legislator instructs that the tribe representatives should hold office after scrutiny in court, and the Pandionis tribe chose Demosthenes as holder of the office of Commissioner for Walls, a task for which he holds almost ten talents from the public funds; another law forbids the crowning of officials [40] subject to audit; you have sworn to vote according to the laws; the public speaker has proposed to crown a man subject to audit without adding "when he presents his account and submits to audit"; and I am going to prove the breach of law with the testimony of the laws, the decrees, and my opponents. How could anyone prove more clearly that a man has drafted an illegal proposal?

[32] I also want to prove to you that the way he orders the announcement to take place in his decree is illegal. For the law gives explicit instructions that if the Council crowns someone, the award is to be announced in the Council chamber, and if the people crown someone, in the Assembly, "and nowhere else." Please read out the law.

[LAW]

[33] This is a very good law, men of Athens. For in my view the legislator did not think a public speaker should parade in front of outsiders but should rest content with being honored within the city itself by the people and not use proclamations for profit. So that's

---

[38] The reference is to the *dokimasia,* the preliminary examination imposed on magistrates before commencement of office to determine eligibility.

[39] The demes of Attica (for which see 1.18n) were gathered into thirty districts (*trittyes,* literally one-third of a tribe).

[40] The Greek says *archē,* "an office," which would cover both individual and collective magistracies.

the view of the legislator. And what about Ctesiphon? Read out the decree.

[DECREE]

[34] You hear, men of Athens, that the legislator instructs that the proclamation of the receipt of a crown from the people is to take place among the people at the Assembly on the Pnyx, "and nowhere else." But Ctesiphon proposed proclamation in the theatre, not only breaching the laws but actually changing the location; and not when the Athenians are in session in the Assembly, but when fresh tragedies are being performed; and not in front of the people but in front of all Greeks,[41] to let them know the kind of man we honor.

[35] Though he has so blatantly drafted an illegal measure, with his ally Demosthenes he will bring his rhetorical tricks to bear on the laws. I shall explain these and tell you about them in advance, so that you won't find you have been deceived.

My opponents will not be able to argue that the laws do not forbid the announcement outside the Assembly of the receipt of a crown from the people. But they will include in their defense case the law dealing with the Dionysia[42] and will use part of it to deceive your ears. [36] They will provide a law that has no bearing on this indictment and argue that the city has two laws in existence to deal with proclamations: the one I am adducing today, which explicitly forbids the proclamation of the receipt of a crown outside the Assembly, and they will say there is another law that opposes this one that has given permission for the proclamation of the crown at the tragic performances in the theatre, "if the people so vote." This is the law under which they will say Ctesiphon drafted his measure.

[37] In response to their tricks, I shall provide your laws to speak in my support, and this I shall do throughout the whole of my speech for the prosecution. If this is the truth and this kind of habit has

---

[41] Unlike the other dramatic festival, the Lenaea, which was held in winter, the Dionysia took place in the spring, when the seas were open. Accordingly it attracted a panhellenic audience. The Athenians exploited this presence to make the festival an exercise in propaganda, both artistic and civic (for instance, with the public parade of the orphans, 3.154).

[42] The point is made briefly by Demosthenes at 18.120–121.

insinuated itself into your political practice, so that there are invalid laws publicly inscribed among the valid laws and there are two laws opposed to one another dealing with a single issue, what term could one use for a constitution[43] in which the laws order one both to do and not to do the same things? [38] But this is not so, and I hope you never reach such a state of confusion in the laws. This issue has not been ignored by the legislator who set up the democracy;[44] no, an explicit duty has been imposed on the Thesmothetae[45] to amend the laws in the Assembly each year after a careful investigation and examination to determine whether there is any inscribed law that contradicts another law or an invalid law among the valid ones or more than one law inscribed to deal with each issue.[46] [39] And if they find anything of the sort, he orders them to inscribe them on boards and display them in front of the eponymous heroes;[47] the Presidents (*pryta-*

---

[43] The text is problematic. The manuscript text literally translated would be: "What should one still call this constitution (*tautēn tēn politeian*) in which," where "still" (*eti*) makes no sense; I have deleted *eti* as a scribal error. The alternative is deletion of *tēn* (literally "why should one still call this a constitution, in which, etc.").

[44] The Athenian democracy, here treated as the product of a single organizing mind, was in fact the result of an evolutionary process that involved an extended series of intermittent constitutional changes. It is typically Greek to think in terms of a single "inventor." The enactment in question does not predate the restoration of the democracy in 403.

[45] See 3.13n.

[46] Despite Aeschines' bluster in 3.40, the existence of this recurring duty for the Thesmothetae suggests that the Athenians were aware of the continuing possibility of internal contradiction in the law code; the attempt to remove or avert contradiction is a recurrent feature in Athenian statutes concerning legislation in the fourth century (Dem. 20.89, 93; 24.18, 33). In fact, Aeschines virtually admits that the laws on the award of crowns were more complicated than his simple account would suggest. He indicates in 3.47 that the Assembly could decree the proclamation of a crown in the theatre; his restriction of the possibility to crowns given by foreign states is based on his own tendentious presentation in 3.45.

[47] The statues (situated toward the southwest corner of the Agora) of the ten heroes after whom the ten Athenian tribes (1.33n) were named were regularly used as a place for posting public notices.

neis) are to hold an Assembly meeting and register its purpose as "for legislators,"[48] and the president of the Chairmen (*proedroi*) is to allow the people to vote by show of hands on the removal or retention of specific laws, in order to have one law on each issue and not more. Please read out the laws.

[LAWS]

[40] Now if, men of Athens, their argument were true and there were two laws on proclamations in existence, it is inevitable, I think, that once the Thesmothetae had discovered them and the Presidents had handed them over to the legislators, one of the laws would have been annulled, either the one giving permission to make the proclamation or the one forbidding it. The fact that neither of these things has happened is clear proof that they are not only telling lies but making claims that are completely impossible.

[41] Just why they are advancing this false claim I shall tell you, after I have explained why the laws concerning announcements in the theatre were passed. At the performance of the tragedies in the city, people were making announcements without the permission of the people, in some cases that individuals were being crowned by their tribe, in others by their demes, and others again would set free their slaves by proclamation, with all Greece as their witness. [42] And the most offensive thing was that people who had been given the position of foreign representative (*proxenia*)[49] in other cities would contrive to have an announcement made that they were being crowned by the people of Rhodes, it might be, or Chios, or some other city, for their virtue and merit. And unlike the individuals crowned by your Coun-

---

[48] Legislation in the democracy of the fourth century was designed to be a more ponderous process than in the fifth. In the fifth century, any collective decision of the Assembly had the force of law. In the fourth century, a distinction was drawn between laws (*nomoi*) and decrees (*psephismata*), roughly between general and abiding enactments and immediate or specific enactments. Although there is some uncertainty about the number of (and relationship between) laws dealing with legislation in the fourth century, what is clear is that legislation consistently required the empaneling of "legislators" (*nomothetai*) made up of individuals who had sworn the judicial oath.

[49] For *proxenia*, see 2.89n.

cil or the Assembly, who win your agreement and have a decree passed out of the gratitude they have earned from you, they did this on their own initiative without any decision from you. [43] The result of this practice was that the audience and producers (*chorēgoi*) and performers were inconvenienced, while the individuals who had their names announced in the theatre obtained more prestige than the ones crowned by the people. For one group the Assembly was specified as the location for the crowning, and it was stated that they should be announced "nowhere else," while the other group had their names proclaimed in front of the whole of Greece; and yet the former were crowned on the strength of a decree, with your agreement, the latter without any decree.

[44] Observing this situation, a legislator drafted a law entirely unconnected with the one dealing with individuals crowned by the people. He neither annulled the latter (for it was not the Assembly that was being inconvenienced but the theatre), nor did he enact a law opposed to the pre-existing ones (which is not allowed).[50] It was a law concerning those individuals who received crowns from their tribe and their deme, without a decree from you, and people who were setting free their slaves and crowns by foreign states. And it explicitly forbids either the freeing of a slave in the theatre or the proclamation of the receipt of a crown from tribe or deme, "nor from any other source," it says, "or the herald is to be disfranchised."

[45] So when the legislator specifies the Council chamber as the place for the proclamation of the receipt of crowns from the Council, the Assembly for crowns from the people, when he forbids the announcement at the tragedies of the receipt of crowns from deme and tribe (to prevent anyone from acquiring spurious prestige by collecting crowns and proclamations) and further forbids in his law the proclamation of an award from any other source, if we take away the Council and the people and the tribes and demes—when one removes these, what is left but the foreign crowns?

[46] To prove the truth of what I am saying, I shall give you convincing evidence from the laws themselves. The law deprives the recipient of the actual golden crown that is announced in the city the-

---

[50] See Demosthenes 18.33, and cf. above, 3.38n.

atre and orders it to be consecrated to Athena. Yet who among you would convict the Athenian people of such mean-spiritedness?[51] To say nothing of cities, there's not a single individual who would be so ungenerous as to announce and at the same moment take away and consecrate a crown that he had personally given. But I think it is because the crown is from abroad that the consecration takes place, to ensure that nobody will take the goodwill of outsiders more seriously than his country and have his mind corrupted. [47] But nobody consecrates the other crown, the one proclaimed in the Assembly. It can be kept, so that not only the individual himself but also his descendants may have the memorial in their home and never be disloyal to the people. And the reason why the legislator added the clause that no crown from outside could be proclaimed in the theatre "unless the people so vote" was to ensure that any city that desired to crown any of our citizens would send envoys and put a request to the people, so that the individual proclaimed would be more grateful to you for allowing his name to be proclaimed than to those who awarded the crown. To prove the truth of what I say, hear the laws.

[LAWS]

[48] So when they try to deceive you by claiming that the law contains the additional clause "if the people so vote," remember to give them the answer: "Yes, if some other city crowns you. But if it is the Athenian people, you have been shown the place where this is to take place, and you have been forbidden to have yourself proclaimed outside the Assembly. You can spend the whole day explaining "and nowhere else"; you won't prove that his proposal is legal."

[49] The remaining part of my prosecution is the one I am particularly concerned about.[52] This is the pretext on which Ctesiphon sees fit to have him crowned. This is what he says in his decree: "And the herald is to announce to Greece in the theatre that the Athenian people are crowning him for his virtue and integrity." And most im-

---

[51] Aeschines presumably hopes that the brevity of the argument will conceal its weakness. In fact, the public consecration of the crown enhances rather than reduces the honor.

[52] This, of course, is the essence of Aeschines' speech, whose purpose is to attack Demosthenes' political record.

portant of all: "Because he consistently speaks and acts in the best interests of the people." [50] The rest of my case is absolutely straightforward and easy for you to evaluate when you hear it. As prosecutor I think what I must prove to you is that the praise devoted to Demosthenes is false, that he neither began his career by "speaking for the best" nor "consistently acts in the best interests of the people." And if I prove this, Ctesiphon will rightly be convicted on this indictment; for all the laws forbid anyone to introduce false proposals among the public decrees. And the speaker for the defense must prove the opposite. It will be for you to act as judges of our arguments.

[51] This is the way it is. In my opinion, an examination of Demosthenes' life would need too long a speech. Why should I tell it all now, either what happened to him over the indictment for wounding,[53] when he indicted Demomeles of Paeania, his own cousin, before the Areopagus, and the way he cut his head; or the business of Cephisodotus' service as general and the naval expedition to the Hellespont,[54] when Demosthenes was one of the trierarchs [52] and carried the general on his ship and shared his table, his sacrifices, and his libations, privileges granted to him because of their fathers' friendship, yet did not hesitate, when Cephisodotus was impeached and on trial for his life, to act as prosecutor; and again that business with Midias and the punches he received in the orchestra when he was chorusproducer, the way he sold for thirty minas the outrage committed against him and the vote the Assembly passed against Midias in the theatre of Dionysus.[55] [53] This and all other matters of the sort I

---

[53] For the allegation, cf. 2.93.

[54] Cephisodotus' command dates to 360/59; he was one of a number of Athenian generals who failed in the 360s and 350s to re-establish Athenian influence in Thrace. He was forced to reach a humiliating accord with the mercenary general Charidemus, at that time in the service of the Thracian king; for his failure he was fined five talents.

[55] Midias had a prolonged quarrel with Demosthenes that culminated in a public assault on Demosthenes when they were competing producers in the choral competition at the Dionysia in 348. Demosthenes used the procedure of *probole*, which involved a hearing before the Assembly, to secure a guilty verdict against Midias. Demosthenes 21, *Against Midias,* was written for the courtroom trial that would normally follow the Assembly verdict. The present passage sug-

intend to pass over. My intention in this is not to betray you or to make a present of the trial to him, but my fear is that your response may be to feel that what I say is true but ancient and all too generally acknowledged. And yet, Ctesiphon, when the worst of a man's disgraceful acts are so certain and familiar to the hearers as to give the impression that the accuser is not telling lies but talking of matters that are ancient and all too readily acknowledged from the start, does he deserve a golden crown or reproach? And should you, the man who has the nerve to draft lying and illegal proposals, be allowed to treat the courts with contempt or be punished by the city?

[54] But on the political crimes of Demosthenes I shall try to give a more detailed account. For I am told that Demosthenes' plan, when he is given his turn to speak, is to reckon up for you that there have been four periods before now in which he has intervened in politics.[56] As one of these, and the first, I hear, he counts the time when we were at war with Philip over Amphipolis, which he defines as ending with the peace and alliance proposed by Philocrates of Hagnus, with Demosthenes' support, as I shall demonstrate. [55] The second he claims is the period when we were at peace, evidently up till the day when

---

gests that Demosthenes reached a compromise; this may have been an out-of-court settlement or (as suggested by Lene Rubinstein) a prior agreement on the penalty assessment (1.15n). Since Midias appears to have been politically associated with Eubulus, it is likely that Demosthenes' decision was part of a temporary informal truce between rival factions in the period leading up to the Peace of Philocrates.

[56] The periods are 357–346, 346–339, 339–338, and 338–330. Demosthenes does in fact make this broad division, but without either the crisp clarity of Aeschines' demarcation or his adherence to continuous chronological presentation. The two writers also differ on the precise boundary between the second and third phases. For Aeschines (see 3.106–158, esp. 106) the boundary is the Amphissa affair of 339, which allows him to blame Demosthenes for the resumption of hostilities with Philip; he suppresses the fact that Athens had declared war on Philip in 340 after he seized the Athenian grain ships (see Introduction to Aeschines, p. 7. Demosthenes (18.53–109, esp. 76) sets the watershed in 340 with the seizure of the ships, which casts the blame on Philip. The emphasis given to the division by Aeschines probably reflects both his habitual desire to present the impression of crisp lucidity and the advantage to be gained from seeming to engage the opponent successfully on his own terms.

this same politician put an end to the peace the city was enjoying and proposed the war. The third is the period when we were at war, up to the events at Chaeronea. And the fourth is the present. On the basis of this arithmetic, I am told, he intends to call on me and ask me which of the four periods forms the basis of my accusation and when it is that I claim he has not pursued a policy in the best interests of the people. And if I refuse to answer and cover my face and run, he says he will come and expose my face, drag me to the platform, and force me to answer.

[56] So to forestall his bravado and enable you to know the facts in advance and for me to give you an answer in front of the jurors, Demosthenes, and in front of all the other citizens who are standing beyond the fence⁵⁷ and all the Greeks who are anxious to hear this trial (for I can see no small number present, indeed, more than anyone can remember attending a public case), my answer is that my accusation concerns all four periods you distinguish. [57] And if the gods so wish and the jurors give us an equal hearing and I am able to recall everything I know against you, I fully expect to demonstrate to the jurors that the responsibility for the city's survival lies with the gods and the individuals who have treated the city's situation with humanity and moderation,⁵⁸ while the responsibility for all our misfortunes lies with Demosthenes. And I shall use in my speech the order that I am told he intends to use and speak firstly about the first period, secondly about the second, thirdly about the next one, and fourthly about the current situation. So then I am going back now to the peace that you and Philocrates proposed.

[58] Now you would have been able, men of Athens, to conclude the earlier peace⁵⁹ together with the general congress of the Greeks, if certain people had allowed you to wait for the embassies that you had sent out to the rest of Greece at that time, calling them to unite against

⁵⁷ I.e., in the public viewing area, separated by a barrier from the jurors' seats.

⁵⁸ That is, Philip and Alexander; Athens had been treated far better than expected (and far better than Thebes was) in the aftermath of the defeat at Chaeronea.

⁵⁹ The Peace of Philocrates of 346 is called "the earlier peace" to distinguish it from the peace following Chaeronea.

Philip,[60] and in the course of time to recover your position of leadership with the agreement of the Greek states. You were robbed of this opportunity by Demosthenes and Philocrates and the bribes they took for plotting against your collective interests. [59] And if such a statement strikes some of you as rather suspect on suddenly hearing it,[61] listen to the rest as follows. When we take our seats at an audit session for expenditure over a long time, we may sometimes come from home with false impressions, but still when the account is reckoned up there is none of you of so grudging a disposition that he leaves without admitting and agreeing that the figure proved by the reckoning is true. [60] This is the way you should listen now. If some of you have left home with the impression that Demosthenes has never yet spoken in support of Philip in collaboration with Philocrates, I ask anyone with this opinion not to decide for or against anything until he hears the facts. That would not be fair. But if you listen to my brief account of the occasions and the texts of the decrees that Demosthenes proposed with Philocrates, and the unadorned reckoning of the facts contains proof that Demosthenes is the author of more proposals for the original peace and alliance than Philocrates, [61] that he has fawned on Philip and his envoys with unparalleled shamelessness, that he is to blame for the fact that peace was concluded without the support of the general congress of the Greeks to the detriment of the people, that he has handed over Cersobleptes, the king of Thrace, a friend and ally of the city, to Philip—if I prove this conclusively to you, I shall make a modest request of you: please concede in heaven's name that his policy for the first of the periods has not been sound. I shall begin at the point that will make it easiest for you to follow.

[62] Philocrates proposed[62] that Philip be allowed to send a herald and envoys here to discuss peace. This proposal was indicted as illegal.[63] The time for the hearing came. Lycinus, the man who had

---

[60] See 2.57n.

[61] Aeschines is aware that he has an uphill task to present Demosthenes as a Macedonian stooge (though Demosthenes' accusers after the Harpalus affair of 324 were happy to reproduce the allegation).

[62] In 348; cf. 2.13.

[63] Cf. 2.14.

brought the indictment, presented the prosecution case; Philocrates
presented the defense, and he was supported in his defense by Demosthenes; Philocrates was acquitted. After this came the archonship
of Themistocles.[64] At that point, Demosthenes became a member of
the Council, not by winning the ballot or as a substitute,[65] but by
buying the office dishonestly, with the aim of supporting Philocrates
on every issue by word and act, as the result showed. [63] For Philocrates was successful with a second proposal[66] in which he directed
that ten envoys be selected to go to Philip and urge him to send ambassadors here with full powers to discuss peace. One of the envoys
was Demosthenes;[67] and on his return from Macedonia he was full of
praise for the peace and gave the same report as the rest of the envoys.
And alone of the Councillors he proposed a truce for Philip's herald
and envoys, a proposal that supported that of Philocrates; for the one
made it possible for the herald and ambassadors to be sent here, while
the other created the truce for the embassy.

[64] Now for what followed please pay very careful attention. Negotiations did not involve the other envoys, the people who have been
the object of a lot of subsequent persecution from Demosthenes since
he changed face,[68] but Philocrates and Demosthenes. Not surprisingly. These were the ones who both served as envoys and proposed
the decrees. The first aim of the negotiations was to prevent you from
awaiting the return of the envoys you had sent out calling for a united
front against Philip so that you would conclude the peace alone and
not in collaboration with the rest of Greece. [65] The second aim was
to ensure that you would vote not just for peace but also for an alliance
with Philip, so that any Greeks who were closely observing your democracy would be reduced to a state of utter despondency as they saw
that you yourselves, while issuing a summons to join the war, had

---

[64] 347/6.

[65] That is, as a replacement for an elected member rejected at his *dokimasia*
(for which see 3.29n). The allegation is absent from Aeschines 2.

[66] In 346.

[67] Aeschines here passes over in silence his own role in the embassy, which is
the subject of Aeschines 2 and Demosthenes 19.

[68] An implicit but unmistakable reference to Aeschines himself, the only participant in the embassies to Philip to be prosecuted by Demosthenes (2.178).

voted in Athens to conclude not just a peace but also an alliance. The third aim was that Cersobleptes the king of Thrace would not be included in the oaths and would be excluded from the alliance and the peace. An expedition against him was already being announced. [66] In all this there was no wrong on the part of the purchaser⁶⁹ (for before the oaths and the compact no one could resent his serving his own interests), but the people who sold off and conspired against the city's power deserved bitter resentment. For the man who now claims to be anti-Alexander and claimed then to be anti-Philip, Demosthenes, the one who reproaches me for my friendship⁷⁰ with Alexander, proposed a decree whose aim was to rob the city of its chances. [67] He proposed that the Presidents (*prytaneis*)⁷¹ convene an Assembly on the eighth of Elaphebolion,⁷² the day of the sacrifice to Asclepius and the opening ceremony (*proagōn*) of the festival,⁷³ on the sacred day, an occurrence without precedent in anyone's memory. And what was his pretext? "So that," he says, "if Philip's envoys are already here, the people may reach a decision as quickly as possible on relations with Philip." He was appropriating the Assembly for the envoys who had not yet arrived,⁷⁴ surreptitiously cutting short the time available and forcing the matter to a hasty conclusion, so that you

⁶⁹ I.e., Philip.

⁷⁰ Greek *xenia,* the relationship that bound host and guest.

⁷¹ For the *prytaneis,* see 2.53n.

⁷² Roughly March in our calendar. The decree in question does not figure in Aeschines' account in speech 2.

⁷³ The Dionysia. Neither the Assembly nor the Council met on festival days. If, as is likely, the festival proper began on the tenth day of the month, Demosthenes' action was not improper, though evidently unusual. At the *proagōn* (literally "preliminary contest/prelude to the contest"), playwrights who had been permitted to compete at the festival appeared with their choruses in the theatre and gave the themes of their plays.

⁷⁴ That is, Demosthenes arranged an Assembly meeting to deal with Macedonian envoys before they arrived, thus eliminating the delay that would result from fixing a date after their arrival. A possible, but less likely, interpretation of the Greek is "pre-empting the [business of] the Assembly against the envoys who had not yet arrived," a reference to the timing of an Assembly meeting to preclude the presence of Athenian envoys returning from the Greek cities (or envoys from the cities in response to Athenian overtures), for which see 2.57n.

would conclude the peace alone and not in collaboration with the rest of Greece on the return of your envoys.

[68] Subsequently, men of Athens, Philip's ambassadors came. Yours were away calling on the Greeks to unite against Philip. At this point, Demosthenes carried another decree in which he proposed that the Assembly should reach a decision not only about peace but about an alliance as well, without waiting for your envoys but immediately after the City Dionysia, on the eighteenth and nineteenth.[75] To prove that I am telling the truth, listen to the decrees.

[DECREES]

[69] So when the Dionysia had passed, men of Athens, and the Assemblies were held, in the first Assembly a joint resolution of the allies was read out, which I shall first summarize for you briefly. First they proposed that you should reach a decision on peace alone; and they omitted the term "alliance," not by oversight,[76] but because they took the view that the peace was more a matter of necessity than something honorable. And then they wisely opposed Demosthenes' venality with a proposed antidote, [70] adding in their resolution that any Greeks should have the right within three months to have their names registered on the same column with the Athenians and be party to the oaths and the treaty. They were taking two precautions of the utmost importance; firstly, they were trying to provide with the three-month period sufficient time for the Greek embassies to arrive, and secondly they were seeking to obtain the goodwill of Greece for our city and the joint congress of the allies, so that if the treaty were breached we would not go to war alone or without resources, which has in fact happened, thanks to Demosthenes. You will discover that I am telling the truth, from hearing the allied resolution itself.

[ALLIED RESOLUTION]

[71] I admit that I spoke in support of this resolution, as did all those who addressed the people in the first of the Assemblies. And the

---

[75] Of Elaphebolion.

[76] The allied resolution cited at 2.60 speaks only of peace, but since it explicitly leaves the final decision to Athens, it leaves Athens free to negotiate an alliance.

people went home essentially in the belief that the peace would be made (the alliance was not an appropriate issue to settle in view of our appeal to the Greeks) and that it would be made in collaboration with the whole of Greece. A night intervened, and the next day we were at the Assembly. Now Demosthenes took control of the platform, leaving no opportunity for anyone else to speak.[77] He said there was no use in what had been said the day before, if Philip's envoys were not persuaded to agree; and he said he could not understand peace without an alliance. [72] He said that we must not—for I remember the term he used, because of the unpleasantness of the speaker as well as the word[78]—"rip" the alliance from the peace nor wait on the indecision of the Greeks but must either fight ourselves or make a separate peace. And finally he called Antipater[79] to the platform and put a question to him (having told him in advance what he would say and coached him in the reply he must give against the interests of the city[80]). And in the end, the proposal was successful; Demosthenes had coerced you with his speech, and Philocrates had drafted the decree. [73] One task remained; they had to hand over Cersobleptes and the area in Thrace.[81] This they accomplished on the twenty-fifth of Elaphebolion, before Demosthenes set off on the second embassy,

---

[77] There is a major inconsistency (more visible to the modern reader who can compare texts in a printed edition than to an Athenian audience hearing the speeches at an interval of thirteen years) between the accounts of speeches 2 and 3. In 2.64–66 Aeschines argues that there were no speeches at the second meeting (because there was no opportunity under the terms governing the meetings), whereas here, like Demosthenes in 343 (19.15–16), he talks of speeches on both days. The account here, in which Demosthenes changes ground overnight, is a mirror image of Demosthenes' allegations against Aeschines in 343 (19.14–16).

[78] For Aeschines on Demosthenes' style, cf. 2.110n, 3.166n.

[79] An astute courtier and distinguished Macedonian general who served both Philip and Alexander, sufficiently trusted for Alexander to leave him as regent in Europe when he invaded the Persian empire, though the two were estranged shortly before Alexander's death. Antipater died in 319.

[80] The allegation looks like an attempt to mimic Demosthenes' charge in 343 (see 2.124–129) that Aeschines coached Philip in the writing of the letter that he sent to Athens with his second embassy.

[81] I.e., to Philip. Again the charge reflects accusations made by Demosthenes in 343 (19.174, 179–181).

the one for the oath-taking—for this speaker of yours, the anti-Alexander, the anti-Philip, served as envoy to Macedonia twice, when he need not have gone even once, this man who now urges us to spit on the Macedonians. Taking his seat in the Assembly on the twenty-fifth, and having connived to serve on the Council, he handed over Cersobleptes with the help of Philocrates. [74] Philocrates unobtrusively inserted in the decree, along with the rest, and Demosthenes put to the vote, a clause that says: "The allied representatives are to swear the oaths to Philip's envoys today."[82] But there was no representative from Cersobleptes at the session.[83] By proposing that the representatives at the session should swear, he excluded Cersobleptes, who was not at the session, from the oaths. [75] To prove I am telling the truth, please read out who proposed this motion and who put it to the vote.

[DECREE]

It is a good thing, men of Athens, a good thing that we preserve the texts of public documents. This record is unchanging and does not shift its ground to suit political deserters but enables the people, whenever they wish, to recognize individuals who have long been dishonest but change tack and claim to be men of principle.

[76] I have still to talk about his servility. For you will find that Demosthenes, men of Athens, during the year he served on the Council, never invited a delegation to take a seat of honor; no, that was the first and only time that he invited envoys to take a seat of honor,[84] and

---

[82] The allegation both incriminates Demosthenes and exculpates Aeschines' audience; in fact, it was the Assembly that decided on the date for oath-swearing. It is the norm for Athenian politicians when criticizing Assembly decisions to present the members of the Assembly as deceived by the opponents rather than at fault themselves.

[83] Since Cersobleptes was not part of the Athenian alliance, he had no right to send a representative to the allied congress. In 343 (2.83), Aeschines states that Cersobleptes had a representative in Athens.

[84] The *proedria*, "front seat," was a position of honor, allowing both the best vantage point for the performance and the greatest visibility to the assembled crowd. Aeschines deals more briefly with the issue at 2.55, 110, where the detail of the mule cart does not appear.

he placed cushions there and spread out rugs and at daybreak led the ambassadors into the theatre, with the result that he was hissed for his undignified and fawning behavior. And when they were setting off for Thebes, he hired three mule teams and accompanied the envoys as far as Thebes, an act that brought ridicule on the city. To prevent me from straying from the subject, please take the decree about the seats of honor.

[DECREE]

[77] Now this man, men of Athens, this consummate flatterer, was the first to learn of Philip's death through the scouts from Charidemus.[85] And he invented a dream of his own and told lies against the gods, claiming that he had not heard of the event from Charidemus but from Zeus and Athena. Though he perjures himself in their name by day, he claims these gods converse with him at night and tell him the future. Seven days after his daughter's death, before he had mourned her and performed the rites custom demands,[86] he put on a crown and white clothing and sacrificed oxen in violation of tradition, when the wretch had lost the first and only child to call him father. [78] And I am not blaming him for his misfortune but exposing his character. For a bad father who hates his children could never be a good public leader; and a man who does not love his nearest and dearest will never feel concern for outsiders like yourselves; nor could a man who is evil in his private life be of use in public life; and a man

---

[85] In 336 Philip was assassinated by a Macedonian noble named Pausanias who had a personal grudge against him. Charidemus was presumably in the north at the time. A native of Euboea whose career as a mercenary began in the 360s, Charidemus served the Thracian king Cotys and then his son Cersobleptes ably and was rewarded with marriage to Cersobleptes' sister. He was given Athenian citizenship, possibly in the early 350s. He fought effectively against Macedonia and had the distinction of being one of the Athenians whose surrender was demanded by Alexander in 335 (see 3.161n). At that point he returned to his career as a mercenary general and served the Persian king Darius against Alexander, but was executed after falling foul of Darius' advisers.

[86] After the formalities of burial, there was a period of mourning of thirty days. The color of mourning was black.

who is worthless at home can never have been a man of honor as envoy in Macedonia—he changed his position, not his disposition.[87]

[79] Now how did he come to change his policy (this is the second period), and why is it that Philocrates has been impeached[88] and exiled for the same policies as Demosthenes while Demosthenes came forward to accuse the others? How has this vile man brought our misfortunes upon us? It is especially important for you to hear these things. [80] As soon as Philip passed Thermopylae and against all expectation destroyed the cities of Phocis and strengthened Thebes beyond what was reasonable or advantageous to you,[89] as you thought then, and you had brought your possessions in from the country in a state of alarm, when the envoys who had negotiated the peace were severely criticized, especially Philocrates and Demosthenes, because they had not only acted as envoys but also proposed the decrees, [81] and, as it happened, at the same time Demosthenes and Philocrates were falling out for more or less the reasons even you guessed lay behind their quarrel[90]—amid all this confusion, he immediately planned the next step, prompted by his innate vices, that is, his cowardice and his competition in corruption with Philocrates. He thought that if he turned accuser against his fellow envoys and Philip, Philocrates would certainly be ruined and the other envoys would be put in danger, while he personally would win respect and (though a traitor to his friends and a criminal) would be thought loyal by the people.

[82] Seeing what he was up to, the enemies of public peace readily called him to the platform, calling him the only incorruptible politician the city had. He came forward and sought to give them the op-

---

[87] The Greek plays with the words *tropos* ("character, disposition") and *topos* ("place, location").

[88] By Hyperides in 343; cf. 3.5n. In his account of the second period, Aeschines ignores the expansion of Macedonian power, concentrating solely on the bellicosity of Demosthenes. Criticism of Philip is muted (3.80); his attempts at conciliation receive more emphasis (3.82–83). Cf. 3.54n, 3.106n.

[89] The settlement following the surrender of Phocis (for which see 2.142n) broke the power of Phocis and deprived Athens of a major ally against Thebes. For Athens' panic, cf. 2.139n.

[90] The vague allegation hints at disagreement between Demosthenes and Philocrates over the profits of treason.

portunities for war and turmoil. This is the man, men of Athens, who first discovered Fort Serrium, Doriscus, Ergisca, Myrtisca, Ganos, and Ganias,[91] places of which we did not even know the names before then. And he pressed so far in distorting the situation that if Philip did not send envoys, Demosthenes asserted that he was showing contempt for the city, while if he did send them, he was sending spies, not envoys. [83] If Philip was willing to submit our complaints to the arbitration of a neutral and disinterested city, Demosthenes asserted that there was no neutral judge between us and Philip. Philip offered to give us Halonnesus; Demosthenes urged us not to accept "if he offers to give, not to give back,"[92] arguing about syllables. And finally, by awarding a crown to Aristodemus and his group, who went on a mission to Thessaly and Magnesia in contravention of the peace treaty,[93] he put an end to the peace and brought about the catastrophic war.

[84] Yes, but he fortified our country with walls of bronze and adamant, he claims,[94] with the Euboean and Theban alliance. But this

---

[91] Fortresses in Thrace captured by Philip in the interval between the Athenians' and his own swearing of the oath under the Peace of Philocrates. Scholars have pointed out that Demosthenes at 18.27 speaks of Myrtenus and have suggested that Aeschines distorts the name for the sake of a derisory jingle; it has also been suggested that Ganias is invented for the jingle with Ganos.

[92] The reference is to the offers brought by Python in 344/3 (see 2.125n) and subsequent negotiations. The insignificant island of Halonnesus had been seized from Athens by pirates; these were then expelled by Philip, who retained possession. The author of the pseudo-Demosthenic speech *On Halonnesus*, probably Hegesippus (1.64n), confirms ([Dem.] 7.2–6) both that Philip was willing to give Athens the island (*didonai*) and that the anti-Macedonian politicians at Athens insisted he must restore it (*apodidonai*). The same author ([Dem.] 7.7–8) shares the impassioned rejection of arbitration attributed to Demosthenes here. The issue in question was in part a matter of prestige. But (as Ed Harris reminds me) it also had practical implications; for Philip, it raised the specter of further demands from Athens for the restoration of territories that they had lost.

[93] In 343/2 (according to the ancient commentators on Aeschines), with a view to stirring up rebellion against Macedonia in the context of worsening relations between Athens and Philip. For Aristodemus, see 2.15n; evidently he had by now become disillusioned with the peace.

[94] The nearest statement to this in Demosthenes' defense speech is 18.299. For Aeschines on Demosthenes' style, see 3.166n.

is actually the greatest wrong done to you, men of Athens, and the one you have least understood. Eager as I am to discuss the marvelous alliance with Thebes, to maintain the proper order I shall speak about the Euboean alliance first.[95]

[85] You had been seriously wronged on many occasions by Mnesarchus of Chalcis,[96] the father of Callias and Taurosthenes[97]—men Demosthenes here, who has taken money from them, now has the nerve to propose for Athenian citizenship—and by Themison[98] of Eretria, who robbed us of Oropus when we were at peace with him. But you voluntarily forgot these wrongs, and when the Thebans crossed to Euboea in an attempt to enslave the cities there,[99] you gave them support within five days with a fleet and a land force. Within thirty days you sent the Thebans back to the mainland under truce and made yourselves masters of Euboea. You honestly and fairly restored the cities themselves with their constitutions to the people who had placed them in your care, because you did not think it right to remember your anger when people had put their trust in you.

[86] Despite receiving assistance on this scale, the people of Chalcis did not repay like with like. In fact, when you crossed to Euboea to support Plutarch,[100] initially at least they pretended to be your friends; but the moment we reached Tamynae and crossed the mountain called Co-

---

[95] Demosthenes replies at 18.95–101.

[96] On the west coast of Euboea, facing Boeotia across the Euripus Strait.

[97] Aeschines' lucid (if biased) narrative of the shifts in the external alignment of Callias of Chalcis here and in what follows is our fullest account of his career. Although Aeschines presents him as unscrupulous, the consistent goal of his policy seems to have been the creation of a fully independent Euboea. The grant of Athenian citizenship (date uncertain) and Demosthenes' role in it are criticized by Dinarchus 1.44 and Hyperides 5.20.

[98] For Themison and Oropus, see 2.164n. Eretria was on the west coast of Euboea, southeast of Chalcis.

[99] In 357, during a brief struggle between Athens and Thebes for control of Euboea.

[100] The campaign in question was both a military and a political disaster for Athens. In 348, Plutarch, the dictator of Eretria in Euboea, sought Athenian aid to put down a revolt. The Athenian army under Phocion enjoyed some initial success, but the situation changed after his recall to Athens; the expeditionary force was eventually defeated, and Athens had to acknowledge Euboean independence and pay a substantial ransom to secure the release of the prisoners-of-war.

tylaeum, then Callias of Chalcis, the man whose praises Demosthenes sang for pay, [87] saw that our army was caught in a confined and dangerous position, from which there was no possibility of withdrawal without a military victory and no hope of relief by land or sea. He mustered an army from the whole of Euboea and summoned additional forces from Philip, while his brother Taurosthenes, the man who now clasps everyone's hand and smiles at them,[101] brought the mercenaries across from Phocis, and they attacked with the intention of destroying us. [88] And but for the fact first that some god rescued the army, and second that your troops, both infantry and cavalry, proved themselves brave men and defeated the enemy in a pitched battle by the hippodrome at Tamynae before sending them away under truce, the city would have been exposed to complete humiliation. For the worst misfortune is not defeat in war, but when someone takes a risk against opponents unworthy of himself and fails, the disaster is naturally doubled.

But still, despite such mistreatment, you were reconciled with them once more. [89] But once pardoned by you, Callias of Chalcis after a short interval could not resist reverting to his natural disposition. On the pretext of assembling a Euboean League at Chalcis, in reality he sought to strengthen Euboea against you and to secure the prize of dictatorship for himself. At this point, in the hope of obtaining the support of Philip, he went off to Macedonia and went around with Philip and was termed one of his "comrades."[102] [90] But he offended Philip and fled from there and hurriedly ingratiated himself with the Thebans. Then he abandoned them, too, and after more changes than the Euripus[103] by which he used to live, he found himself caught between the hatred of the Thebans and that of Philip. At a loss what to do with himself, with a campaign now being declared against him, the sole remaining hope of survival he could see was to bind the Athenian people with an oath to come to his aid under the title of ally, if anyone attacked him. This was clearly what would happen, unless you were

---

[101] The manuscripts are divided here; some have only "who smiles at everyone."

[102] For Philip's *hetairoi*, see 2.34n.

[103] The Euripus, the narrow stretch of water separating Euboea from the mainland, is known for its rapidly shifting currents; it was applied proverbially to changeable individuals. The image is taken up by Hyperides *Against Demosthenes* (5.20), a speech that shows the influence (conscious or otherwise) of this one.

to prevent it. [91] With this in mind he sent Glaucetes, Empedon, and Diodorus [104] the former long-race runner here as representatives, bearing false hopes for the people and money for Demosthenes and his associates. There were three things he was trying to buy at once. First, to be sure to conclude the alliance with you—for he had no middle course, if the people remembered his earlier offenses and rejected the alliance; his certain fate was either exile from Chalcis or death if he was caught there, so great were the combined forces of Philip and Thebes marching against him. Second, payment was being delivered for the man who would propose an alliance that would exempt Chalcis from a place on the allied council at Athens. [105] The third aim was to avoid paying any contributions. [92] Callias failed in none of these aims. No, Demosthenes the anti-tyrant (so he pretends), the man Ctesiphon claims speaks in your best interests, sold the opportunities open to the city and wrote into the decree that you should support Chalcis. As for the return you would get, he drafted mere words, adding for the sake of appearance, "And Chalcis is to give support if anyone attacks Athens." [93] As to seats on the allied council and financial contributions, which would strengthen the war effort, he sold these off entirely, proposing the most disgraceful course of action in the most noble words and leading you on with the assertion that the city must first give aid to any Greeks who asked for it and only later conclude alliances, after bestowing benefits. [106] To show you that I am

---

[104] In 341. The envoys are otherwise unknown, though the description of Diodorus suggests that he was a distinguished athlete.

[105] The second and third objectives together amount to political independence from Athens for the cities of Euboea and freedom from the obligation to make financial contributions to its league. In a context of worsening relations with Macedonia in the late 340s (Introduction to Aeschines, p. 7), the terms of the alliance made sense as a means of aligning the whole of Euboea with Athens and were probably the most Athens could expect after the debacle of 348 (3.86n). Here and in his account below of the Euboean League, Aeschines expects his audience to forget the political realities twelve years earlier.

[106] Aeschines here picks up on a strand of Demosthenes' rhetoric reflected in the heroic vision of Athens projected in his defense speech (18.95–101, 190–210), a vision derived from the epideictic tradition, specifically the funeral orations for Athenians killed in war (see 3.152n). Demosthenes maintains that his policy was not only honorable but also expedient (18.95).

telling the truth, take the alliance proposed with Callias and read out the decree.

[DECREE]

[94] Now the fact that such important opportunities and the membership of the allied council and the financial contributions have been sold off is not yet the worst thing. You will find what I am about to tell you far more monstrous than this. So far did the insolence and greed of Callias of Chalcis progress, together with the venality of Demosthenes, the man praised by Ctesiphon, that while you still had breath and mind and sight, they managed, without being noticed, to rob you of the contributions from Oreus[107] and Eretria, ten talents in all, they caused the council members from those cities to abandon you, and they brought them together in Chalcis at the so-called Euboean council. By what dishonest means this was done deserves to be told to you right now. [95] Callias stopped using messengers and approached you directly.[108] He came before the Assembly and gave you an account that had been fabricated by Demosthenes. He claimed that he had just come from the Peloponnese, where he had negotiated a contribution that would produce 100 talents for use against Philip and calculated how much each city would pay, the whole of Achaea and Megara sixty talents, the cities of Euboea collectively forty. [96] These sums would furnish a fleet and a land army. And there were, he claimed, many other Greek states willing to contribute to the collection, and so there would be no shortage of money or troops. This was the public part. But he also stated that he was engaged in other secret measures, which some of your citizens could attest, and finished by calling on Demosthenes and asking him to speak in his support.

[97] Now Demosthenes came forward with great solemnity and lavished exaggerated praise on Callias, pretending that he knew of Callias' secret, and said that he wanted to give you an account of his mission to the Peloponnese and Acarnania.[109] The essence of his ac-

---

[107] Oreus was in northern Euboea.

[108] In 340.

[109] In northwest Greece. Philip's campaign in Epirus in 343/2 had alarmed the Greeks of the area, and Athens had aligned itself with the opponents of Macedonia.

count was that the whole of the Peloponnese was ready and all of Acarnania had been drawn into an alliance against Philip thanks to him, that there was a financial fund sufficient for the crews of 100 fast ships, 10,000 infantry, and 1,000 cavalry. [98] In addition, the citizen armies would be available, more than 20,000 hoplites from the Peloponnese, and as many again from Acarnania. The command of all these forces had been granted to you. All this would not be delayed but would be completed by the sixteenth of Anthesterion,[110] since he had given instructions in the cities and invited all of them to join a congress in Athens at the full moon. This, you see, is the peculiarity that distinguishes Demosthenes from other men. [99] All other braggarts, when telling lies, try to make vague and imprecise statements, because they fear refutation. But Demosthenes, when making grandiose claims, firstly adds an oath to his lies, calling destruction down on himself, and secondly has the nerve to give a date for events he knows will never happen and provides the names of people he has not seen in person, deceiving his hearers and mimicking the manner of people telling the truth. And for this he deserves fierce hatred, because as well as being a criminal, he also obliterates the signs that distinguish honest men.

[100] After this speech, he gave the clerk a decree to read out that was longer than the *Iliad* and emptier than the speeches he likes to make and the life he has led, but full of hopes that would not be fulfilled and armies that would never be mustered. After diverting your attention well away from the swindle and raising you up with hopes, he at last gathered his confidence and proposed the appointment of envoys to Eretria to ask the Eretrians (they really needed to be asked!) to cease giving us their contribution of five talents and give it to Callias, and another group of envoys to Oreus to ask them to consider the friends and enemies of Athens theirs. [101] Then he reveals that his purpose throughout the decree is the fraud, proposing in addition that the envoys should also ask the people of Oreus to give the five talents not to us but to Callias. To prove that I am telling the truth, omit the pomp and triremes and boasting and read out

---

[110] Anthesterion corresponds roughly to February in our calendar; the year is 340.

specifically the theft perpetrated by this vile and unholy man, the man Ctesiphon says in his decree "consistently speaks and acts in the best interests of the people."

[DECREE]

[102] So you see that what you heard was a verbal promise of the triremes, the army, the deadline of the full moon, and the representatives at the congress, while what you lost in reality was the financial contributions of your allies, the ten talents.

[103] I still have to add that Demosthenes was paid three talents for drafting this proposal, a talent from Chalcis, from Callias, a talent from Eretria, from the dictator (*tyrannos*) Clitarchus,[111] and a talent from Oreus, which was what exposed him, because Oreus is a democracy and conducts all its business through public decrees. Since their funds had been exhausted by the war and they were without any resources, they sent Gnosidemus, the son of Charigenes who was once ruler of Oreus,[112] to him with a request that he forego the talent due from the city and an offer to erect a bronze statue of him in Oreus. [104] Demosthenes answered him that bronze was the last thing he needed and used Callias to exact the talent. Under pressure and lacking the resources, the people of Oreus mortgaged their public revenue to him for the talent and paid Demosthenes interest of a drachma per mina per month[113] for the bribe due to him until they had paid off the capital due to him. [105] And this was approved through a democratic decree. To prove I am telling the truth, please take the decree of the people of Oreus.

---

[111] Clitarchus with his colleagues Hipparchus and Automedon held power in Eretria from 343 until dislodged by Phocion in 341. Since Clitarchus was leader of the pro-Macedonian faction at Eretria and his fall from power cleared the way for the creation of the Euboean League, the alleged bribe from him is implausible.

[112] Otherwise unknown.

[113] 12% per annum, the normal rate for well-secured loans in Athens. There is no reason to doubt that Oreus was in debt to Demosthenes, in view of what looks like documentary confirmation. But there is no good reason to suppose that the debt related to an unpaid bribe rather than a loan toward the war effort.

[DECREE]

This is the decree, men of Athens, a disgrace to our city, substantial proof of the policies of Demosthenes, and an explicit accusation against Ctesiphon. For it is impossible that the person who so engaged in such disgraceful corruption could have proved himself a man of integrity, as Ctesiphon has had the nerve to draft in his decree.

[106] Now we have the third of the periods, more accurately the most bitter time of all, in which Demosthenes destroyed the interests of Greece and our city,[114] by committing impiety against the temple at Delphi and proposing an unjust and completely unequal alliance with Thebes. I shall begin my account with his offenses against the gods.

[107] There is a place called the plain of Cirra,[115] men of Athens, and a harbor that is now termed "consecrated and cursed." This region was once settled by the Cirraeans and the Cragalidae, lawless peoples, who behaved impiously toward the temple at Delphi and its dedicated offerings and wronged the Amphictyons.[116] They say that this aroused the indignation in particular of your ancestors and also of the other Amphictyons, who sought an oracle from the god, asking about the punishment they should inflict on these people. [108] And the Pythia[117] answered them that they should make war day and night without cease against the Cirraeans and Cragalidae, they must lay waste their territory and their city, enslave the inhabitants, and consecrate the land to Pythian Apollo, Artemis, Leto, and Athena Pronaia[118] to be unworked in any way, and they must neither work

---

[114] In setting the boundary between the second and third periods in 339 over the Amphissa affair, Aeschines ignores the fact that Athens had technically been at war with Macedonia since Philip seized the Athenian grain ships in 340 (Introduction to Aeschines, p. 7). This enables him to place all the blame on Demosthenes' belligerence. Cf. 3.54n, 3.79n.

[115] On the coast of the Corinthian Gulf, southwest of Delphi.

[116] For the Amphictyonic League, see 2.94n. The events narrated belong to the First Sacred War, c. 590.

[117] The priestess of Apollo at Delphi, who prophesied under the influence of the god.

[118] Athena "Before the Temple," a title under which she was worshipped at Delphi. Throughout this section of the narrative, the manuscripts give Pronoia,

this land themselves nor allow anyone else to work it. On receiving the oracle, the Amphictyons voted, on the motion of Solon [119] of Athens, a man both skilled in legislation and versed in poetry and philosophy, to make war on the cursed peoples according to the god's oracle. [109] They assembled a large force from among the Amphictyons and enslaved the inhabitants and demolished their city and harbor and consecrated their land as instructed by the oracle. In addition, they swore a binding oath that they would neither work the land themselves nor allow anyone else, but would aid the god and the consecrated land with hand and foot [120] and every means. [110] Not satisfied with swearing just this oath, they added a curse, a strong imprecation, on the subject. The curse contains the following clause. "If anyone," it says, "city or individual or people, contravenes this, let them be cursed by Apollo, Artemis, Leto, and Athena Pronaia." [111] And a prayer is included that their land should not produce crops nor their women bear children that resemble their parents but monsters, nor their livestock bring forth natural offspring, but they should be defeated in war, lawsuits, and debates, and both they themselves and their households and their race should perish utterly. "And may they never," it says, "offer pure sacrifice to Apollo or Artemis or Leto or Athena Pronaia, and may the gods not accept their offerings." [112] To prove I am telling the truth, read out the god's oracle. Listen to the curse; remember the oaths your ancestors swore together with the Amphictyons.

"Athena Forethought," a title found at Athens. It is conceivable that we have here not a scribal error but either confusion by Aeschines or a deliberate attempt to associate the goddess at Delphi with Athenian cult. But since Aeschines goes on to cite an inscription, which presumably will contain the Delphic title, it is unlikely that he would either err himself or confuse his audience in this way. The fact that the later lexicographer Harpocration (who refers to this passage) seems to have had Pronaia in his text speaks for scribal error, though if so the error is an old one, since it was in the text read by the commentaries (*scholia*) found in the manuscripts of Aeschines.

[119] For Solon, see 1.6n. Here, as in 3.107, Aeschines strives to present the issue as one of particular interest to Athens in tacit justification of the stance he took (3.113–124).

[120] On the basis of 3.120 editors usually add here "and voice."

[ORACLE] *You will never seize and bring down this city's tower until at the god's sanctuary blue-eyed Amphitryte's wave breaks with a roar on sacred shores.*[121]

[OATHS, CURSE]

[113] Though this curse and the oaths and the oracle are publicly inscribed to this day, the Locrians of Amphissa,[122] or rather their leaders, men without any concern for law, were cultivating the plain, and they had refortified and established themselves in the harbor that was consecrated and cursed; they were exacting duties from people putting in there and had bribed some of the delegates (*pylagoroi*)[123] who came to Delphi, including Demosthenes. [114] Although he was your elected delegate (*pylagoros*), he accepted 2,000 drachmas from the people of Amphissa to prevent any mention of them at meetings of the Amphictyons. An agreement also was made with him that for the future he would receive in Athens twenty minas every year from the consecrated and cursed income on condition that he give every kind of support to the Amphissaeans at Athens. The result of this has been that even more than before, to whomever he touches, private citizen or ruler or democratic state, he brings incurable disaster in every single case.

[115] Now observe the complete superiority of god and fortune over the impiety of Amphissa. In the archonship of Theophrastus,[124] when Diognetus of Anaphlystus was sacred envoy (*hieromnēmōn*),[125] you elected as delegates (*pylagoroi*) the well-known Midias from An-

---

[121] The oracle cited does not match the preceding text. From the blatant forgeries in Aeschines 1, it is clear that no ancient text of Aeschines had the documents cited in court; a later scholar has inserted the wrong oracle (evidently derived from Pausanias 10.37.5).

[122] Chief city of Ozolian Locris, west-northwest of Delphi.

[123] There were two kinds of state representative at the council, the *hieromnē-mōn* and the *pylagoros*. The former held office for longer and had a vote on the Council. At the date in question, Athens evidently sent three *pylagoroi*. How the numbers of *pylagoroi* were distributed among the relevant states is not clear.

[124] 340/39.

[125] Diognetus is known only from this passage. For the *hieromnēmōn*, see 3.114n.

agyrus[126]—who I wish was still alive for many reasons—and Thrasycles of Oe, and third with them myself. As it happened, the moment we arrived in Delphi, Diognetus developed a fever, and the same thing happened to Midias. [116] The rest of the Amphictyons were in session, when we received a message from people who wanted to demonstrate their loyalty to our city that the Amphissaeans, who had come under the influence of Thebes at that period and were trying desperately to ingratiate themselves with them, were proposing a motion against our city;[127] they wanted the Athenian people fined fifty talents because we had dedicated gilded shields in the new temple before it was consecrated and added the appropriate caption: "The Athenians, from the Medes and the Thebans, when they fought on the opposite side to the Greeks."[128] The sacred envoy sent for me and asked me to go to the council and address the Amphictyons on behalf of the city, something I had myself already decided to do. [117] As I was beginning to speak, having entered the council chamber perhaps rather impatiently,[129] since the rest of the delegates (*pylagoroi*) had withdrawn,

---

[126] For Midias, see 3.52n. Presumably Thrasycles is the man associated by pseudo-Plutarch ([Plut.] *Lives of the Ten Orators* 842e) with the attack on the sons of the politician Lycurgus after the latter's death in 325/4; given Lycurgus' anti-Macedonian inclinations, this would agree with Thrasycles' association with Aeschines and Midias here. In view of the difficult position in which the Athenian representatives were placed, the sudden illness of both, though clearly not impossible, is suspiciously convenient.

[127] Demosthenes at 18.145–155, esp. 149–150, offers a lame denial of Aeschines' version. The threat was real enough. The Amphissaean charge meant that Athens was faced with the prospect of a humiliating fine or, if the people refused to pay, the declaration of a sacred war by the Amphictyons against Athens.

[128] Evidently a rededication (during the Phocian occupation of Delphi) of shields from the second Persian invasion (480), when Thebes had fought on the Persian side.

[129] In the account that follows, Aeschines displays the same ability for devastating retaliation when attacked that he had shown against Timarchus in 346 (Aeschines 1). Despite the overall confidence of his presentation of the incident, Aeschines here appears to show some discomfort. His oratorical coup offered Athens the opportunity to take the lead in a religiously sanctioned campaign and to improve relations with Philip, the power behind the Amphictyonic scenes, but it was risky, since it depended on his ability to induce the Athenians to follow

one of the Amphissaeans cried out. He was a thoroughly gross individual and, it seemed it me, a man with no education; perhaps, too,
he was led into error by some superhuman force. He said: "Fellow
Greeks, if you had any sense you would not mention the Athenian
people at all during these days, but bar them from the temple as
people under a curse." [118] He went on to mention the alliance with
Phocis proposed by the illustrious Crobylus,[130] and made many other
offensive statements against our city that I could neither bear to listen to then nor find it pleasant to recall now. As I listened, I was
enraged to a degree I had never experienced before in my life. I shall
omit most of what I said. But it occurred to me that I should speak of
the Amphissaean impiety against the consecrated land, and I stood up
right there and pointed it out to the Amphictyons—for the plain of
Cirra lies below the temple and can easily be seen. [119] "You see," I
said, "fellow Amphictyons, this plain worked by the Amphissaeans
and potteries and farm buildings built on it. You see with your eyes
the consecrated and cursed harbor fortified. You know yourselves, and
have no need of other witnesses, that these people exact duties and
derive an income from the sacred harbor." At the same time I ordered
that the god's oracle, the ancestors' oath, and the curse that had been
uttered be read out to them. And I declared: [120] "Personally, for the
sake of the Athenian people, my life, my children, and my household,
in keeping with the oath, I intend to support the god and the sacred
land with hand and foot and voice and every means I can, and I release
our city from impiety against the gods. As for you, you must now
make your own decision. The sacrificial baskets are ready,[131] the victims are standing at the altars, and you are about to ask the gods for
collective and individual good fortune. [121] Ask yourselves—what

---

through on his initiative. And by driving a wedge between Thebes (an ally of
Amphissa) and the Amphictyons, he offered those Athenians who favored war
with Macedonia the possibility of a Theban-Athenian axis against Philip. He may
have felt after Chaeronea that his response was precipitate, and that it might have
been possible to rebut the charge without the potential for destabilization created
by inciting a sacred war against Amphissa.

[130] For Crobylus (Hegesippus), see 1.64n. The words are sarcastic.

[131] The sacrificial baskets contained barley grain for sprinkling on the victim
and (hidden underneath) the knife for cutting its throat.

will be your voice, your state of mind, your expression, what confidence will you possess as you make your requests, if you allow these men who are damned and under a curse to go unpunished? The fate that the men who have actually committed the impiety and those who have let them must suffer is written not in riddles but explicitly in the curse, and at the close it says: 'And may they never offer pure sacrifice to Apollo or Artemis or Leto or Athena Pronaia, and may the gods not accept their offerings.'"

[122] After I had said this and much else besides, when I had finished and left the council chamber, there was a great deal of shouting and uproar among the Amphictyons, and the talk was no longer about the shields that we had dedicated but now about punishing the Amphissaeans. The day was already far advanced, when the herald came forward and announced that all Delphians two years into adulthood, slave and free alike, should assemble at daybreak at the spot there called the Thyteum,[132] bringing spades and picks. And again the same herald announced that the sacred envoys and the delegates should assemble at the same spot to protect the god and the sacred land, adding: "Any city that does not attend will be barred from the temple and damned and under the curse."

[123] Next day, we went to the appointed place at dawn, descended to the plain of Cirra, and demolished the harbor and burned the houses, and then we withdrew. While we were doing this, the Amphissaean Locrians, who live sixty stades[133] from Delphi, came at us fully armed with all their forces; and but for the fact that we just managed to escape to Delphi at a run, we would have been in danger of our lives.

[124] The following day, Cottyphus,[134] whose duty it was to put proposals to the vote, called an assembly of the Amphictyons. They use the term "assembly" when not only the delegates and sacred envoys are summoned but also the people who are there to sacrifice or to consult the god's oracle. At this meeting there were many accusa-

---

[132] Location uncertain; etymology connects it with sacrifice (Greek verb *thyein*).

[133] The stade was approximately 200 yards, giving a distance here of about seven miles.

[134] One of the Thessalian representatives at the Amphictyonic Council from 343 to 337.

tions made against the Amphissaeans, and there was widespread praise
for our city. The upshot of the whole story is that they voted that the
sacred envoys should come to Thermopylae on an appointed day before the next Amphictyonic meeting (*Pylaia*)[135] with a motion on the
punishment the Amphissaeans should receive for their offenses against
the god and the sacred land and the Amphictyons. To prove I am
telling the truth, the clerk will read you the decree.

[DECREE]

[125] This resolution was reported by us in the Council and again
in the Assembly, and the people approved our actions, and the whole
city was minded to behave piously. Demosthenes spoke in opposition[136] for the sake of the money he had negotiated from Amphissa,
while I exposed him clearly in front of you. When the fellow could
not manage to dupe the city by open argument, he came into the
Council chamber and, after having the nonmembers removed,[137] obtained a draft motion that he brought to the Assembly, taking advantage of the inexperience of the drafter. [126] He contrived to have

[135] The Amphictyonic Council met twice yearly, in spring and autumn. The
vote approved an extraordinary meeting outside the normal calendar.

[136] Athenian participation in a campaign against Amphissa would create a rift
with Thebes at a time when Athens was already at war with Macedonia, and
Demosthenes viewed a showdown with Philip as inevitable and an Athenian-
Theban alliance as vital for success. Demosthenes' motion effectively deprived
Athens of influence on the outcome of the campaign and on any settlement, while
setting them in opposition to the Amphictyons. Aeschines does not substantiate
the allegations that Demosthenes exploited the ignorance of a fellow member of
the Council when getting the preliminary motion (*probouleuma*) for the Assembly
drafted, and that attendance was sparse at the point in the Assembly meeting
when Demosthenes' motion was ratified. Despite the emphasis on Demosthenes'
deceit in what follows, it is clear that Demosthenes had majority support for his
stance at this point; it is difficult to believe that the Athenians were unaware that
the motion was a snub to the Amphictyons and, through them, to Philip.

[137] Council meetings were public, but meetings could be held in secret when
necessary. The claim (not substantiated) implies that Demosthenes did not want
the alleged maneuvering in Council to become public knowledge, which would
weaken his prospects for success in the Assembly.

this same motion ratified and turned into a popular decree in the Assembly, when it was adjourning and I had left (for I would never have allowed it) and the majority of the people had dispersed. Its essence is as follows: "The sacred envoy," it says, "of Athens and the delegates in office at any time are to go to Thermopylae and Delphi at the times appointed by our ancestors," on the face of it a reasonable measure but in reality disgraceful. For it prevents attendance at the conference at Thermopylae, which had to take place before the regular date. [127] And again, in the same decree, in much clearer and more malicious words, he proposes: "The sacred envoy," he says, "of Athens and the delegates in office at the time may not engage in any discussion, act, resolution, or venture with the people gathered at that meeting." What does "not engage in" mean? Shall I speak the truth or what is most pleasing to hear? I shall speak the truth; it is the constant practice of saying what is pleasing that has reduced the city to this condition. It does not permit you to remember the oaths that our ancestors swore or the curse or the god's oracle.

[128] So we stayed behind because of this decree, while the other Amphictyons assembled at Thermopylae, except a single city whose name I will not utter,[138] and I hope that disasters like hers may not befall anyone in Greece. Once assembled they voted to march against Amphissa and elected as general Cottyphus of Pharsalus,[139] the man whose duty it was to put proposals to the vote. Philip was not at home in Macedonia, and indeed was not even in Greece but in Scythia, so far away, though very shortly Demosthenes will have the nerve to claim that I brought him against Greece. [129] Once they reached Amphissa on this first campaign, they treated the Amphissaeans generously. For crimes of the worst kind they punished them with a fine and instructed them to pay this to the god within a stipulated time; they exiled the individuals under a curse, the ones responsible for the acts, and restored the people who had been in exile for their piety. But the Amphissaeans persistently failed to pay the money to the god and

[138] Thebes. The disaster mentioned is the destruction of Thebes by Alexander after the unsuccessful revolt of 335.

[139] For Cottyphus, see 3.124n.

restored the cursed men, exiling the pious ones who had been brought back by the Amphictyons. And so in these circumstances they conducted a second campaign against Amphissa, much later, after Philip's return from his campaign against the Scythians. The gods had handed the championship of the cause of piety to us, but Demosthenes' corruption had prevented it.

[130] But didn't the gods warn us, didn't they signal us to be on our guard, doing everything but speak in human voices? Never before have I seen any city more clearly being rescued by the gods but ruined by some of the public speakers. Was not the sign that appeared at the Mysteries [140] enough, the way the celebrants died? Didn't Aminiades [141] warn you to be cautious in the light of this and advise you to send to Delphi to ask the god what should be done, and didn't Demosthenes oppose it, claiming the Pythia was on Philip's side—a lout enjoying to the full and abusing the indulgence you showed him? [131] Didn't he finally send the troops out to face unmistakable danger with the sacrifices missing or inauspicious? And yet the other day he dared to claim that the sole reason Philip did not attack our country [142] was that the sacrifices he made were not favorable. What punishment do you deserve, you curse on Greece? For if the victor did not invade the territory of the defeated because his sacrifices were not favorable, and you without knowing the future sent out the troops before auspicious sacrifice was made, should you be crowned as a result of the city's misfortunes, or cast beyond the borders? [143]

---

[140] According to the ancient commentators, a shark seized one participant, and possibly two, as they bathed in the sea as part of the ritual cleansing that began the Eleusinian Mysteries (for which see 2.133n). In a world permeated by divine signs, this would inevitably be seen as an omen. Plutarch (*Phocion* 28.3) relates a similar incident not long afterward, likewise taken as a portent, and it has been suggested that the ancient commentators mistakenly imported the shark from Plutarch.

[141] The ancient commentators identify him without further detail as "an Athenian seer," perhaps an intelligent guess.

[142] After his resounding victory at Chaeronea, when Athens was at his mercy. The settlement he imposed was, in the event, remarkably generous.

[143] Probably not merely exiled but executed and then denied burial in Attica, the punishment for treason.

[132] And so what unimaginable or unexpected event has not occurred in our time? We have not lived a normal human life but were born to be a source of marvelous stories for future generations. Is it not the case that the king of Persia, the man who dug through Mount Athos,[144] who yoked the Hellespont, who demanded earth and water from the Greeks, who dared to write in his letters that he was master of all mankind from the rising to the setting sun, now struggles not to be lord of others but already to save his life?[145] And don't we see that the people who were rewarded with this glory and the leadership against the Persians were the same ones who also liberated the temple at Delphi?[146] [133] And Thebes, Thebes, our neighbor city, has been snatched from the middle of Greece in a single day;[147] justly, it may be, since their whole policy was mistaken, but their blindness and folly came not from a human but from a superhuman source. And the poor Spartans, who became involved in these events only at the beginning with the seizure of the temple,[148] who once claimed to be leaders of Greece, are about to be sent to Alexander[149] as hostages and make an exhibition of their calamity, to suffer, both individually and as a country, whatever he chooses, and to have their fate decided by the mercy of a victor they have wronged.

---

[144] I.e., in the preparation for the invasion of 480. Aeschines treats the successive Persian kings as a single entity.

[145] The year before the trial, Alexander had decisively defeated the forces of the Persian king at the battle of Gaugamela, and Darius III had fled the field. He was murdered not long before the date of the trial, but evidently the Athenians had not yet heard.

[146] Macedonia. For the second campaign against Amphissa, under Philip, cf. 3.129; Aeschines may also be referring to the surrender of Phocis to Philip.

[147] This lament finds an echo in Dinarchus 1.24.

[148] In 355 the Spartan king Archidamus (cf. 2.133n) supplied money and mercenaries to the Phocian leader Philomelus, enabling him to seize the temple, which led to the Sacred War.

[149] In 331 the Spartan king Agis headed a revolt against Macedonia, aided by Arcadia and most of Achaea. The rest of Greece, including Athens, felt that the timing was not right, and the revolt was confined to the Peloponnese. Agis had an initial success against the Macedonian general Corrhagus but was decisively defeated by Alexander's regent Antipater at the battle of Megalopolis.

[134] And our city, the universal refuge of the Greeks, which previously received embassies from the rest of Greece, each looking to find protection for their individual cities from us, now no longer competes for the leadership of Greece but is already struggling for our country's soil. And this has been our fate since Demosthenes came to political prominence. The poet Hesiod expresses himself well on situations like this. He says at one point, as he seeks to educate the masses and advise the cities, that they should not tolerate corrupt demagogues. [135] I shall pronounce the verses; the reason I think we learn by heart the poets' thoughts as children is to make use of them when we are men.

> Often enough the whole city has paid for an evil man
> who does wrong and devises deeds of wickedness.
> Upon them from heaven Cronus' son brings great woe,
> famine and plague together, and the people perish.
> He may destroy their vast army or their walls
> or take vengeance on their ships at sea, far-seeing Zeus.[150]

[136] If you remove the rhythm and examine the poet's sentiments, I think you will see that they are not Hesiod's poetry but an oracle directed at Demosthenes' political career. For indeed, army and fleet and whole cities have been obliterated as a result of his policies.

[137] But I think that neither Phrynondas nor Eurybatus[151] nor any other criminal of old was such a charlatan and trickster[152] as this man, who— O earth and gods and powers and all you men who wish

---

[150] Hesiod *Works and Days* 240–245.

[151] The comparison is hurled back at Aeschines in Demosthenes 18.24. Of these two proverbial criminals, Phrynondas was said to have been an unscrupulous Athenian, Eurybatus an Ephesian entrusted with money by the Lydian king Croesus in the sixth century who joined his Persian enemy Cyrus.

[152] Greek *magos kai goēs*, "magician and sorcerer/conjurer." The language of magic is used repeatedly by Aeschines of Demosthenes; it is difficult to determine the resonance of the words for the audience, that is, whether they connote sinister power or merely superficial display. Possibly the words carry elements of both qualities, presenting Demosthenes simultaneously as casting a malign influence over his audience and as having nothing of substance to offer. Demosthenes rejects the terminology at 18.276. It is picked up by Dinarchus at 1.66, 92, 95.

to hear the truth—dares to maintain, looking you [153] full in the face, that the Thebans concluded the alliance with you not because of the crisis, not because of the danger in which they were immersed, not because of your reputation, but because of Demosthenes' speeches. [138] And yet many times the men most closely associated with Thebes undertook embassies to them, first of all Thrasybulus of Collytus,[154] a man more trusted in Thebes than anyone else, and again Thrason of Erchia, who was representative (*proxenos*) for Thebes, [139] Leodamas of Acharnae, as skillful a speaker as Demosthenes, in my view indeed more pleasing, Archedemus of Peleces, both an able speaker and a man who has often run risks in political life for the sake of Thebes, Aristophon of Azenia, who faced the charge of favoring Boeotia longer than anyone, and Pyrrhander of Anaphlystus, who is still alive. But still nobody managed to draw them into friendship with you. As to the reason, though I know it, I need not say in view of their misfortunes. [140] In my opinion, it was only when Philip took Nicaea [155]

---

[153] The manuscripts (as often) are divided between "us" and "you" (literally "looking into our/your faces") here and later in the sentence. Any decision is highly subjective, but the second person more effectively isolates Demosthenes from the audience, here as often in forensic oratory representing the Athenian people.

[154] Thrasybulus of Collytus, less distinguished than his namesake Thrasybulus of Steiria, was politically active in the last decade of the fifth and first quarter of the fourth century and was one of the exiles who restored the democracy in 403. He served as envoy to Thebes in 378/7. Thrason, his nephew, was probably (Dinarchus 1.38) instrumental in helping the Theban exiles after the Spartan seizure of the Cadmea (see 2.117n). For Leodamas, see 1.69n. Archedemus was politically active at the close of the fifth and the opening of the fourth century. For Aristophon, see 1.64n. Pyrrhander served on the embassy to Thebes in 378/7 and was still politically active in the 340s (1.84). Aeschines overstates the failure of previous attempts to win over Thebes; the embassy of 378/7 drew Thebes into alliance with the newly created Second Athenian League.

[155] In 339 Philip, invited by the Amphictyons to take the lead in the second campaign against Amphissa (3.129), marched south, but after marching through Thermopylae, instead of proceeding westward toward Amphissa, he seized and fortified the Phocian site of Elatea. He then asked Thebes, still at this stage a Macedonian ally, either to join him in attacking Athens or to allow his army to pass through Boeotia; he also demanded that they relinquish control of Nicaea, one of the sites controlling access to the pass at Thermopylae.

from them and gave it to the Thessalians and restarted the war, directing it against Thebes through Phocis—the same war he had previously driven beyond the borders of Boeotia[156]—and finally seized and fortified Elatea and brought in a garrison, only then at last, when danger was upon them, did they send for Athens. Then you marched out and entered Thebes fully armed, infantry and cavalry, before Demosthenes had drafted a single syllable about alliance. [141] What brought you to Thebes was the crisis, their fear, and their need for an alliance, not Demosthenes.

Indeed, in this business Demosthenes is guilty of the three worst offenses against you. Firstly[157] because though Philip, while ostensibly at war with you, in reality was much more hostile to Thebes, as events themselves have shown (need I say more?), Demosthenes concealed this fact, which is of fundamental importance, by pretending that the alliance was about to be concluded not because of the crisis but because of his diplomacy. [142] First of all he persuaded the Assembly to dismiss the question of the terms on which the alliance should be concluded and to be satisfied with the mere fact of its creation; once he had secured this, he handed over the whole of Boeotia to Thebes[158] by stating in the decree: "If any city secedes from Thebes, the Athe-

---

[156] The war was the same (as that against Phocis) only in the sense that both were fought in the name of the Delphic temple. But both the target state and its relationship with Thebes were different. Although he is right to stress that it was ultimately self-interest that decided Thebes' position, in his desire to minimize Demosthenes' achievement Aeschines understates the Theban freedom to choose. Although a weakened Athens (if Thebes sided with Macedonia) would have reduced Philip's need for Thebes as a counterweight and so left Thebes exposed, with a Macedonian force on their doorstep at Elatea, the Thebans were risking immediate war on their own territory. There was a substantial faction in Thebes that preferred the safer option of siding with Macedonia.

[157] Though as usual he lays out his points with clinical precision, Aeschines' account here is a little confusing. The main list of alleged crimes is interrupted by a subsidiary list in 3.142–144, before being resumed in 3.145.

[158] Athenian policy had been to support the independence of Boeotian cities to prevent Thebes from achieving the degree of consolidation that Athens had achieved in Attica. According to Aeschines, the illusion of continuity with past policy is created by terming the Thebans "Boeotians" and suppressing the identity of the potential rebel cities.

nians are to support the Boeotians in Thebes." He used the wording to conceal and distort the situation, as usual, as though, when the Boeotians were suffering real mistreatment, they would be happy with Demosthenes' verbal formulation rather than feel resentment at their mistreatment. [143] Secondly he set down two-thirds of the war expenses to you,[159] though the dangers for you were more remote, and one-third to the Thebans, all of this in return for a bribe. And he made the naval command a joint one but the cost yours alone, while in contrast the land command, not to mince words, he took and gave in its entirety to Thebes. As a result, in the war that followed, your general Stratocles[160] had no authority to decide on the safety of his troops. [144] And this is not a charge brought by me but ignored by everyone else. No, I make it and everyone else hurls it at him, too; and you know it and feel no anger. This is what Demosthenes has done to you; you are already habituated to hearing of his crimes, and as a result you feel no surprise. This is not the right way; you should be indignant and punish them, if the city is to prosper in the future.

[145] A second crime he committed, much worse than this, was that at a stroke he surreptitiously spirited away our city's Council chamber and the democracy and transferred them to Thebes, to the Cadmea, when he agreed to give the Boeotarchs[161] joint control of our policy. And he appropriated so much power for himself that right then he came to the platform and declared that he would go to negotiate wherever he saw fit, [146] even if you did not send him. And in an attempt to make the officials his slaves and train them not to op-

---

[159] The terms on which the alliance were negotiated were very favorable to Thebes. But Thebes was the stronger land power (and the war would inevitably be fought on land and, indeed, on Theban soil), and Thebes, unlike Athens, still had a choice between peace and war.

[160] Apart from his command at Chaeronea (confirmed by Polyaenus 4.2.2), Stratocles is merely a name to us. It has been suggested that the treaty allowed for the city that summoned the expedition to take command, as in the treaty quoted at Thucydides 5.47.

[161] The Boeotarchs were military and political officials of the Boeotian federation. Their numbers varied at different times during the classical period, with Thebes usually supplying a significant proportion (and between 478 and 338 the majority, 4 out of 7).

pose him, if any of the generals spoke against him, he threatened to bring a suit (*diadikasia*) [162] against the generals' office on behalf of the speakers' platform. For he claimed that you had profited more from his activity on the platform than from the generals in their office. By profiting from empty places in the mercenary force [163] and defrauding the military fund and hiring out the 10,000 mercenaries to Amphissa [164] despite my protests and complaints at Assembly meetings, with the destruction of the mercenaries he hastened the danger and brought it on the city when it was unprepared. [147] What do you think Philip would have prayed for at that point? Surely to fight separately against our citizen army and at Amphissa against the mercenaries and catch the Greeks while they were dispirited from suffering such a heavy blow at the start? And Demosthenes, though responsible for calamities on this scale, is not content to have escaped punishment; no, he is angry that he might be denied a golden crown. And it is not enough for him to have it proclaimed in front of you; no, he is angry, too, if it is not announced in the presence of all Greece. So true is it, evidently, that a base nature, when given great indulgence, generates public disasters.

[148] The third and worst of the crimes of which I spoke is the one I am coming to. Philip had no slight regard for the Greeks and was well aware (he was no fool) that in a small portion of a day he would risk all he possessed in battle. For this reason he wanted to make peace and was proposing to send envoys. The authorities at Thebes were

---

[162] The duties of the generals included command in war; any opposition to Demosthenes' plans from that quarter would carry weight. The suit allegedly threatened is puzzling. The term used, *diadikasia,* describes a private suit to determine the appropriate allocation of property, rights, or responsibilities among two or more claimants. Either (on Aeschines' account) Demosthenes is proposing to extend the use of this action (normally between individuals) to obtain a formal jury vote on the demarcation of responsibilities between offices or functions, or (more probably) the term is metaphorical and Demosthenes expresses an intention to use public actions with severe penalties as a means of resolving his power struggle with officials who oppose him.

[163] The accusation is that Demosthenes has conspired to fill out the mercenary list with nonexistent soldiers in order to pocket the relevant portion of the pay provided by the public exchequer.

[164] These were dispatched to help defend Amphissa.

afraid of the imminent danger—and rightly so, for their advice came not from a politician who evaded service and deserted his post;[165] no, the ten-year Phocian War had taught them an unforgettable lesson. [149] And Demosthenes, seeing that was how matters stood and suspecting that the Boeotarchs were about to make a separate peace in exchange for money from Philip with no share for him, decided that life was not worth living if he was left out of any chance of bribery. He leapt up in the Assembly, though nobody in the world was arguing either for or against the need to make peace with Philip—rather, his aim was to give advance notice to the Boeotarchs that they must allocate a share of the profits to him. And he swore by Athena, [150] whose statue it seems Phidias[166] created to serve Demosthenes' profiteering and perjury, that in truth if anyone said we must make peace with Philip he would grab him by the hair and haul him off to prison, imitating the policy of Cleophon,[167] who during the war against Sparta (we are told) brought the city to ruin. But the authorities in Thebes ignored him and sent back your troops who had marched there in order to allow you to debate the issue of peace. [151] At that point he at once panicked completely and, mounting the platform, he called the Boeotarchs traitors to Greece. And he said he would propose a decree—this man who has never looked the enemy in the face in battle—requiring you to send envoys to Thebes to ask the Thebans for the right of passage to march against Philip. The authorities in Thebes, ashamed that it might be thought that they really were traitors to Greece, abandoned the thought of peace and turned to preparations for battle.[168]

---

[165] The evasion of service referred to is probably Demosthenes' failure to serve in the Euboean campaign of 348; he had exemption as a festival chorus producer, but this did not prevent his enemies from prosecuting him for failure to serve. The desertion relates to Chaeronea itself; Aeschines repeatedly charges Demosthenes with having abandoned his shield and run (152, 159, 175, 181, 187, 244, 253); the charge is repeated by Dinarchus (1.12) and later biographers.

[166] The colossal statue of Athena Promachos, which dominated the Acropolis, was the work of the fifth-century sculptor Phidias.

[167] For Cleophon, see 2.76n.

[168] There is an inconsistency between the earlier claim that Demosthenes did little to influence the Thebans (3.137–141) and the claim here that he shamed their officials into precipitate action.

[152] At this point it is appropriate to mention the brave men whom this man sent out to unmistakable danger with the sacrifices missing or inauspicious, yet he had the nerve (mounting the dead men's tomb with those runaway feet that deserted their post)[169] to speak in praise of their courage. Of all men in the world the most useless when it comes to important and serious business but most marvelous when it comes to verbal bravado, will you choose shortly to look these men in the face and try to claim that you deserve to be crowned for the city's calamities? And if he does say it, will you men tolerate it? Are we to suppose your ability to remember will die along with the dead men? [153] Please imagine yourselves for a moment not in the court but in the theatre, and suppose that you see the herald coming forward, the announcement in the decree about to take place, and ask yourselves whether the relatives of the dead will shed more tears over the tragedies and sufferings of the heroes that will be staged after this or at the city's insensitivity. [154] What Greek with a free man's education would not feel pain to recall this, if nothing else, that once on this day, when as now the tragedies were about to take place, when the city was better governed and had better champions, the herald would come forward and, with the orphans whose fathers had died in war beside him, young men decked out in full armor, would make a proclamation, one that brought most honor and was most calculated to inspire courage, that these young men, whose fathers had died in war displaying their valor, were reared to adulthood by the people, who, having equipped them with this hoplite armor, now send them off to their own affairs with their blessing and invite them to a seat of honor.[170] [155] This was the proclamation in those days, but not now.

---

[169] It was a distinctive Athenian tradition to hold a public burial of the cremated remains of all those who had died in war and to have a distinguished orator make a formal and elaborate speech in their praise. Demosthenes was selected to make the oration for the dead at Chaeronea, an indication that he was not held responsible by most Athenians for the disaster there. A speech purporting to be the one delivered on that occasion survives as number 60 in the modern editions of Demosthenes.

[170] That is, at the performance which followed the announcement. For the treatment of the sons of the war dead, cf. Thucydides 2.46; Plato *Menexenus* 248e; Isocrates *On the Peace* 82; Aristotle *Politics* 2.8.5 (1268a), *Constitution of Athens*

No, with the man responsible for the children's orphan state beside him, what announcement will the herald make? What will he say? For if he goes through the actual announcement ordered by the decree, shame prompted by the truth will not stay silent but will seem to proclaim in opposition to the herald's voice that this man, if man he really is, is being crowned by the Athenian people for his virtue when he is utterly base, and for his manly excellence when he is a coward who has deserted his post. [156] No, in the name of Zeus and the gods, I beg you, men of Athens, do not set up a trophy to your own defeat in the orchestra of the theatre of Dionysus. Do not convict the Athenian people of madness in the presence of all of Greece. Do not remind the wretched Thebans, who were exiled because of him and who have been given refuge in our city, of their incurable and irreparable sufferings, when their temples and children and tombs have been destroyed by Demosthenes' corruption and the king's gold. [157] But since you were not there in person, witness their disasters with your mind's eye and imagine that you can see their city being captured, the demolition of the walls, the burning of the houses, the women and children being led away to slavery, old men, old women learning late in life to forget their freedom, weeping, begging you, angry not at the people who were taking revenge on them but at the men responsible for these events, solemnly instructing you under no circumstances to crown the curse of Greece but to be on your guard against the evil destiny and the bad luck[171] that dogs the man's footsteps. [158] For no city nor private individual ever turned out well for relying on the advice of Demosthenes. As for yourselves, men of Athens, in the case of ferrymen who carry people to Salamis, you passed a law that if any of them accidentally capsizes a boat during the crossing, he is barred from working as a ferryman again, to prevent anyone from taking

---

24.3; Diogenes Laertius 1.55; according to the fragments of Lysias *Against Theozotides*, the provision was extended to the (legitimate) children of those who died fighting against the Thirty at the end of the fifth century.

[171] Demosthenes replies at 18.252–255, 270–275. The same point is made against Demosthenes by Dinarchus at 1.31, 41. In a society where good and bad fortune may reflect divine favor or hostility, which in turn from Homer onward (*Od.* 3.375–376) reflect individual merit or its opposite, good luck can be claimed as a laudable asset (Thuc. 6.17.1, 7.77.2) and bad luck held against a man, as here.

chances with Greek lives; so are you not ashamed at the prospect of allowing this man, who has totally capsized Greece and our city, to steer public policy again?

[159] Turning to the fourth period, the situation in which we now find ourselves, I want to remind you of the fact that Demosthenes deserted not only his military post but also his post as citizen. He took control of one of your ships and exacted money from the Greeks.[172] And when our unexpected survival brought him back to the city, initially the man was all aquiver, and, coming to the platform half-dead with fear, he urged you to vote him "guardian of the peace."[173] And though in the initial period you would not even allow Demosthenes to attach his name to decrees but assigned this task to Nausicles,[174] now he demands to be crowned.

[160] When Philip died[175] and Alexander became ruler, once more Demosthenes was up to his posturing. He had a shrine created to Pausanias and exposed the Council to the charge of making sacrifice for good news; he gave Alexander the nickname "Margites"[176] and

---

[172] An attempt in the aftermath of the battle of Chaeronea to seek the aid of the allies for the supply of Athens (see Dem. 18.248). Aeschines nimbly presents this as flight from the city on a specious pretext (so did Dinarchus later, 1.80–81). For the emergency measures passed after Chaeronea, see 3.252n.

[173] That is, Athenian representative at the Congress of Corinth in 338 at which Philip imposed a settlement on Greece. The (implied) rejection may reflect fluctuation in Demosthenes' popularity after Chaeronea; but equally it may reflect a pragmatic recognition by the Assembly that Demosthenes would not be a welcome negotiator at any conference convened by Philip. The decrees referred to here (if Aeschines is telling the truth) may likewise have dealt with relations with Macedonia.

[174] For Nausicles, see 2.18n. I take Aeschines to be saying that Nausicles' name was added to decrees proposed by Demosthenes (presumably to conceal Demosthenes' influence from Macedonia); it has, however, been suggested that "this task" refers back to the preceding sentence, in which case Nausicles was elected to the Congress of Corinth.

[175] Cf. 3.77n.

[176] An insulting nickname derived from the eponymous hero of an archaic epic (now lost) who was famous for his stupidity.

had the nerve to maintain that he would not stir from Macedonia. He claimed that Alexander would be content to stroll around[177] in Pella observing the entrails.[178] He said this was not based on guesswork but on accurate knowledge that the price of valor is blood, though he himself has no blood in him and was judging Alexander not by Alexander's nature but by his own cowardice. [161] The Thessalians had already voted for a campaign against our[179] city, and the young man was initially enraged,[180] not surprisingly. And when the army was near Thebes, Demosthenes, elected envoy by you, turned tail[181] halfway through Cithaeron[182] and came back, a man equally useless in peace and in war. The worst thing of all is that, though you did not betray him or allow him to stand trial in the Greek congress,[183] this man has now betrayed you, if what we hear is true. [162] For according to the

---

[177] It has been suggested that the Greek (*peripatounta*) is a sneer at Alexander's training by Aristotle, who taught at Athens at the Lyceum, whose colonnade (*peripatos*) gave the name "Peripatetic" to his school of philosophy.

[178] The Greek, *ta splanchna phylattonta,* is ambiguous; it could mean "watching carefully for the (sacrificial) entrails" (i.e., to be favorable), or just possibly "guarding his entrails" (i.e., avoiding putting his life at risk in war, or merely watching out for assassins). The ancient commentators favor the latter.

[179] As often, the manuscripts here are divided between the second and third persons, the majority favoring "your."

[180] The death of Philip encouraged hope of independence in many parts of Greece, which Alexander moved rapidly to dispel. Although Athens did not overtly break with Macedonia, it opened negotiations in a number of directions intended to pave the way for revolt.

[181] Dinarchus (1.82) says that Demosthenes refused to serve at all. Either way, Demosthenes' nonparticipation made sense. Quite apart from the obvious threat to his personal safety, an embassy that included Demosthenes would not warm Alexander to Athens.

[182] The main road from Athens to Thebes led over Cithaeron.

[183] I.e., the League of Corinth set up by Philip after Chaeronea. In 335, after Alexander's capture and sack of Thebes, he demanded that Athens surrender the politicians (including Demosthenes) who had agitated against Macedonia. An Athenian delegation, including the rising politician Demades, persuaded Alexander to withdraw the demand.

crew of the *Paralus* [184] and the envoys who went to Alexander (and the incident is entirely credible), there's a certain Aristion of Plataea, [185] the son of Aristobulus the pharmacist, no doubt known to some of you. This young man was once outstandingly beautiful and lived for a long time in Demosthenes' house—as to what he did and what was done to him, the allegations vary, and it would be quite improper for me to discuss the matter. This man, so I am told, is trying to ingratiate himself with Alexander, who does not know his background and his way of life, and is seeking out his company. And through him Demosthenes has sent letters to Alexander and so has achieved some immunity and a reconciliation for himself and has engaged in a great deal of flattery.

[163] Now see how the facts fit the allegation. If Demosthenes' thoughts were as he claims and he was hostile to Alexander, as he maintains, he has had three opportunities up to now, none of which he has used. The first of these was when Alexander had recently come to power, and while his personal situation was still unsettled he crossed to Asia. [186] The Persian king was at the peak of his strength, with his navy, his wealth, and his land army, and would readily have concluded an alliance with you because of the danger bearing down on him. Did you make any speech at that point, Demosthenes, or propose any decree? Shall I suppose you took fright and followed your natural inclinations? Yet a public crisis does not wait on a politician's cowardice. [164] But when Darius had brought all his forces to the coast and Alexander was cut off in Cilicia [187] and short of everything, so you claimed, and according to your account he was on the point of being trampled

---

[184] One of the two state triremes of Athens reserved for special ceremonial and political duties.

[185] According to the later lexicographer Harpocration (evidently on good authority), Aristion was from his youth an associate and agent of Demosthenes. The people of Plataea were given Athenian citizenship after the city was destroyed by Sparta in the Peloponnesian War. The inhabitants were restored to Plataea in the 380s but driven out again by Thebes in 373, when they took refuge in Athens.

[186] In 334.

[187] Aeschines refers to the period before the battle of Issus in the autumn of 333, when Darius succeeded in outflanking Alexander but at the cost of moving on to terrain more favorable to the Greek army.

underfoot by the Persian cavalry, and the city was not big enough for your arrogance and the letters you dangled from your fingers [188] as you went around pointing out to people my expression as a sign of amazement and dismay, calling me a gilded ox [189] and claiming I was garlanded, ready for any failure suffered by Alexander, even then you did nothing but put it off for some more opportune moment.

[165] Anyway, I will pass over all this and speak about the current situation. The Spartans and the mercenary force in a successful engagement destroyed Corrhagus' army,[190] and the people of Elis and Achaea, with the exception of Pellene, and the whole of Arcadia except Megalopolis joined their cause. Megalopolis was under siege, and its capture was expected every day. Alexander was in the far north [191] and virtually outside the inhabited world. Antipater was taking a long time assembling his army, and the future was uncertain. Set out for us, Demosthenes, just what it was you did and what it was you said at that juncture. If you like, I am ready to give up the platform to you while you have your say. [166] You are silent; I can understand your confusion. But as for what you said then, *I* shall give an account now. Don't you remember his vile and incredible statements? How could you bear to listen to them—are you made of iron? I mean when he came forward and said: "There are people who are pruning the city like a vine, people who have cut back the shoots of democracy. The sinews of state policy have been cut. We are being stitched up like a blanket. There are people pressing us into tight places like needles." [192]

---

[188] The point is repeated in similar words by Dinarchus 1.36. The letters are presumably from foreign powers (though Dinarchus accuses Demosthenes of writing them himself).

[189] That is, an ox ready for sacrifice, with its horns gilded and its head garlanded.

[190] For the Spartan revolt and the defeat of Corrhagus, see 3.133n.

[191] Greek "beyond the bear" (i.e., the constellation); the Greeks located Asia broadly to the east, stretching from the northeast to the south.

[192] The text here is uncertain on points of detail (quotations in later authors differ from the text presented by the manuscripts), but the broad thrust of Aeschines' criticism is clear. For Aeschines on Demosthenes' style, cf. 2.110n, 3.72n. From Demosthenes' response at 18.232, it is clear that Aeschines accompanied his mockery in 3.166–167 with mimickry of Demosthenes' performance (cf. 1.25n).

[167] What are these, you sly fox, words or wonders? And again, when whirling yourself around on the platform, you said, as though you were maneuvering against Alexander: "I admit that I contrived the Spartan revolt; I admit that I am inciting insurrection among the Thessalians and Perrhaebians." *You*—incite revolt in Thessaly? Could *you* incite revolt in a village? Would you approach even a house, let alone a state, where there is danger? But if there is money on offer anywhere, you will be sitting right there, but you will never act like a man. And if there is any chance of success, you will lay claim to it and attach your name to it after the event; but if any danger turns up, you will take flight; then if we find cause for confidence, you will ask for rewards and demand to be honored with gold crowns.

[168] Oh yes, but he's loyal to the people. Well, if you keep your eyes on his fine words, you will be tricked; but if you keep them on his natural character and the reality, you won't be. This is how you should hold him to account. I shall reckon up together with you the qualities a democrat and decent man should naturally possess, and then I shall set against them the character to be expected of an oligarch and a base man.[193] You should compare the two and examine him to see which side he belongs to, not in his words but in his way of life.

[169] Now I think that you would all agree that a democrat should possess the following qualities: first of all, he should be a man of free birth on both his father's and his mother's side, so that the misfortune of his birth will not make him hostile to the laws that keep the democracy safe; second, he should be able to claim good services toward the people from his ancestors, or at the very least no enmity toward them, so that he will not try to harm the city in an attempt to avenge the disasters of his ancestors. [170] Third, he should show a decent and moderate disposition in his daily life, so that he will not be led by excessive spending to take bribes against the interests of the people. Fourth, he should have sound judgment and ability to speak. For it is a fine thing when the intellect chooses the best course and the speaker's training and skill at speaking persuades his audience. Failing this, sound judgment must always be preferred to skill at speaking. Fifth,

---

[193] Demosthenes at 18.122 dismisses Aeschines' definition of the democrat here as pedantic and divorced from the real world.

he must have a courageous spirit, so that he will not desert the people in the face of threat and danger. The oligarchic man should possess the complete opposite of these qualities. Why bother to list them in turn? Observe now which of these qualities Demosthenes can claim. And let the appraisal be entirely fair.

[171] This man's father was Demosthenes of Paeania, a man of free birth—I must tell no lies. But on his mother's side and that of his maternal grandfather, I shall tell you how things stand with him. Gylon came from Cerameis.[194] This man betrayed Nymphaeum in the Black Sea, a position the city held at that period, to the enemy;[195] he was impeached and went into exile from the city, where he was condemned to death, without facing his trial. He arrived at the Bosporus[196] and was given the place called The Gardens by the dictators (*tyrannoi*) there. [172] And he married a rich woman who brought him a large dowry in gold but was of Scythian birth. By her he had two daughters, whom he sent here with a large sum of money. He married one of them to someone or other (I am trying to avoid making a number of enemies), while Demosthenes of Paeania married

---

[194] Even if the account that follows is broadly true (after discounting the inevitable exaggerations and distortions to be expected in Athenian political abuse), this would not necessarily affect Demosthenes' citizenship. The citizenship decree of Pericles of 451/0 restricted citizenship to males with Athenian parents on both sides. This law seems to have been quietly set aside during the latter part of the Peloponnesian War (431–404, with intermissions) but was reinstated after the restoration of democracy in 403. Provided that Demosthenes' mother was born before 403, his citizen status was technically unaffected. It is perhaps worth adding that Aeschines' term "Scythian birth" would cover anything from pure Scythian stock to mixed Athenian-Scythian; since The Gardens was a Greek (but not Athenian) colony, Aeschines may simply be exploiting the fact that the woman was of non-Athenian stock. Demosthenes makes similar play with Aeschines' birth qualifications in his defense speech (18.129–131).

[195] Nymphaeum was on the Tauric Chersonnese (modern Crimea). The alleged incident probably belongs in or after 410. Demosthenes (28.1–4) admits only that Gylon was fined; either Aeschines exaggerates or the sentence was subsequently commuted.

[196] The Bosporan kingdom occupied the eastern part of (what is now) the Crimea, together with part of the Taman Peninsula facing it. The rulers referred to are Satyrus and his descendants.

the other in contempt of the city's laws. And her son is the nuisance and sykophant Demosthenes. So then, from his grandfather he would naturally be an enemy of the people (you condemned his ancestors to death), while on his mother's side he is a Scythian barbarian who speaks Greek. Hence his dishonesty, too, is of foreign extraction. [173] And in his daily life, what sort of man is he? He suddenly turned from trierarch to speechwriter [197] after squandering his inheritance in a ridiculous way. After losing his credibility even in this trade by handing speeches over to the opposing side,[198] he leapt onto the speaker's platform. Though he had gotten an enormous income from politics, he saved very little. For now, however, the king's gold has submerged his extravagance. But even this will not be enough; for wealth never yet got the better of a bad character. The sum of it all is that he pays for his way of life not with his private income but with your dangers.

[174] And in the matter of sound judgment and skill at speaking, what is his nature? Clever in argument, evil in way of life. His treatment of his own body and his siring of children have been such that I refuse to discuss what he has done. For before now I have seen the hostility toward people who speak too explicitly about the shameful conduct of their neighbors. And then what is the outcome for the city? His words are fine, but his acts are worthless. [175] On the subject of courage there's little I need to say. If he denied being a coward or you did not know the facts, my account would have taken some time. But since he himself admits it in Assembly meetings and you are fully informed, I need only remind you of the laws in existence to deal with this offense. The ancient legislator Solon believed that the same penalty should apply to the man who fails to serve and the man who has deserted his post and the coward alike.[199] For there are indictments for cowardice, too. Some of you might be amazed that there are indictments for natural defects. But there are. Why is that? So that each of us will fear the legal penalties more than the enemy and so fight

---

[197] For Demosthenes' career as speechwriter, see 1.94n.

[198] See 2.165n.

[199] The penalty for military offenses was *atimia,* loss of citizen rights (some of the restrictions are listed in 3.176). The terms "coward" and "cowardice" here refer specifically to the act of throwing away one's shield in battle.

more bravely for his country. [176] Well then, when the legislator bars the man who fails to serve, the coward, and man who has deserted his post from entering the purified[200] area of the Agora and does not allow him to wear a ritual crown, or enter the public temples, *you*[201] order us to crown the man who cannot wear a crown by law, and with your own decree you invite into the orchestra at the tragic competition a man who has no place there—you invite into Dionysus' temple the man who through his cowardice has betrayed the temples.

But I do not want to distract you from my theme. So remember this, when he claims to be a democrat. Examine not his words but his way of life, and consider not who a man claims to be but who he is.

[177] But since I have mentioned crowns and awards, while I still remember, I warn you, men of Athens, that if you do not put a stop to these extravagant awards and the crowns you bestow with abandon, the men receiving the honors will not feel any gratitude, nor will the city's policies prosper. For you will never make rogues honest, but you will reduce decent men to utter despair. I think I can give you convincing proof I am telling the truth. [178] If anyone were to ask you whether in your opinion the city is more renowned at the present time or in our ancestors' time, you would all agree that it was in our ancestors' time. And were men better then or now? Then they were outstanding, now they are far inferior. And were the awards and crowns and proclamations and free meals in the Prytaneum more plentiful then than now? In those days distinctions were scarce in our city, and the name of virtue was an honor. Now the whole practice has been completely discredited, and you give your crowns out of habit, not on purpose. [179] Is it not odd, when you look at it this way, that the awards are more plentiful now but the city's situation was stronger then, and the men now are inferior but were better then? I shall try to explain it to you. Do you think, men of Athens, that anyone would ever choose to train for the Olympics or any other of the crown games,[202] in the pancratium[203] or any of the other tough events, if the

---

[200]For the sacred character of the Agora, cf. 1.21n.

[201]I.e., Ctesiphon.

[202]That is, the games in which the sole prize is the crown and attendant prestige.

[203]See 1.33n.

crown was given not to the strongest but to the man who schemed to win it? Nobody would ever choose to train. [180] As it is, I think it is because of its rarity, the fierce competition, the honor, and the immortal renown that come from victory, that people choose to risk their bodies, endure most extreme hardship, and face the danger through to the end. Now imagine you are umpires in a contest in political excellence and recognize the fact that, if you give your awards to few men, those who deserve them, according to the laws, you will have many competitors for excellence, while if you give them to anyone who wants one and gratify those who scheme for them, you will corrupt even decent natures.

[181] I want to show you a little more clearly that I am right to say this. In your opinion, who was the better man, Themistocles,[204] who served as general when you defeated the Persians in the battle of Salamis, or Demosthenes, who recently deserted his post? Was Miltiades,[205] who won the battle of Marathon against the barbarians, or this man? Or again, the men who brought back the people from exile from Phyle?[206] And Aristides,[207] known as "the just," whose nickname is quite different from Demosthenes? [182] In my own opinion, by the Olympian gods, it is not right even to mention this beast and those illustrious men on the same day. Now let Demosthenes demonstrate in his speech whether there is any record of a decree to crown any of these men. So were the people ungrateful? No, they were great-hearted, and those men were worthy of the city. They thought their honor should reside not in written words but in the memory of those they had aided, and this memory from that day to this has remained immortal. And it is worthwhile recalling what rewards they did receive.

[183] There were those who in that period, men of Athens, endured

---

[204] See 2.9n.

[205] The celebrated Athenian general, son of the colonist and tyrant of the Thracian Chersonnese (the Dardanelles), also named Miltiades. He returned to Athens after the unsuccessful revolt of the Greek cities of Ionia (modern Turkey and the islands) from Persia of 499–494 and led the Athenian forces at Marathon in the battle against the Persian invasion force of 490.

[206] See 2.176n.

[207] See 1.25n.

much labor and great dangers and defeated the Medes at the river
Strymon.[208] When these men returned home, they asked the people
for a reward, and the people gave them great honors by the standards
of the day, namely the right to set up three stone Herms in the Portico
of the Herms,[209] on condition that they did not inscribe their own
names on them, so that the inscription would be perceived as belonging to the people, not the generals. [184] And you will recognize the
truth of what I say from the actual verses. For the inscription on the
first Herm is:[210]

> Stouthearted indeed were those men, too, who once on the sons
> of the Medes at Eion on Strymon's stream
> brought to bear blazing famine and the force of Ares,
> and first found how to bring the foe to impotence.

And on the second:

> The commanders received from the Athenians this reward
> for their good service and great courage.
> And seeing this, men in ages to come, too, will wish the more
> to bear labors for the common good.

[185] And on the third Herm is inscribed:

> Once from this city with Atreus' sons, Menestheus[211]
> led his men on the holy plain of Troy.
> Homer once said, of the linen-clad Danaans

---

[208] In 476/5 the forces of the Delian League under Cimon (see 2.172n), son of
Miltiades (see 3.181), captured the Persian fortress of Eion on the river Strymon
in Thrace after a prolonged siege.

[209] Situated at the northwest corner of the Agora.

[210] The three inscriptions recur in Plutarch *Cimon* 7 in an account that seems
to be based on Aeschines, though Plutarch's text of the inscriptions differs in a
number of details from that offered by the Aeschines manuscripts. The connection between the inscriptions made by Aeschines has been doubted.

[211] Menestheus was in myth the son of Theseus. The reference is to Homer
Iliad 2.552–554. The effect of the third inscription is to locate the recent victory
against Persia within the same heroic tradition as the epic struggle against Troy.
This assimilation of modern to ancient warfare between Greek and Asiatic is typi-
cal of the iconography and verse of the period.

he was supreme in ordering the battle.
Not unfittingly, then, are the Athenians called
marshals of war and manly courage.

Is the name of the generals anywhere? Nowhere; just the name of the
people.

[186] Now approach the Painted Portico[212] in your imagination.
For the memorials of all your noble deeds are set up in the Agora.
Well then, what is there relevant to my theme in that building? There
is a painting of the battle of Marathon. Who then was the general?
When asked this question, you will all answer "Miltiades," but it is
not inscribed there. How is this? Didn't he ask for this reward? He did
ask, but the people did not give it.[213] Instead of mention by name,
they allowed him to be painted at the front urging on the soldiers.
[187] Then in the Mother's shrine[214] one can see the reward you gave
to the men who restored the people from exile from Phyle.[215] The
man who proposed and carried the decree was Archinus of Coile,[216]
one of the men who restored the democracy. He proposed that they
be given 1,000 drachmas for sacrifices and dedications (this is less
than ten drachmas per man). And then he gives instructions that each
of them should receive a crown of olive, not gold. In those days the
crown of olive was prized, while now even the gold crown has come
to be despised. And he directs that even this should not be done casually, but after careful inquiry by the Council to establish all those who

---

[212] The Painted Portico (*Stoa Poikilē*) was in the north of the Agora. It contained paintings by the celebrated artist Polygnotus of Thasos, including a depiction of the battle of Marathon.

[213] Since Miltiades died in the early 480s and the Painted Portico belongs to
the early 460s, he was in no position to make this request. It is possible that the
request was made by his son Cimon, who was in the ascendant at this time, but
since the narrative pattern (request and refusal) runs throughout this section and
is one that suits Aeschines' rhetorical purpose, we should not take it seriously.

[214] This building, which stood in the Agora, was the original Council chamber.
When the new Council chamber was built immediately behind it in the last two
decades of the fifth century, the old Council chamber was not demolished but
was used instead as the sanctuary of the Mother of the Gods. From the end of the
fifth century this shrine was the repository of texts of Athenian laws.

[215] See 1.39n.

[216] For Archinus, see 2.176n.

were under siege [217] when the Spartans and the Thirty attacked the forces that had seized Phyle, not all those who deserted their post at Chaeronea when the enemy advanced. To prove I am speaking the truth, he will read out the decree to you.

[DECREE ON THE REWARD FOR THE MEN FROM PHYLE]

[188] Now read out in comparison the decree proposed by Ctesiphon for Demosthenes, the cause of the most serious disasters.

[DECREE]

This decree erases the reward for the men who restored the democracy. If this one is right, the other one is a disgrace; if those great men deserved their honor, this man is being given a crown he does not deserve.

[189] Yet I am told he intends to say [218] that it is unfair of me to compare his deeds with those of our ancestors. He will explain that Philammon the boxer was crowned at Olympia not for beating Glaucus, [219] the famous boxer of old, but the competitors of his own day, as though you were not aware that, while boxers are measured in contest against each other, men who ask for a crown are measured against virtue itself, since this is the justification for crowning them. For the herald must be telling the truth when he makes the proclamation to Greece in the theatre. So don't demonstrate to us that you have been a better politician than Pataecion, [220] but attain excellence and on this basis ask for the people's gratitude.

---

[217] The manuscripts here add "at Phyle," which I have omitted as otiose, since the location is specified later in the sentence.

[218] This argument is actually advanced by Demosthenes (18.314–319, esp. 319). The anticipation of Demosthenes' defense is so precise that we must suppose either that Aeschines' sources of information were very good or that in revising he added detail on the basis of Demosthenes' spoken or published speech.

[219] Philammon was a successful contemporary Athenian boxer; Glaucus of Carystus in Euboea was a distinguished boxer of the late sixth century whose many successes included two Olympic victories.

[220] Who Pataecion was and what made him a negative example are unknown. Equally unclear is whether he was merely a criminal or a dishonest or insignificant politician. Later attempts at explanation make him a thief and sykophant, but their lack of detail argues guesswork.

[**190**] But I do not want to distract you from my theme; so the clerk will read out to you the inscription for the men who restored the people from exile from Phyle.

[INSCRIPTION]

These men for their virtue were honored with crowns by the ancient
people of Athens, because once when men with unjust
ordinances ruled the city, they were first to check them
and lead the way, accepting mortal danger.

[**191**] It was because they overthrew the men who ruled illegally that they were honored, the poet says. For the thought echoed in all men's minds that it was when certain people annulled the indictments for illegal legislation that the democracy was overthrown.[221] For I tell you that, as I heard from my own father, who died at the age of ninety-five and had taken part in all the city's struggles,[222] which he would often relate to me when he had time to spare—he said that when the democracy was newly restored, if anyone brought into court an indictment for illegality, word was as bad as deed.[223] For what could be more vile than a man who speaks or acts against the laws? [**192**] And they did not listen, so he would tell me, in the same way they do now; no, the jurors were far more harsh toward men whose proposals breached the laws than the actual prosecutor and would often check the clerk and order him to read again the laws and the decree. And men whose proposals breached the laws were convicted not for by-passing all the laws, but for transgressing a single syllable. But what happens now is utterly preposterous. The clerk reads out the ille-

---

[221] Cf. [Demosthenes] 58.34. The oligarchic revolutionaries of 411 (2.176n) certainly abolished the indictment for illegal legislation, *graphē paranomōn* (Thuc. 8.67.2; Arist. *Constitution of Athens* 29.4), as an obstacle to wholesale constitutional change. (For the *graphē paranomōn,* see 1.34n.) Aeschines is our sole authority for its formal abolition again in the revolution of 404 (1.39n).

[222] For the democratic credentials of Aeschines' father Atrometus, see 2.78.

[223] The Greek (literally "the word was the same as the deed") could mean "the word was as much as the deed," that is, the utterance of the term was enough to establish guilt, or "the term [i.e., *graphē paranomōn*] was the same as the reality," that is, the *graphē paranomōn* was more than just a name.

gal proposal, while the jurors have their mind on something else, as though they were hearing an incantation or some issue of no concern to them.

[193] Already, thanks to Demosthenes' tricks, you admit a shameful practice in your courts. The city's approach to justice has been inverted: the prosecutor defends himself, while the man facing the indictment acts as prosecutor, and the jurors forget what they are there to decide and are forced to cast their vote on issues they are not there to decide. And the defendant argues, if ever he actually touches on the issue, not that his proposal is legal but that at some point before now someone else has been acquitted after making a similar proposal. And this is the source of the confidence I hear Ctesiphon now feels.

[194] The celebrated Aristophon of Azenia [224] once dared to boast in court that he had been acquitted seventy-five times on indictments for illegal legislation. This was not the way, though, with the famous Cephalus of old,[225] who was considered outstandingly loyal to the people; in fact, his source of pride was the opposite, for he claimed that, though he had proposed more decrees than anyone, he had never been indicted for illegal legislation; this was a worthy boast in my view. For indictments for illegality were brought not just by active politicians against each other, but by friends against friends, if they committed any offense against the city. [195] This I can prove to you. Archinus of Coile brought an indictment for illegal legislation against Thrasybulus of Steiria,[226] one of the group who returned with him from Phyle, and he secured his conviction, despite the fact that his

---

[224] For Aristophon, see 1.64n.

[225] Cephalus of Collytus was a politician from a mercantile background. We first catch sight of him as supporting speaker for Andocides in 400 (Andoc. 1.50). In the early 370s at least, he favored rapprochement with Thebes against Sparta (Dinarchus 1.39). The respect expressed by Aeschines here is echoed by Dinarchus (1.76) and Demosthenes (18.219).

[226] For Archinus and Thrasybulus, see 2.176n. Though it suits Aeschines' purpose to present the two as "friends" (*philoi*), the statement is true only to the extent that they formed a brief alliance opposed to the Thirty. The incident in question is Archinus' prosecution of Thrasybulus for his proposal to extend citizenship to the noncitizens who had helped to restore the democracy (Aristotle *Constitution of Athens* 40.2).

good services were fresh. The jurors took no account of these. They reckoned that just as Thrasybulus had restored them from exile from Phyle, so now he was attempting to exile them when they were home by bringing a proposal that contravened the laws. [196] It is not like that now; in fact, the reverse is the case. Your good generals and individuals who have been rewarded with meals in the Prytaneum plead for acquittal in indictments for illegality.²²⁷ And you would be right to see them as ungrateful. For if anyone who has won honor under a democracy has the nerve under such a constitution, which is defended by the gods and the laws, to help people who bring illegal proposals, he is trying to overthrow the constitution that has honored him.

[197] I myself will tell you the appropriate argument for a supporting speaker with a sense of propriety. The day is divided into three parts when an indictment for illegal legislation comes to court.²²⁸ The first portion of water is poured into the urns for the prosecutor, the laws, and the democratic constitution, the second portion of water for the man facing the indictment and supporters who speak to the main issue. And once the illegal proposal is overturned by the initial verdict, at this point the third portion of water is poured in for the penalty assessment and deciding the extent of your anger. [198] Now anyone who asks for your vote²²⁹ at the assessment stage is seeking to placate your anger. But anyone who asks for your vote in the first speech is asking you to make a gift of your oath, of the law; of democratic rule. None of these can rightly be asked by anyone, nor can they rightly be given to another when asked. So tell them to leave you to cast your initial vote according to the laws and then approach you at the assessment stage. [199] In sum, I personally would almost say, men of Athens, that a law should be passed applying solely to indictments for

---

²²⁷ That is, they use their influence to secure the acquittal of men on trial.

²²⁸ For the "measured out" day, see also 2.126, and Aristotle *Constitution of Athens* 67. The arrangement described here applied to public cases; in private cases the jurors tried several cases in a day. For the water-clock (*klepsydra*) used to time legal hearings, see 2.126n. Aeschines' account of the process skillfully aligns the prosecution with the law code and the democracy, and presents conviction as a foregone conclusion.

²²⁹ That is, by using his own public record as the basis for an appeal to the jurors to vote for the defendant without speaking to the issue.

illegal legislation forbidding either the prosecutor or the man facing the indictment to bring up supporting speakers. For the issue of justice is not something imprecise but is defined by your laws. As in carpentry, when we want to know what is straight and what is not, we apply a ruler, which determines the issue, [200] in the same way in indictments for illegality we have at hand as the ruler of justice this board here containing the proposed decree and the laws next to it. Demonstrate that these agree with each other and then step down, and why do you need to call on Demosthenes? But when you bypass the defense based on justice and call on a rogue and a verbal craftsman, you are deceiving your audience, harming the city, and overthrowing the democratic constitution.

[201] I shall tell you how to protect yourselves against arguments such as this. When Ctesiphon comes forward here and goes through the preamble in front of you according to his instructions,[230] and then wastes time without offering a defense, remind him quite calmly to take the board and read out the laws together with the decree. And if he pretends not to hear you, then don't you listen to him either. You have not come here to listen to people who avoid giving a just defense but to people who are ready to defend themselves as justice demands. [202] And if he bypasses the defense based on justice and calls on Demosthenes, ideally you should not listen to a sophist who thinks he will annul the laws with clever phrases, and none of you should count it virtuous, when Ctesiphon asks if he may call Demosthenes,[231] to be the first to shout out: "Call him, call him." You are calling him against yourself, against the laws, against the democratic constitution. But if in fact you decide to listen to him, order Demosthenes to present the

---

[230] That is, what is technically the main defense speech delivered by the defendant Ctesiphon will in effect be a brief introduction to what is formally the supporting speech but in reality the main defense speech from Demosthenes, Aeschines' real target. Ctesiphon is presented as Demosthenes' puppet.

[231] Although litigants sometimes ask the jurors' permission to call a supporting speaker, the practice is not invariable (cf. Aeschines 2.184). Presumably, therefore, either the request was a courtesy or a rule requiring the jurors' permission for the introduction of a supporting speaker had come to be applied less rigorously. Either way, the present passage suggests that the request could be a useful way of attracting the goodwill of the jurors.

defense as I have presented the prosecution.²³² And how have I presented the prosecution? Let me remind you.

[203] I neither started with an account of Demosthenes' private life nor spoke first about any of his crimes against the state, though clearly I had a plentiful supply of things to say, or I would be the most inept man alive. Instead I began by demonstrating that the laws forbid the crowning of men subject to audit; then I proved that the public speaker in question proposed to crown Demosthenes when he was subject to audit, without any excuse and without adding the clause "when he has presented his account," but with complete contempt for you and the laws. And I told you of the excuses that would be offered for this, which I also urge you to keep in mind. [204] Secondly, I gave you an account of the laws governing proclamations, in which it is expressly forbidden for a man receiving a crown from the people to be proclaimed outside the Assembly. The public speaker facing the indictment has not only breached the laws but also the time of the proclamation and the place, when he orders the proclamation to take place not in the Assembly but in the theatre, when the Athenians are not even holding an Assembly²³³ but the tragic performances are about to begin. After saying this, I spoke briefly about his private life, but most of what I said concerned crimes against the state. [205] This, then, is the way you should expect Demosthenes, too, to present the defense, first of all with the law dealing with men subject to audit, second with the law dealing with proclamations, third and most important, the argument that he is in no way unworthy of the award. If he asks you to make a concession to him on the order of his argument, with the firm promise that he will refute the charge of illegality at the end of the defense, don't make any concession and don't fail to recognize that this is a feint to trip up the court. For he will never voluntarily offer a defense later against the charge of illegality; in fact, since he has no

²³² Demosthenes opens his speech (18.2) by insisting on his right to arrange his defense as he wishes.

²³³ The normal place of Assembly was the Pnyx hill. The Assembly held a meeting in the theatre of Dionysus after the Dionysia in the spring (Aeschin. 2.61, Dem. 21.8) and (by the 320s) a meeting at which the ephebes (see 2.167n) gave a military display (Aristotle *Constitution of Athens* 42.4).

justification to offer, he wants to make you forget the prosecution case by introducing irrelevant issues. [206] So be like the boxers in athletic contests you see competing with each other for position; in the same way, you, too, must spend the whole day fighting with him about the disposition of his argument, and you must not let him step outside the limits of the issue of illegality; you must sit there on guard, lying in wait for him as you listen, and drive him back to the argument about illegality, and watch out for his attempts to divert the case. [207] But it is my duty now to tell you in advance what you will experience, if you listen in the way I have described. He will bring onstage this conjurer,[234] this pickpocket,[235] who has carved up the constitution. This man weeps more easily than other men laugh, he finds perjury the most natural thing in the world. It would not surprise me if he changes tack and insults the viewing public, claiming that the partisans of oligarchy, marked out by the truth itself, have come to support the prosecutor's platform,[236] while the partisans of democracy have come to support the defendant's. [208] Now when he says that sort of thing, in response to his divisive claims, you should give him the following answer: "Demosthenes, if the men who restored the people from exile from Phyle had been like you, the democratic constitution would never have been re-established. As it is, after great disasters, they saved the city by pronouncing the noblest words an enlightened education can provide: 'No recriminations.'[237] But you inflict wounds and are more concerned with the arguments of the moment than with the safety of the city."

And when, perjurer that he is, he falls back on the trust that oaths inspire, remind him that a man who perjures himself repeatedly yet always demands to be trusted because of his oaths must rely on one of two things, either new gods or a different audience, neither of which Demosthenes has. [209] As to his tears and his shrill voice, when he

---

[234] Greek *goēs;* for the language of magic, cf. 3.137n, 2.124n.

[235] Greek *ballantiotomos,* "cutpurse."

[236] Demosthenes does not in fact take this line; the attribution, whether arising from erroneous anticipation or calculated invention, allows Aeschines to present Demosthenes as a source of political division.

[237] *mē mnēsikakein;* for the amnesty of 403, see 1.39n.

asks you: "Where shall I find refuge, men of Athens?[238] Shut me out of public life and there's nowhere for me to fly," you must answer him in turn: "And the Athenian people—where are they to find refuge, Demosthenes? With what allied support? With what financial resources? What protection have you created for the people by your policies? We can all see how you have planned for yourself. Having abandoned Athens[239] you do not so much live in the Piraens, it seems, but are at anchor off the city, and you have provided financial support for your craven escape with the king's gold and the bribes you have taken in public life." [210] But anyway, why the tears? Why the noise? Why the shrill voice? Isn't Ctesiphon the man under indictment? Isn't this trial one with the penalty assessed?[240] As to you, you are not on trial for your property, your life, or your citizen status. But what is it that so concerns him? Gold crowns and illegal proclamations in the theatre. [211] Yet what he ought to do, supposing the people in a fit of madness, or forgetful of the current situation, wanted to crown him at such an inopportune moment, is go before the Assembly and say: "Men of Athens, the crown I accept, but I do not approve of the occasion of the proclamation. It is not fitting that I should receive a crown for events that made the city cut its hair in mourning."[241] In my view these would be the words of a man who really had lived a life

---

[238] Presumably the point is that having alienated Macedonia, Demosthenes can find safety nowhere. The point is picked up by Dinarchus 1.43. The text in the next sentence is problematic. I have followed the reading of most manuscripts. The alternative is "You have shut me out. . . ." This would be inaccurate but intelligible as a rhetorical presentation of potential as actual; some editors would remove "from public life," giving "You have confined me," or the like.

[239] Demosthenes' house in the Piraeus is mentioned by Dinarchus (1.69) and Hyperides (5.17), who repeats Aeschines' jibe in identical words.

[240] For assessed actions, see 1.15n. The point is that even if convicted, Ctesiphon can propose a lenient penalty. The argument is not without force, though matters were not as simple as Aeschines implies. Each party had to gauge the jurors' mood carefully at the assessment stage, try to predict his opponent's bid, and pitch his proposal accordingly; too lenient a proposal might incline the jurors to accept the alternative.

[241] That is, for Chaeronea and its aftermath. The personification is an echo of the funeral speech ascribed to Lysias (Lys. 2.60).

of virtue. Your words will be those one might expect from trash mimicking virtue. [212] For I tell you, by Heracles, one thing at least none of you will worry about is that Demosthenes, great-hearted man and outstanding warrior, if he fails to win the prize for valor, will go home and kill himself.[242] So great is his contempt for an honorable reputation in your eyes that ten thousand times he has cut open this vile head of his, still subject to audit, which this man has proposed against all the laws to crown, and made money from bringing indictments for intentional wounding;[243] and he has had it punched—indeed, I think he still bears the visible marks of Midias' knuckles.[244] What the man has is not a head but a source of income!

[213] I want to say a little about Ctesiphon, the proposer of the motion, though I shall omit most of what I could say, to test if you can recognize real villains even without advance warning. One thing I will tell you, which is common to the two of them and which it is my duty to report to you. They are wandering round the Agora expressing accurate opinions and making statements against each other that are not untrue. [214] Ctesiphon says that he is not afraid on his own account (he says he expects to be seen as an ordinary man), but that what makes him afraid is Demosthenes' venality in political life, his capriciousness and his cowardice. Demosthenes, on the other hand, says he is confident for himself but is deeply worried by Ctesiphon's unscrupulousness and his pimping. When people have actually convicted each other of crimes, you in your role as impartial judges of the charges must under no circumstances acquit them.

[215] And I want to warn you briefly about the slanders against me personally. I am informed that Demosthenes will claim that the city has received many benefits from him but has been harmed by me and will use Philip and Alexander and the accusations arising from them

---

[242] The implied contrast is with the hero Ajax, who fought at Troy. After Achilles' death, Ajax and Odysseus competed for his weapons. When Odysseus won, Ajax went mad and plotted the murder of the Greek leaders. He was thwarted by Athena and on recovering his sanity killed himself. The comparison is well chosen, since Demosthenes adopts a heroic view of Athenian political destiny in his defense speech (3.93n).

[243] See 2.93n.

[244] See 3.52n.

against me. He is such a rhetorical expert, it seems, that he's not satisfied to bring charges against any political activity of mine among you
or any speeches I have made, [216] but he even slanders the very qui-
etness of my way of life and makes my silence ground for accusation
against me in order to leave no area free from his false charges.[245] And
he reproaches me for the time I spend in the gymnasia with younger
men,[246] and right at the start of his speech he brings a complaint
against this prosecution,[247] saying that I brought the indictment not
for the city's sake but as a gesture to Alexander because of Alexander's
hatred for him. [217] And by Zeus, so I am told, he intends to ask me
why I criticize his political career as a whole when I did not prevent
any specific actions or indict them,[248] but have brought the indictment after an interval in which I have not engaged much in political life. Personally, I have not emulated Demosthenes' habits, nor am
I ashamed of my own; nor would I wish the speeches I have made
among you unsaid, and if I had made the same speeches he has, I
would not choose to live. [218] My silence, Demosthenes, is the product of my restrained way of life. I am satisfied with little and have no
desire for greater wealth acquired shamefully; as a result, I both keep
silent and speak with a set purpose, not under the pressure of an extravagant nature. But you, in my opinion, keep silent when you receive money and shout when you have spent it. You do not speak
when you decide or say what you choose, but when your paymasters

[245] Demosthenes does in fact attack Aeschines' silence (18.198, 308), though his
point is that Aeschines makes no positive contribution and is silent unless there
is a disaster, at which point he comes forward to criticize others.

[246] Presumably the suggestion is that Demosthenes portrays Aeschines as a
predatory homosexual (cf. 1.135n), though the allegation may be that Aeschines
corrupts the youth by offering them unscrupulous rhetorical training (a charge
Aeschines makes against Demosthenes); the two are of course not mutually exclusive. The allegation does not appear in the text of Demosthenes 18 as we have it.

[247] The charge is not made in Demosthenes 18 as we have it. The explanation
may be revision of the defense speech by Demosthenes, inaccurate speculation by
Aeschines on Demosthenes' defense, or deliberate misstatement by Aeschines.

[248] For this argument, see Demosthenes 18.13, 22, 117, 124, 191, 242. Aeschines
could be sure that Demosthenes would use this inevitable rejoinder; he had used
it himself in 343 (2.123). Aeschines does not answer the question.

order. And you are not ashamed to make grandiose claims that are proved false on the spot. [219] The indictment against this proposal, which you claim I made not for the city's sake but as a gesture to Alexander, was brought while Philip was still alive, before Alexander came to power, before you had had your dream about Pausanias[249] or had conversed in the night with Athena and Hera. How, then, could I have been making gestures in advance to Alexander? Unless, of course, Demosthenes and I had the same dream!

[220] But you criticize me for not coming before the people continually, but at intervals. And you think we won't notice that you are borrowing this requirement not from democracy but from a different constitution. In oligarchies it is not the volunteer[250] who speaks but the man with power, while in democracies it is the volunteer, at a time of his choosing. And speaking at intervals is the mark of a man who engages in politics at the right occasion and when it is beneficial, while missing not a single day is the mark of a professional and a hireling. [221] As to the fact that you have not been brought to trial by me before or been punished for your crimes, when you fall back on arguments like these, you either take your hearers to be forgetful or you are misleading yourself. As to your impious crimes in relation to Amphissa[251] and your corruption in connection with Euboea,[252] crimes for which you were unambiguously exposed by me, perhaps you hope the people have forgotten because of the long interval. [222] But what length of time could obscure your robbery in the matter of the triremes and the trierarchs, when you legislated about the Three Hundred[253] and persuaded the Athenians to appoint you overseer of the

---

[249] That is, about the assassination of Philip; cf. 3.77.

[250] Greek *ho boulomenos,* the standard term for the prosecutor or (less frequently) the speaker in the Assembly who comes forward on his own initiative.

[251] See 3.114, 125.

[252] See 3.91–105.

[253] For the system of maintaining warships in the fifth and early fourth centuries, see 3.19n. In 357 the system was changed so that the 1,200 richest citizens (between 4% and 6% of the population), divided into groups (*symmoriai,* "symmories") of differing sizes, were collectively responsible for the fleet. In 340 Demosthenes carried a reform that placed either the whole or the bulk of the cost on the 300 richest citizens, making the system both more equitable and potentially more efficient. Demosthenes defends his measure at 18.102–109. Dinarchus

fleet, you were exposed by me as having deprived us of trierarchs for sixty-five fast ships, thereby doing away with a bigger fleet for the city than the one with which the Athenians defeated Pollis and the Spartans at the battle of Naxos?[254] [223] But you so effectively protected yourself from punishment with your accusations that the danger threatened not you, the guilty party, but your prosecutors. You made much of Alexander and Philip in your slanders, and alleged that certain individuals were blocking the city's opportunities (forever discrediting the present and making promises for the future). And finally, when you were about to be impeached by me, did you not contrive the arrest of Anaxinus of Oreus, who was making purchases for Olympias?[255] [224] And this same man you tortured twice with your own hand and proposed that he be punished with death, the same man you lodged with at Oreus and ate, drank, and poured libations from the same table and clasped right hands and treated him as a friend with ties of hospitality—this man you killed. And when you were exposed for these acts by me among the whole Athenian citizenry and were declared your host's murderer, you did not deny your impious crime but gave an answer that made the people and all the foreign

---

(1.42) accuses Demosthenes of taking bribes of three talents to introduce amendments, whereas Demosthenes (18.312) makes a similar accusation against Aeschines, claiming (18.103–104) that he himself was offered but refused bribes. The manuscript tradition is divided between "the Three Hundred" and "three hundred ships"; the latter would refer to the target numbers for the fleet, the former to the 300 richest citizens who headed the symmories before Demosthenes' reforms. I have preferred the former, since the term "the Three Hundred" appears to be a stereotyped expression for the leaders of the symmories.

[254] In 476, when the Spartan fleet sought to cut off the grain ships coming to Athens from the Black Sea. As the first major (unaided) Athenian naval success against Sparta since the Peloponnesian War, the battle had a significance beyond its scale. The figure represents a confusion (probably deliberate) between the Spartan fleet of sixty and the Athenian fleet of eighty-three.

[255] Mother of Alexander. Date uncertain but possibly to be linked to the period preceding the declaration of war in 340. Demosthenes replies at 18.137 that Anaxinus was a spy and repeats the allegation cited by Aeschines (3.225) that Aeschines was implicated. Anaxinus may well have been engaged in purchasing for Olympias, but it would be surprising if the opportunity to gather information on Athens was passed over.

observers at the Assembly cry out: you said you valued the city's salt²⁵⁶ more than the shared table of hospitality. [225] I say nothing of your forged letters and the arrest of spies and the torture based on fictitious charges to the effect that I was planning revolution in collusion with certain individuals in the city.²⁵⁷

And then he intends, so I am told, to ask what kind of a doctor it would be who gave no advice to a sick man during the course of his illness, but on his death went to the funeral and explained to the relatives the treatment that would have restored him to health.²⁵⁸ [226] But you do not ask yourself what kind of a politician it would be who had the ability to ingratiate himself with the people but sold off the opportunities to make the city secure, used slander to prevent men of sense from giving advice, and after running away from danger and immersing the city in incurable catastrophe demanded a crown for virtue, when he had done nothing of benefit and was to blame for every disaster; who asked the men he had driven out of public life with false prosecutions at those moments when security could have been achieved why they did not prevent his crimes; [227] and who concealed the last thing of all, that when the battle had taken place, we had no time for punishing you but were negotiating the city's survival. It was when you were not satisfied to have escaped punishment but were actually asking for rewards and making the city a laughing-stock in the sight of Greece that I objected and brought the indictment.

[228] And by the gods of Olympus, of all the things I hear Demosthenes will say, the one I am about to tell you enrages me the most. He compares my natural gifts with the Sirens,²⁵⁹ it appears. He says

---

²⁵⁶ Cf. 2.22n.

²⁵⁷ Though he does not mention this incident, at 18.133–135 Demosthenes associates Aeschines with another alleged spy, Antiphon, and accuses him of treason.

²⁵⁸ See Demosthenes 18.243. The anticipation is so accurate that some scholars are disposed to attribute its presence to revision; equally (Usher 1993: 253), Demosthenes may already have used the metaphor in an unpublished speech.

²⁵⁹ The comparison with the sweet-sounding but destructive Sirens is not in the text of Demosthenes 18 as we have it. It is possible that Demosthenes omitted it in revision for publication; but equally, Aeschines' advance information may be

that their hearers were not enchanted but destroyed by them and this is why the Sirens' singing is not admired; that likewise my experience in speaking and natural talent have proved disastrous for those who listened to me. Yet this claim is one that nobody under any circumstances can properly make against me; it is disgraceful when someone makes an accusation and cannot prove the fact. [229] But if it had to be said, it was not Demosthenes who should make this claim, but a general who has done great deeds for the city but lacks skill as a speaker and whose reason for admiring his opponents' natural talent is that he is aware both of his inability to express any of his achievements and of his accuser's ability to present to his hearers even acts he has not performed as vividly as though he had done them. But when a man fashioned from words, and bitter and contrived words at that, takes his stand on simplicity and action, who could bear it? When if you took out his tongue, like the reed of a pipe, there is nothing left.

[230] I wonder about you, men of Athens, and I ask myself what reasons you could have for acquitting on this indictment.[260] Possibly because the decree is lawful? But there has never been a more illegal proposal. Or because the man who drafted the decree does not deserve to be punished? Then there will be no prospect of making men accountable for their lives, if you let him go. Does it not grieve you that in former times the orchestra was filled with gold crowns awarded to the people by other Greeks, because that day had been set aside for crowns from foreign states, but thanks to Demosthenes' policies you have no crowns and proclamations, while he will have his name proclaimed? [231] And if any of the tragic poets whose works are performed afterward were to present Thersites being crowned by the Greeks, none of you would tolerate it, because Homer describes him as a coward and slanderer (*sykophantēs*).[261] But when you yourselves

---

inaccurate or he may be inventing, since the alleged charge serves to introduce an attack on Demosthenes.

[260] The device of suggesting and demolishing possible objections, *hypophora*, is a commonplace of ancient oratory. It is especially common, as here, where the prosecutor reviews and rejects grounds for acquittal, and regularly occurs toward the end of a speech.

[261] Thersites is the obstreperous commoner who criticizes Agamemnon in Homer and is punished by Odysseus; cf. *Iliad* 2.212ff. The comparison neatly balances the contrast between Demosthenes and Ajax in 3.212.

crown a man like this, don't you think you are being hissed [262] in the minds of the Greeks? Your fathers gave the credit for the glorious and brilliant achievements to the people but blamed humiliations and failures on shabby politicians, but Ctesiphon thinks you should remove the stigma from Demosthenes and place it on the people. [232] And when you claim to be blessed by fortune, as thank heavens you really are, will your vote declare that you have been abandoned by fortune and Demosthenes is your benefactor? And most bizarre of all, in the same courtrooms where you disfranchise men convicted of corruption, will you crown a man you yourselves know pursues policies for pay? You punish the judges of the Dionysia, if they do not judge the dithyrambic choruses [263] honestly; yet when you yourselves are serving as judges not of dithyrambic choruses but of the laws and of virtue in public life, will you give the prizes, not as the laws dictate or to the deserving few, but to the man who has schemed to get them? [264]

[233] When he leaves the court, a juror who behaves like this will have weakened himself and strengthened the politician. In a democratic city, the ordinary man has a king's power through the law and his vote. [265] But when he hands these over to someone else, he has subverted his power of his own accord. And then the jurors' oath [266] he swore pursues and torments him; for this oath, I think, is what makes his act wrong. But the favor he has done goes unnoticed by the recipient, because the vote is cast anonymously. [234] It is my personal view, men of Athens, that because of our lack of sense, our political situation is both fortunate and precarious. The fact that in the present circumstances, you the masses are abandoning the bastions of democracy to the few, I cannot approve. But the fact that we have not had a

---

[262] Dilts accepts an emendation that would translate as "you would be hissed." The manuscript text presents the threat to Athens' reputation more vividly. The metaphor is derived from audience response to bad writing or performance in the theatre and is designed to emphasize that the jurors (and through them Athens) no less than the litigants are on show.

[263] Greek "circular (*kyklios*) choruses"

[264] For the comparison, cf. 3.179–180.

[265] The claim recalls the position sustained by Philocleon in the debate in Aristophanes' *Wasps* (esp. 548–549).

[266] Cf. 1.154n.

rich crop of unscrupulous and reckless politicians in our day is our good fortune. In the past, our public life bred the sort of characters who found it the easiest thing in the world to overthrow the democracy. The people enjoyed being flattered, and the result was that it was overthrown not by the men it feared but by the ones it entrusted itself to. [235] Some of them even joined the Thirty.[267] These killed more than 1,500 citizens without trial, before the victims could even hear the charges on which they were to be executed, and they would not even let the relatives attend the funerals of the dead.[268] Won't you keep the politicians under your control? Won't you send home humbled the men who now are so confident? Won't you keep in mind that nobody in the past ever attempted to overthrow the democracy until he had made his power greater than that of the courts?

[236] Personally, men of Athens, in your presence I would be happy to reckon up with the decree's proposer the services for which he demands the crown for Demosthenes. If you say, as you said at the beginning of your decree, that he made a good job of digging the trenches around the walls, you amaze me. The charge of being responsible for their construction carries more weight than the successful completion of the task. The honest politician should not ask for rewards because he has put up a stockade around the walls or has destroyed the public tombs[269] but because he has performed some good service for the city. [237] If you move on to the second part of the decree, where you have had the nerve to state that he is an upright man who "consistently speaks and acts in the best interests of the Athenian people," then abandon the bluster and pomp of your decree and deal with real acts—show us what you mean. I leave aside the corruption in the matter of Amphissa and Euboea. But when you give Demosthenes the credit for the alliance with Thebes,[270] you may deceive the ignorant, but you insult people who know the facts and are

---

[267] For the Thirty, see 1.39n.

[268] Cf. Lysias 12.18, 87, 96.

[269] I.e., in the process of improving the fortifications (either by removing them to make way for the ditch or by using the masonry for the walls); cf. Lycurgus *Against Leocrates* 44 (speaking of the defensive measures taken immediately after Chaeronea).

[270] For Amphissa and Euboea, see 3.90–105, 114, 125; for the alliance with Thebes, see 3.137–151.

alert. You omit the crisis and the renown of the men here, which brought about the alliance, and you imagine we do not notice that you are transferring the city's prestige to Demosthenes. [238] I shall try to show the scale of this confidence trick with a convincing piece of evidence. Not long before Alexander crossed to Asia, the Persian king sent the Athenian people a very arrogant letter worthy of a barbarian. In it, among various insensitive statements, he added at the end: "I shall not give you gold. Do not ask me," he says, "for you won't get it." [239] Yet this same man, when caught in his current dangers, without any request from the Athenians, voluntarily sent the people 300 talents[271] of his own accord, which they wisely refused.[272] What brought us the money was the context, his fear, and his need for allies. It was the same combination that brought about the Theban alliance. But you bore us constantly with mention of the name of Thebes and this ill-fated alliance, while you are silent about the seventy talents of the king's gold that you intercepted and filched. [240] Wasn't it for lack of money, five talents in this case, that the mercenaries refused to hand over the citadel to the Thebans?[273] And because of nine silver talents, when the Arcadians had taken to the field in full force and their leaders were prepared to give aid, nothing came of it?[274] Yet you are rich and can fund[275] your personal pleasures. The upshot is that you get to keep the king's gold while we get to keep the dangers.

[241] It is also worth noting their bad taste. If Ctesiphon has the

---

[271] See 3.132n. With "his current dangers" Aeschines alludes to the whole sequence of events beginning with Alexander's invasion of Asia. The money was offered before Alexander crossed over as a classic diversionary maneuver to keep Alexander busy by stirring up revolt in Greece.

[272] Aeschines' account suggests that after failing to obtain support from the Assembly, the Persians had entrusted Demosthenes with a portion of the 300 talents to enable him to exert covert influence on their behalf. Cf. Dinarchus 1.18.

[273] In 335, when Thebes revolted, the Cadmea was held by a Macedonian (mercenary) garrison. Aeschines' point is that Demosthenes could have used the Persian money to buy off the mercenaries and save Thebes.

[274] Dinarchus (1.18–21) says that the Arcadian forces were prepared to intervene in support of Thebes for ten talents, which Demosthenes refused.

[275] Greek *chorēgein*, a metaphor from the role of chorus-producer, for which see 1.11n.

nerve to call on Demosthenes to address you, and Demosthenes has
the nerve to take the stand and speak in praise of himself, listening to
him is more infuriating than our actual misfortunes. For we refuse to
accept it when men of real worth, whose many fine achievements we
know, speak in their own praise; so when a person who has been a
disgrace to the city speaks in praise of himself, who could endure listening to this kind of thing?

[242] So you will avoid this disgraceful practice, if you have any
sense, Ctesiphon, and offer your own defense. One excuse you surely
won't offer is that you are not a good speaker. It would be preposterous, if just recently you allowed yourself to be elected envoy to Philip's
daughter, Cleopatra, to express condolences on the death of the Mo-
lossian king, Alexander,[276] but you now say you have no speaking
ability. So you have the skill to console someone else's wife in her grief,
but when you have been paid to propose a decree you won't offer a
defense? [243] Or is the man you have proposed to crown the sort
whose merit won't be recognized by his beneficiaries unless someone
speaks in your support? Then ask the jurors if they recognized the
merit of Chabrias and Iphicrates and Timotheus,[277] and ask them
why they gave them their rewards and set up statues of them. They
will all answer you with one voice that Chabrias was rewarded for the
sea battle off Naxos,[278] Iphicrates for destroying a Spartan division,[279]
Timotheus for his voyage round the Peloponnese to Corcyra,[280] and
there are others, who each have many fine achievements in war to their

---

[276] Brother of Olympias and husband of Philip's daughter (by Olympias) Cleopatra, and king of the Molossians in Epirus; he died on campaign in southern
Italy in 331.

[277] Chabrias was one of the great Athenian generals of the fourth century, associated with the remarkable renaissance of Athenian power in the early decades
of the century. His military career lasted from the late 390s until his death in battle
at Chios (during the Social War) in 357. For Iphicrates, see 2.27n; for Timotheus,
see on 2.70.

[278] See 3.222n.

[279] A reference to the successful attack on a Spartan hoplite force by light-
armed troops under Iphicrates near the Corinthian Port of Lechaeum in 390.

[280] In 376 Timotheus sailed round the Peloponnese and won over a number of
states to the Athenian alliance.

credit. [244] Then ask instead: "Why are you going to reward Demosthenes?" Because he's corrupt, because he's a coward, because he deserted his post? And will you be honoring him or leaving yourselves and the men who died in the battle[281] for your sake unavenged? You should imagine you see them complaining, if this man receives a crown. Men of Athens, if a piece of wood or stone or iron falls on someone and kills him, we remove these mute and senseless objects beyond our borders,[282] and when someone kills himself, we bury the hand that did the deed separately from the body. So it would be monstrous, [245] men of Athens, if you proceed to honor Demosthenes, the man who proposed that final expedition and then betrayed the troops. In that case, the dead are insulted and the living lose heart, when they see that the prize for courage is death and the memory of it fades; and most important of all, the younger men ask you by what model they should live their lives. [246] For rest assured, men of Athens, it is not just the gymnasia or the schools or musical training that educate young men, but far more the public proclamations. It is announced that some man is receiving a crown in the theatre for virtue and merit and loyalty, when he is an evil person with an unseemly way of life, and the younger man who sees this is corrupted. Some criminal and pimp like Ctesiphon is punished, and the rest receive a lesson. A man who votes against decency and justice goes home and tries to educate his son, and the son naturally does not obey, but calls this guidance pestering, quite rightly.[283] [247] And so you should cast your vote not just as men giving judgment, but as men under observation, with an eye to your defense before those citizens who are not here but will ask you about your verdict. You are certainly aware, men of Athens, that the city's character is judged by that of whoever is proclaimed. It is a source of shame that you should be associated not with your ancestors but with Demosthenes' cowardice.

How, then, could this disgrace be avoided? [248] If you are sus-

---

[281] I.e., at Chaeronea.

[282] For this procedure, see Demosthenes 23.76; it reflects the importance of blood pollution in homicide cases. The provision (ascribed to Draco by Pausanias 6.11.2) is echoed by Plato (*Laws* 873d). Aeschines is our only source of the classical period for the regulation concerning suicides.

[283] Cf. 1.186–187.

picious of people who appropriate for themselves the language of equality and generosity but whose character is suspect. The terms "loyalty" and "commitment to democracy" are open to all, but in general the people who are quickest to resort to them in argument are the ones furthest removed from them in their conduct. [249] So when you find a public speaker yearning for crowns and proclamations before the eyes of Greece, tell him to base his speech on his honorable life and a decent character, in the same way that the law instructs us to give warranties for property we sell. And if anyone has no testimony for this sort of life, do not confirm the praise he seeks, but protect the democratic constitution that is already slipping away from you. [250] Or don't you think it monstrous that the Council chamber and the Assembly are ignored, while the letters and embassies come to private houses,[284] not from people of no consequence but from the leading men of Asia and Europe? Some people do not deny they are engaging in practices for which the lawful punishment is death, but they admit to them in the Assembly and read out the letters to each other for comparison. And some of them urge you to look at their faces, as guardians of democracy, while others ask for rewards as the city's saviors. [251] And the people are discouraged by their experiences, like someone senile or out of his mind; they preserve only the name of democracy, while they have surrendered the real thing to others. Then when you go home from Assembly meetings you have not decided policy, but like men coming from a picnic you have been given a share of the leftovers. [252] To prove this is no idle claim, consider my statement in the light of the following. A disaster befell the city (I am sorry to mention it so often). At that point, an ordinary citizen who had tried merely to sail off to Samos was sentenced to death the same day by the Council of the Areopagus as a traitor to his country. Another ordinary man sailed to Rhodes, and because he did not handle his fear like a man he was just recently impeached, and the votes in his trial were equal.[285] If a single vote had fallen the other way,

---

[284] As when Demosthenes (rather than the city as a whole) was allegedly courted for money to help the Theban revolt (Dinarchus 1.20).

[285] One of the emergency measures passed in the wake of Chaeronea was a prohibition on anyone leaving Attica at a time when (it was anticipated) everyone would be needed for its defense. The second individual mentioned here is Leocrates, who fled Athens and, on returning after eight years, was prosecuted by the

he would have been put beyond our borders or condemned to death.[286] [253] Let's compare what is now happening. A public speaker, the man to blame for all our troubles, deserted his post in the army and fled the city. This man asks to be crowned and thinks he deserves a proclamation. Won't you get rid of him as a general catastrophe for Greece? Or won't you seize and punish him as a political pirate who sails through public life on a ship of words? [254] Remember, too, the situation in which you are casting your vote. In a few days' time the Pythian festival will be celebrated, and the Greek congress will meet.[287] Our city has become an object of suspicion through Demosthenes' policies at this time. If you crown him, others will think that you agree with the breakers of the common peace,[288] but if you do the opposite, you will release the people from censure.

[255] So deliberate like men dealing with your own city, not some foreign state. And don't just hand out honors, but give them with judgment and reserve the rewards for better persons and more deserving men. And before you decide, don't just use your ears, but turn your eyes to yourselves to see who among you will support Demosthenes. Are they his companions in hunting or in the gymnasium when he was young? No, by Olympian Zeus—he has passed his time not in hunting wild boar nor in tending to his physical fitness but in practicing verbal techniques for use against men with property.[289] [256] Be aware of his bluster, when he says that as envoy he snatched

---

politician Lycurgus; the speech for the prosecution is the only complete speech by Lycurgus to survive. The other unnamed individual is known only from this passage. Cf. 1.81n. Where votes were equal, the defendant was acquitted.

[286] Some editors delete "or condemned to death," in which case the preceding verb would refer not to exile but to the refusal of burial in Attica (imposed in cases of treason) following execution.

[287] Aeschines may refer to the Amphictyons (though this would not naturally be termed "the congress/synod [synedrion] of the Greeks") or simply the gathering of representatives of the Greek states at Delphi (including members of the League of Corinth established by Philip after Chaeronea) for the festival. The Pythian Games, which took place every four years, included competitions in music and athletics.

[288] That is, those who had breached the common peace established by Philip in 338 either by outright revolt or by agitation or manipulation.

[289] That is, as a sykophant.

Byzantium[290] from Philip's hands, detached Acarnania,[291] and stunned Thebes with his oratory. He thinks you are so far gone in stupidity now that you will actually believe this, as though you have the goddess Persuasion in the city and not some slanderer (*sykophantēs*).

[257] And when, just near the end of his speech, he calls on his partners in corruption to speak in support, imagine that you see on the platform where I now stand as I speak the city's benefactors ranged against their impudence. See Solon,[292] who equipped the democracy with the most noble laws, a philosopher and a worthy legislator, urging you in the restrained manner that befits him[293] under no circumstances to set more value on Demosthenes' arguments than on your oaths and the laws. [258] See Aristides, who set the tribute for the Greeks,[294] on whose death the people gave his daughters dowries, expressing his anger at the insult to justice and asking if you are not ashamed that, when Arthmius of Zelea[295] brought gold to Greece from the Medes and visited the city, your fathers came close to killing him, even though he was representative (*proxenos*)[296] of the people of Athens, and barred him by proclamation from our city and every city ruled by Athens, [259] but you are proposing to give a golden crown to Demosthenes, who did not bring gold from the Medes but took bribes from them and still has the money even now. Don't you think

---

[290] In 340, when Athens aided Byzantium when Philip was besieging it. Demosthenes claims the credit at 18.88–89.

[291] See 3.97.

[292] For Solon, see 1.6n.

[293] Cf. 1.25.

[294] For Aristides, see 1.25n. The public dowering of his daughters is mentioned by Plutarch (*Aristides* 27).

[295] Arthmius was an agent sent to Greece by Persia with money to bribe Greeks, but the date and purpose of his mission are unclear; purposes that have been suggested include bribery of Greeks as a prelude to the invasion of 480–479, an attempt to support the ambitions of Pausanias in Sparta in the early 460s, or an attempt to stimulate a Peloponnesian attack on Athens in the 450s when Athens was supporting the revolt of Egypt from Persia. He was evidently a favorite example with the orators; the Athenian decree against him is also cited by Demosthenes at 9.42; Demosthenes 19.271–272; Dinarchus 2.24–25.

[296] See 2.89n.

Themistocles and the men who died at Marathon and Plataea [297] and the very graves of our ancestors will groan aloud, if a man who admits to plotting with the barbarians against the Greeks receives a crown?

[260] O earth and sun, virtue, intelligence, and education,[298] through which we distinguish what is noble and shameful, for my part I have spoken and supported my cause. If I have presented the prosecution effectively and as the crime deserves, I have spoken as I wanted to; if I have been inadequate, I have spoken as best I could. It is for you yourselves on the basis of what has been said and what is omitted to reach a just and advantageous verdict for the city's sake.

---

[297] For Marathon, see 3.181n; at Plataea in 479 the Greek forces defeated the land forces of the second Persian invasion, the fleet having been defeated the previous year at Salamis.

[298] Demosthenes (18.127) sneers at this exclamation, which he regards as being at odds with the career and character of Aeschines.

Index

graphē paranomōn, 36, 98, 130, 167, 230
Gylon of Cerameis, 223
gymnasia, 69

Halonnesus, 193
Halponus, 138, 140
Harmodius and Aristogiton, 68, 70, 138
Harpalus, 185
Harpocration, 174
Hector, 72
Hegemon, 174
Hegesander, 44–49, 56, 61
Hegesippus ("Crobylus"), 47, 49, 204
Hera, 239
Hermes ("herm"), 65–66
Hesiod, 67, 210
Hestia, 109
hetaira. See courtesan
hetairos: member of political club, 81; associate of Philip of Macedonia, 106, 140, 148, 195
Hipparchus, 68
Hipparchus of Eretria, 199
Hippias, 68
ho boulomenos. See volunteer
Holy Mountain, 124
Homer, 67, 70, 71, 72, 227, 242
homicide, 54, 123, 124, 247
homosexuality, 20–21, 69
hospitality, 102
hybris, 28–29
Hyperides, xvii, 89, 100, 145, 166, 192, 194, 195, 236
hypophora, 242

Iatrocles son of Pasiphon, 99, 135
illegal proposals, indictment for. *See graphē paranomōn*

Imbros, 117, 119
inexpedient laws, indictment for, 36
interest rates, 60, 199
Ionians, 132
Iphicrates, 75, 103, 144, 246
Isaeus, xviii
Isocrates, xviii
Issus, 220

jurors, xxv; oath of, 74, 80, 94, 168; voting, 51

kakourgoi, xxvi, 54
kinaidos, 83, 145
klepsydra, 136, 232
klēteusis, 40, 116
kyrios, 84

laws, revision of, 37
legal actions, xxvi
legislation, 178–179
legislators (*nomothetai*), 179
leitourgia. See liturgy
Lemnos, 117, 119
Lenaea, 177
Leocrates, 248
Leodamas of Acharnae, 49, 61, 210
Loedias, 135
Leontini, 119
Leosthenes, 101, 135
Leto, 200, 201
Leuconides, 62
Leuctra, 150
Liparus, 142
liturgy, xxiii, 27, 171
Locrians, 132
logistēs, 60, 62, 172
logographos. See speechwriters
Long Walls, 119, 154
lōpodytai. See *kakourgoi*
Lycinus, 98, 185